WORDS
A STRUCTURAL A
OF BRITISH SIGN LANGUAGE

Mary Brennan
Martin D. Colville
Lilian K. Lawson

Edinburgh BSL Research Project
Moray House College of Education

©1984 Mary Brennan, Martin D. Colville, Lilian K. Lawson.
Edinburgh British Sign Language Research Project,
Moray House College of Education,
Holyrood Road,
Edinburgh EH8 8AW.

Reprinted 1990

ISBN 0 9509750 0 1.

 British Library Cataloguing in Publication Data

    Brennan, Mary
      Words in hand.
      1. Deaf — Means of communication
      2. Sign language
      I. Title II. Colville, Martin D.
      III. Lawson, Lilian K.
      419   HV2474

      ISBN 0 9509750 0 1

BSDCS7

WORDS IN HAND
second edition

revised with the
assistance of Gerry Hughes

Typescript

Ruth Simpson

Illustrations and Cover Design

Martin Connell

Design

Linda Herd

Preface to First Edition

This book describes the regular components of the words of British Sign Language (BSL), including the main handshapes, positions and movements. It also provides a notation system which should be of use to all those who would like to write down BSL signs. We hope the book will be helpful to teachers of the deaf, sign language teachers, sign language interpreters and sign language learners, as well as other researchers.

While Words in Hand contains several hundred signs to illustrate the structure of signed words, it is not a dictionary of BSL. The first major BSL dictionary, Sign It, will be published in the near future by the BDA and we hope that the two books will complement each other. The notation system presented here should be appropriate for use with all the signs in Sign It, as well as for entries in future supplements to the dictionary.

Words in Hand is the product of a number of important developments in the last few years. Firstly, the granting of financial support to several major projects relating to communication and the deaf community shows a new awareness of the status and worth of sign language. Secondly, deaf people themselves are playing an increasingly important part in this 'renaissance' of BSL. All the major research groups have deaf people involved as full-time research workers and our own work would have been impossible without the generous and enthusiastic support of over thirty deaf people.

This account is also an indication of the close co-operation which exists among sign language researchers. Initially, our analysis developed out of a series of workshops organised by the Bristol Sign Language Research Group. These workshops brought together researchers from all over Britain to tackle common issues. The first major need was identified as the development of an adequate notation system and in response to this need the Bristol team produced Coding British Sign Language after the first workshop. At a subsequent meeting, Lilian Lawson presented modifications to the system based on her analysis of over 1,500 BSL signs. This analysis then formed the basis of our revision of the system, although in the year it has taken us to produce the book, we have used many more signs and information from a variety of sources.

Co-operation has also extended to liaison and discussion with researchers in other parts of the world, particularly Sweden, Denmark, Germany and the USA. A glance through these pages will show one name recurring again and again, that of William Stokoe. While we have taken a number of decisions which are at variance with his descriptive framework, there is little doubt that William Stokoe's original and innovative account forms the basis of our whole approach. We owe much not only to his many books and articles but also to his generous and friendly encouragement.

Finally, we would like to say a special thank you to our colleagues in the Edinburgh BSL Research Team, Ruth Simpson, Jim Campbell and Martin Connell, for managing to create order out of chaos.

MB MDC LKL
December 1980

Preface to Second Edition

In the period since the first publication of Words in Hand, work on BSL has continued and our knowledge of the structure of BSL has increased substantially. Here in the Edinburgh BSL Project, it is difficult for us to imagine how this work would have fared without the help of the Stokoe Notation System (SNS) in the form modified for use with BSL. It has been an essential means of recording precise information and freeing us from a distorting dependence upon English glosses. We have been able to transcribe even those BSL signs which are difficult to translate into English and whose function is still under investigation. The system has also been used in the development of a computer file of signs which can output both individual transcriptions of signs and written English descriptions.

It is important to stress that the notation system presented here can be used not only for individual signs, but also within transcriptions of BSL discourse. Once one is familiar with the system, it is just as easy, and far more satisfactory, to use the notation on a regular basis. This then becomes one element in an overall transcription which includes a range of other information such as non-manual features, location, modifications, dynamic aspects and so on.

Over the years, in both using and teaching the original notation system, we inevitably became aware of some of its inconsistencies and we decided to use the opportunity of a second edition to remedy at least some of these. We would like to thank all those learners of the system, particularly students here in Moray House College, who have noted and discussed with us specific problems. The main changes in this second edition are:

1. regularisation of the use of diacritics resulting in some changes to the labels of individual handshapes (see the beginning of Chapter 4 and the pull-out section containing handshape illustrations)

2. abolition of the third 'finger orientation' rule, thus allowing both rules for finger orientation to apply without exception (see Chapters 2 and 5)

3. an attempt at greater consistency in the transcription of circular movement and the different types of contact by establishing conventions for the placing of symbols (see pull-out section and Chapter 6)

4. the use of the contact symbol × as a hand arrangement symbol occurring centrally in two-handed signs (see Chapter 6)

5. the separation of the category 'short and sharp' into two separate categories symbolised as follows:
   short °

   sharp •

While these alterations do result in a substantial number of changes to the transcriptions of individual examples in the book, the majority of symbols and the basic formulae for transcribing signs remain unchanged. Indeed, whenever possible we have tried to use the same examples and have avoided any unnecessary changes.

Despite this concentration on detail, Words in Hand is not simply about notation. Our aim is to provide a structural analysis of the signs of BSL. We believe that this analysis not only remains valid but can be supported by a wealth of further evidence from more recent research. Greater understanding of the role of iconicity, the use of classifying handshapes and the nature and function of non-manual features do require us to provide further types of description and analyses, but they do not invalidate the structural account presented here. Our aim in recent work on non-manual features has been helped enormously by insights gained from this structural account of manual signs. Moreover, we have been delighted at the extent to which learners can benefit from this type of account.

This new edition contains a completely new set of drawings. We hope that by using a real model, Gerry Hughes, we are able to give a better sense of the reality of sign production and in particular a clearer presentation of the relationship between the hands and the body.

Finally we would like to thank all those who have made this edition possible, in particular the Scottish Education Department, the Manpower Services Commission and the British Deaf Association. At a personal level we would like to thank Gerry Hughes for his patience and good humour in demonstrating and discussing many hundreds of signs; Martin Connell for the care he has exercised in translating dynamic three dimensional signs into static illustrations; Linda Herd for detailed work on arrows and for tackling some extremely awkward problems of layout and, of course, Ruth Simpson for actually being able to read our writing and transform it into neat print. We would also like to thank all those who have helped us to check and recheck transcriptions, indexes, etc, particularly Nan Anthony and the Gateshead Brennans. Finally we would like to acknowledge once again the enormous support we have received from deaf people in Scotland.

MB MDC LKL
March 1984

Contents

1
THE WORDS OF BSL

25
THE NOTATION SYSTEM

35
TABULATION

73
DESIGNATION

123
ORIENTATION

139
SIGNATION

163
MINOR PARAMETERS

173
DESCRIPTION AND USE

191
REFERENCES

197 & 199
INDEXES

203
INDEX OF GLOSSES

        oh, better
the word in hand than a thousand
spilled from the mouth upon the hearless ear.

Extract from TO A DEAF CHILD by kind permission of DOROTHY MILES.

CHAPTER ONE

The Words of BSL

Introduction

British Sign Language (BSL) is one of several natural human languages which are produced in a visual-gestural medium. The language user, the signer, makes gestures, including movements of the hands, arms, eyes, face, head and body, which are watched and decoded by the other participants in the communication. If we do not know the significant types of patterning within the gesturing activity of the signer, we cannot decode, and hence understand, the linguistic information imparted by the signer. Thus the major task of a linguist in describing a virtually unanalysed sign language, such as BSL, is to try to discern the patterns which carry the meaning. This is a huge task as different kinds of patterning operate at different levels of language.

The Word

One traditional point of entry to the study of a new language is the word. Like many other linguistic concepts, there are difficulties in providing a precise and comprehensive definition of a word. We all assume we know what words are until we are asked some rather awkward questions. If "meet" and "meat" are pronounced in exactly the same way, how can they be different words? Are "cut" and "cutting" simply different forms of the same word? Is "blackbird" one word or two? These questions are a useful reminder that we can look at words from several different perspectives, including the phonological, the morphological, the syntactic and the semantic.

We can examine a word to see how it is structured internally, to discover its component parts: both "meet" and "meat" are composed of three speech sounds which can be identified as consonant /m/, vowel /i/ and consonant /t/: this is the phonological perspective. We can note how the 'base' forms of words may be changed, for example, to express grammatical categories such as tense (like:liked) or to change lexical meaning (child:childless): the morphological perspective. We can analyse how words are organised into larger linguistic units such as phrases, clauses, sentences and texts: the syntactic approach. Finally, we can examine words in terms of their meaning: the semantic perspective. In the semantic approach, we may need to take account not only of the referent of the word, ie the idea, object or person it represents, but also of related words in the language which may give us a clue as to exactly how the word is used.

This book is mainly concerned with the signed word from the first point of view, the phonological. We are concerned with the internal make-up or structure of the sign and the principles of organisation inherent in its composition. However, the nature of sign language is such that we may need to make some reference to word meaning even when taking a primarily phonological view of the signed word.

2

ENOUGH

FED UP

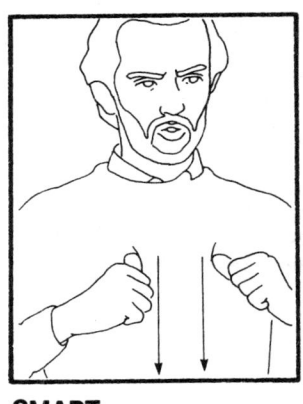
SMART

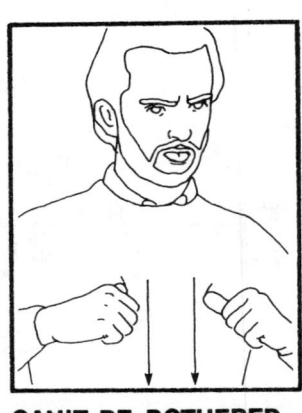
CAN'T BE BOTHERED

Manual/Non-Manual

The focus here is on the manual sign and hence on the organised and meaningful activity of the hands. Much recent work on sign language (Baker and Padden, 1978; Liddell, 1978; Bergman, 1979; Wikström, 1979; Lawson, 1983; Vogt-Svendsen, 1983) has shown that other types of gestural activity, particularly movements of the eyes, the eyebrows, the mouth, the face muscles, the head, the shoulders and the body, can carry specific and complex linguistic information. Baker (1980) has suggested that some signs of American Sign Language (ASL), eg NOT YET and Swedish Sign Language (SSL), eg DON'T KNOW may involve no specific manual activity at all. The lexical meaning is carried entirely by non-manual behaviour. It has also been shown that in SSL and ASL some manual signs must be accompanied by specific non-manual activity. Thus Baker (1980) shows that some pairs of ASL signs have identical manual components and are differentiated only by non-manual activity such as facial gestures. This is also the case in BSL. The signs ENOUGH and FED UP are distinguished only by facial gesture. While it could be argued that FED UP is simply a stronger version of ENOUGH, there are other examples in which there is no semantic link whatsoever between the two signs. SMART and CAN'T BE BOTHERED make use of exactly the same action of the hands, but in the latter case a distinctive mouth pattern is used. This phenomenon is comparable to the use of pitch to distinguish otherwise identical strings of sound segments in tone languages. In a tone language such as Thai, the sequence /naa/ said with a low tone means "nickname"; the same sequence said with a falling tone means "face". SMART and CAN'T BE BOTHERED use exactly the same manual sign, /[ ] Å$_{b>}$ Å$_{D<}$ ^{x} /, but markedly different facial expressions. In this particular case it is the mouth pattern (tongue protrusion) which is the distinguishing feature.

Although, in the case of BSL, the role of non-manual features in the production of both individual signs and signed utterances awaits more detailed investigation, there seems little doubt that such features play an essential part in the language. The following analysis of signs in terms of the significant manual aspects in no way implies that non-manual features are unimportant. In future years, it should be possible to provide equally thorough accounts of both manual and non-manual elements.

Manual Signs/Spoken Words

The pioneering work of William Stokoe on the structure of ASL (Stokoe, 1960, 1965, 1972) provided a way of approaching the analysis of individual signs that still forms the basis of current research in many countries. While using the analogy of the phonological level in spoken languages, Stokoe was careful to emphasise the ways in which the signs of a sign language differ from the words of spoken language. Spoken words occur in time and can be analysed in sequential terms: /kæt/ is made up of three phonemic segments /k/, /æ/ and /t/. Although in actual production the boundaries between each segment may be blurred, nevertheless the notion of segments in ordered sequence does seem to have some perceptual reality for spoken language. If asked how many sounds there are in the word "phone", the English speaker is likely to say three. The speaker's perception of the significant sounds of the utterance will take precedence over both orthographic information (the fact that there are five letters) and phonetic information (the fact that, for many speakers of English, the vowel segment is a diphthong /əu/ and acoustically the word is one continuous flow of sound).

The manual sign, however, occurs in both <u>time</u> and <u>space</u>. Indeed it could be suggested that spatial organisation frequently takes priority in sign language structure. At any one point in time there are several different aspects of sign production which must be regarded as significant. These aspects are significant, or phonemic, in that a change in any one of them may constitute a change in meaning. The BSL sign I is formed by bringing the tip of the extended index finger of one hand into contact with the signer's chest. The handshape used is the same as that of the letter *g* in the American one-handed manual alphabet. If the handshape is changed to the *a* configuration, ie a closed fist, then the meaning of the sign changes to MY. The G hand and the A hand are two possible realisations of one of the significant aspects of BSL, namely hand configuration.

In the transcription system developed by Stokoe and adapted here for use with BSL, the names and symbols for many of the significant handshapes are taken from letters with similar shapes in the American manual alphabet. This alphabet can be found on page 17 and a full discussion of the notation system can be found in Chapter 2. From now on, all BSL signs mentioned in the text will be provided with a transcription within oblique strokes. While newcomers to the system will find such transcriptions impossible to decipher, the notated examples will ensure that other researchers have precise information on the production of each sign. As readers become more familiar with the system, the transcriptions should provide additional information on the internal structure of the signs. All English glosses of BSL are given in capital letters and finger-spelled items are given in lower-case italic script.

I /[]G̈$_{T<}$^{x}/   MY /[]A$_{T<}$^{x}/

Significant Aspects

The original analysis of ASL by William Stokoe distinguished three significant aspects:

> the position of the sign in space, labelled "tabulation" but normally shortened to <u>tab</u>;
>
> the handshape or hand configuration of the hand or hands forming the sign, labelled "designator" and normally shortened to <u>dez</u>;
>
> the movement or movements involved in the production of the sign, labelled "signation" and shortened to <u>sig</u>.

In Stokoe's account (1978):
> <u>tab</u> is where the activity occurs
>
> <u>dez</u> is what acts
>
> <u>sig</u> is the action.

Other authors, particularly Klima and Bellugi (1979), refer to these same aspects as:

    place of articulation (PA)

    hand configuration (HC)

    movement (MOV)

However, throughout this book the original terms, tab, dez and sig will be used.

Just as in spoken languages a relatively small number of significant sound elements may be used for the creation of an unlimited number of words, so a relatively small number of handshapes, positions and movements can combine simultaneously to produce an unlimited vocabulary of signs. Of course, the choice of significant realisations of these parameters may vary from language to language. (In this chapter, the terms parameter and aspect are used interchangeably, and the theoretical distinction between the two terms will be discussed in later sections.) The dental fricatives θ and ð do not occur in German but are significant in English, while many languages, including French and German, make use of the high front rounded vowel [y] which is not significant in English. Even where the same significant contrasts are exploited the rules of co-occurrence may differ. The combination /nz/ is allowable in word final position, eg "tins": /tɪnz/ in English, but the sequence /nz/ at the beginning of a word, is unacceptable in English. However, for many African Bantu languages, such as Chinyanja, the initial sequence /nz/ is quite normal, eg /nzeru/, meaning "wisdom".

In sign languages we can expect comparable differences. Some handshapes, positions and movements appear to be common to all sign languages, at least to those sign languages so far analysed. However, other realisations of these three parameters may be language specific. The handshape in which the middle finger is extended from the closed fist is phonemic in BSL but not in ASL. Gestures which are classified in the wider American culture as obscene also make use of this hand configuration and this may have limited the exploitation of this handshape in ASL except for taboo signs. In BSL the handshape is used without any obscene connotations in such signs as HOLIDAY /∅λ̈ₐ₁ λ̈ₐ₁ ɇ̈/ and LAZY /∅λ̈ₐ₁ λ̈ₐ₁ ˜/.

Even if exactly the same patterns occur in two languages, it is not necessarily the case that two lexical items with the same phonological composition will have identical meaning. Both English and German speakers make use of the word "gift". The individual sound segments and the arrangement of these segments are quite familiar to speakers of each language. However, the English word has the meaning of "something given, a present" while the German word means "poison". Similar examples can be found in sign language comparisons. The BSL sign SWEAR /⊃Iₜ∧ˣ⊥/ is made by moving the extended little finger forward from the mouth. Exactly the same manual activity in Danish Sign Language (DSL) has the meaning "ice".

SWEAR /⊃Iₜ∧ˣ⊥/   **ICE (DSL)** /⊃Iₜ∧ˣ⊥/

The major task attempted in this account of sign formation in BSL is that of isolating the significant phonemic contrasts available to BSL users. The aim is to provide detailed evidence to indicate which handshapes, positions and movements are essential for the production of BSL signs. We can expect that some of our findings will link closely with the formational realisations already discovered in other sign languages; however, it is clear that BSL sign formation does have unique features which we hope to elaborate in the following pages.

How Many Parameters?

A more fundamental problem however concerns the adequacy of the theoretical and descriptive framework developed by Stokoe. Several researchers (Battison, 1974; Friedman, 1975; Frishberg, 1975) have suggested that a fourth parameter, orientation, must be distinguished if an adequate description of sign formation is to be established. Orientation is the relationship of the hand configuration to the signer's body. The same handshape (dez) may be held with palm facing up, (supinating), or held facing down, (pronating); the palm may be facing right or left or held facing the signer or away from the signer. It may also be relevant to provide information on the direction of the fingers, eg the G hand may be held with palm facing left and finger pointing up, or palm facing left and finger pointing away from the signer or in any one of a series of similar combinations.

The basic issue here is whether orientation should be seen as a separate distinguishing parameter or merely a further, more exact elaboration of dez. The move towards regarding orientation as a separate parameter has been influenced by two factors:

1. The fact that orientation may be the only feature which distinguishes certain pairs of signs. Thus the only difference between the BSL signs HEAVY and WAIT is that in the first case the palms face up (supinating) and in the second the palms face down (pronating).

2. For many signs descriptive adequacy demands that orientation should be clearly indicated. Thus when testing out sign descriptions with sign language learners, it became clear to us that correct reproduction of the sign was only possible if full information on orientation was given.

HEAVY /∅ B̈ₐ⊥ B̈ₐ⊥ˇ/   **WAIT** /∅ B̈ᴅ⊥ B̈ᴅ⊥ˇ/

Klima and Bellugi (1979) propose orientation as one of three minor parameters of hand use, the other two being contacting region and hand arrangement. In a sign which involves contact, the part of the sign which actually touches the body may play a significant role in distinguishing that sign from all other signs. Sometimes the point of contact may be obvious from other parameters, especially if information on orientation and hand arrangement is given. Moreover there may be rules or constraints governing the possible points of contact. Some of these constraints may be physical, and thus probably universal; others may be specific to particular sign languages.

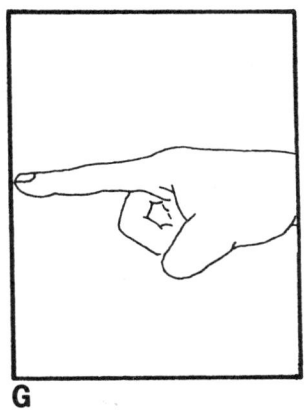 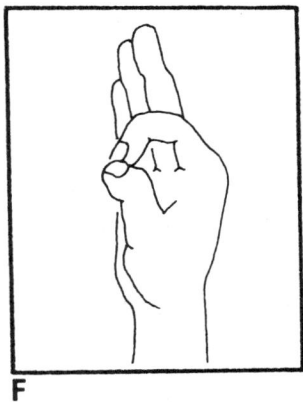

G   F

Thus the F dez (the handshape in which the index finger and thumb tip form a circle and the other fingers are extended) is used in ASL, BSL and Chinese Sign Language (CSL). However, CSL uses the extended fingers for contact in signs such as TOPIC, MENU and SUMMARY (Klima and Bellugi, 1979, p156), while for BSL and ASL the extended fingers are not used for contact. Hand arrangement includes the number of hands used and, if two hands are used, the relationship of one hand to the other. The two hands may be held side by side, one above the other, one behind the other, and so on.

Klima and Bellugi suggest that these minor parameters can be viewed as subclassifications of hand configuration (dez):

> *"whereas the major parameters distinguish very large classes of signs, minor parameters distinguish only a small number of minimal pairs, yet further differentiate signs."*
>
> *(Klima and Bellugi, 1979, p45)*

This account appears to hold good for BSL too. Relatively few sets of minimal pairs are distinguished by one of the minor parameters, yet an adequate descriptive account demands information related to all these three areas. Some of the issues involved here will be discussed further in the relevant chapters. In the account of BSL sign formation which follows, it is assumed that information relating to orientation, contacting region and hand arrangement is necessary for a fully adequate description of BSL signs. The extent to which such information is expressed explicitly within the transcription system may vary. (See particularly the discussion on point of contact in Chapter 7.)

Methodology

A traditional, structuralist approach is taken here to the task of establishing the significant realisations of the basic parameters. At the heart of this approach is the notion of contrast: phonemes in spoken language are contrastive elements which serve to bring about a change in meaning. By substituting one sound segment for another it is possible to discover <u>minimal pairs</u>, ie pairs of words which differ in respect of only one sound segment. The following are minimal pairs in English:

son : soon	/sʌn/ : /suːn/
sight : sign	/saɪt/ : /saɪn/
sin : bin	/sɪn/ : /bɪn/
drown : frown	/draʊn/ : /fraʊn/

In a sign language we look for those handshapes, positions, movements, orientations, hand arrangements and contacts which are contrastive by trying to discover minimal sign pairs. A simple example is the pair SEE:SAY. These two

SEE /ᴜsG_TΛ^xꞱ/   **SAY** /ᴜG_TΛ^xꞱ/

BSL signs are distinguished only by position (tab). In SEE the G hand (extended index finger) moves outwards from the eye, in SAY the same handshape (dez), movement (sig), orientation (ori) and point of contact are used but the position (tab) is different in that the sign begins at the side of the mouth. Throughout this account of BSL sign composition, minimal pairs of signs will be cited to show the necessity for establishing the specific phonemes of BSL.

It is important to recognise that not all observable variations are necessarily phonemic or distinctive. Thus the realisations of /l/ appearing at the beginning and end of the word "lull" are phonetically different: in English different 'l' sounds are used according to the position within the word or syllable. However, although it is possible to hear this difference and to measure it acoustically, the substitution of one 'l' sound for the other would not produce a change of meaning, it would merely sound slightly odd to the native speaker. The 'k' sounds in "king" /kiŋ/ and "car" / kɑː / are phonetically different: the initial sound is affected by the nature of the following vowel. The exact quality of the 'k' sound depends very much on the phonetic context, ie the particular sounds it occurs with in a given word. The various 'k' and 'l' sounds described above are <u>allophones</u> of the two phonemes /k/ and /l/. Allophones are the phonetic realisations of specific phonemes. It may be possible, as with the 'k' and 'l' examples above, to specify the conditions under which one allophone rather than another is likely to be produced. The /A/ phoneme in BSL is commonly known as the closed fist handshape. The closed fist with extended thumb constitutes a quite separate phoneme, /Ȧ/, because /A/ and /Ȧ/ can be used contrastively to distinguish pairs of signs, eg MINE /[ ]A_{T<}^{x}/ and RIGHT /[ ]Ȧ_{T<}^{x}/ . The /A/ phoneme has a number of possible realisations or allophones which make use of variant but non-contrastive thumb positioning. The thumb may be held loosely at the side of the fingers or across the bent fingers as in the American finger-spelling of *s*.

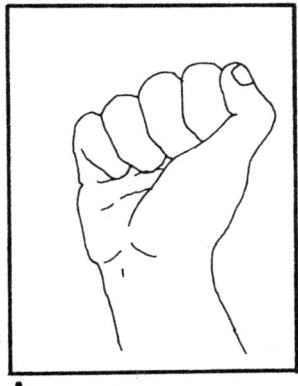
A

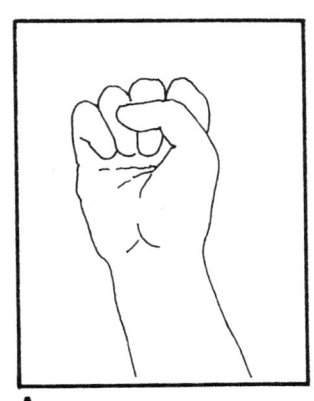
A_S

In ASL this form is contrastive, and thus phonemic, in a number of borrowed signs: compare ATTEMPT /∅A_{>v} A_{<v} $\frac{p}{1}$/ and STRIVE /A_{s>v} A_{s<v} $\frac{p}{1}$/ .

ATTEMPT /∅A_{>v} A_{<v} $\frac{p}{1}$/   **STRIVE** /∅A_{s>v} A_{s<v} $\frac{p}{1}$/

While the use of one allophone rather than another may sometimes be idiosyncratic, in other cases the phonetic environment will allow us to predict which allophone will be preferred. In the BSL sign MAKE /Ā_{T>} A_{T<} $\overset{<}{\dot{\epsilon}}$/ which demands placing one A hand on top of the other, the A_s allophone will be used, at least for the lower handshape. However, in the BSL sign PRINT /B̄_{a>} A_{DꞱ}^{vxɑ}/ which involves bringing the closed fist, palm down onto the flat palm of the other hand, the thumb will be held loosely at the side to allow for a smooth contact between the two hands. Although the use of A_s would make the sign awkward to produce, it would not actually bring about a change of meaning.

MAKE /Ā_{T>} A_{T<} $\overset{<}{\dot{\epsilon}}$/   **PRINT** / B̄_{a>} A_{DꞱ}^{vxɑ}/

Phoneticians have noted that no two realisations of a phoneme are exactly the same. Not only may one speaker's

8

phonetic realisation of a phoneme differ from another speaker's, but the same speaker's repeated articulations of the same word may involve slight phonetic variations. For the most part, native speakers ignore such phonetic variations and note only the contrastive elements within the word. It is only when, for example, a non-native speaker comes too close to the phoneme boundaries or includes unfamiliar phonetic features that the native speaker becomes alert to phonetic characteristics. Native speakers of English tolerate a wide variation in the production of the vowel sound /æ/ of "cat". Although a relatively high articulation of /æ/ is found in some types of English, the boundary between /æ/ and /e/ is always maintained. Foreign learners, for example, native German speakers, may tend to heighten the front vowels of English to the extent of confusing such pairs as "pan:pen" or "pen:pin".

Similarly, in BSL, while a considerable range of variation is permitted from signer to signer, the phonemic boundaries are normally maintained. A sign which has as its tab a position at the side of the eye, may in actual usage be produced much lower than this. However, if the production is too low then the sign may be confused with similar signs produced on the cheek or mouth. Actual observable differences between contrasting handshapes may be very slight, eg the difference between a B hand with fingers and thumb parallel, B̿, and a C hand, yet nevertheless, because such differences serve to distinguish minimal pairs of signs, the boundaries between the handshapes are important.

Specific phonetic features of the sign may demand the choice of a particular variant of the handshape phoneme. If we examine the choices available for the realisation of the B (flat hand) phoneme, it becomes clear that in signs which do not involve any contact, several allophones are in free variation. In these cases, the exact positioning of the thumb is linguistically non-significant. The thumb may be held loosely at the side, across the palm or raised so that it is at right angles to the first finger. In signs such as NIGHT /⊂B_T∧ B_T∧ ⊥/ and ROAD /∅B_>v B_<v ?/ these allophones are in free variation. If the sign demands contact between the thumb of the B hand and the other hand or any part of the body, clearly the B hand with a prominent thumb, ie /Ḃ/, must be chosen. Typical examples are PREPARE /⌐¬Ḃ_D> Ḃ_D< ˣ˙/ and FOOLISH /⌒Ḃ_⊥∧ ӧ˙ /. Unfortunately, we are at too early a stage in the analysis of BSL to be able to provide a comprehensive account of conditions of occurrence for specific variants. However, it is hoped that the following chapters may provide the basis for future analyses.

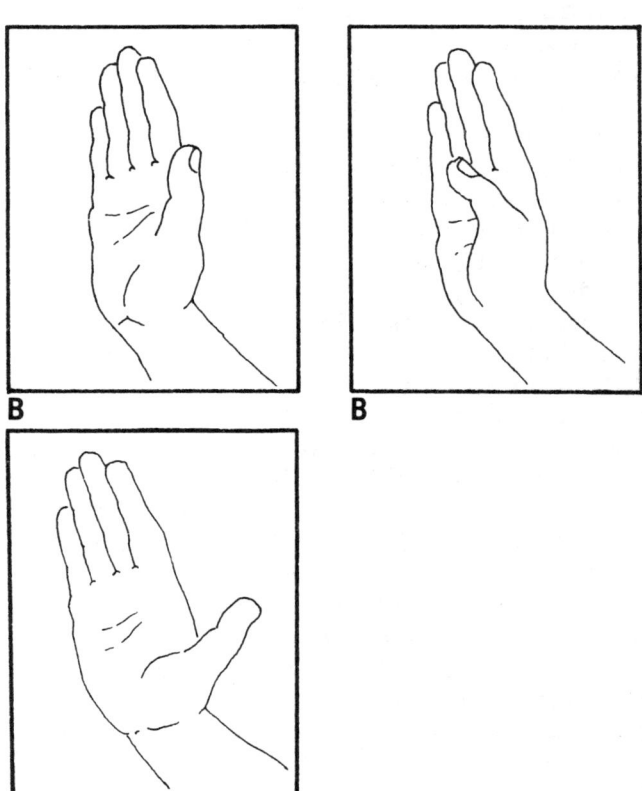

B B

Ḃ

Phonology/Cherology

In the original account of ASL sign structure, Stokoe used a new set of terms to refer to that level in sign language which is analogous to the phonological level in spoken language. Where in spoken language we refer to phonology, phonemes and allophones,

Stokoe referred to cherology, cheremes and allochers in sign language. By using a new set of terms linked to the existing set but derived from a different source (ie the Greek word meaning "hand") Stokoe was able to encapsulate the complex interplay of similarities and differences between two mediums, spoken and sign. In the last decade of sign language research there has been an increasing tendency to revert to the terminology prevalent in spoken language research. This change has been widespread despite the irony of using terms deriving from the Greek word "sound" for languages whose primary distinguishing characteristic is that they are produced in a gestural medium, and thus have no level of sound structure at all. The main advantage of using terms such as phonology and phoneme is that they belong to a tradition of language study which can be a rich source of information and understanding whatever the language medium. Many of the recent developments in the phonology of spoken languages may be relevant to the study of sign production too. Already several linguists have attempted distinctive feature analyses of handshape and position in sign languages and have provided glimpses of the application of a generative approach to the phonological level of sign languages. Cross-linguistic comparisons certainly become easier if there is some common framework for analysis. Therefore, in this account of BSL sign structure, we have decided to use the traditional terms derived from the study of spoken language.

Typology of Signs

In the study of ASL and other sign languages, it has been possible to distinguish specific classes or types of sign. This classification is an important step toward developing a more adequate account of sign formation in that it may be possible to specify general rules or constraints which may be applicable to one class of signs but not to another. Battison (1978) provides a six-fold classification which appears to have some general validity for BSL too. The signs which exemplify the classes are all taken from BSL.

Class A   One-handed Signs

Type 1
(Battison's Type Ø)

Non-Contact

One-handed signs performed in space and not involving contact with any part of the body.

GO /ØG̈_{DL} ᵇ/

WHAT /ØG_{⊥∧} ᵇ/

Type 2
(Battison's Type X)

Contact

One-handed signs in which there is contact with any part of the body except the other hand.

WHY /[]G_{D<} ˣ/

KNOW /⌒Ȧ_{<∧} ˣ/

Class B   Two-handed Signs

Type 1

Double Dez

Two-handed signs in which <u>both</u> hands are active and moving.

AGREE /ØȦ$_{>⊥}$,Ȧ$_{<⊥}$ $^×$/

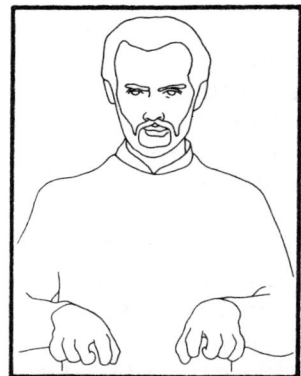
BAKE /Ø5̈$_{ᴅ⊥}$ 5̈$_{ᴅ⊥}$ $^{ɯ·}$/

Type 2
Symmetrical
Single Dez

Two-handed signs in which one hand acts upon the other. The dominant hand is an active dez. Both hands have the same handshape.

QUICK /Ḡ$_{⊤>}$ G$_{<⊥}$ $^{⋰×λ}$/

TRUE /B̄$_{ɑ>}$ B$_{<⊥}$ $^{v×}$/

Type 3
Asymmetrical
Single Dez

Two-handed signs in which one hand acts upon the other, but unlike Type 2, the two hands have different handshapes.

CAKE /B̄$_{ᴅ>}$ 5̈$_{ᴅ⊥}$ $^{×·}$/

REGULAR /B̄$_{ɑ>}$ Ȧ$_{ᴅ⊥}$ $^{×}$/

Class C   Compound Signs

Signs which involve combinations of the above types.

REMEMBER /⌒G$_{<∧}$$^{×}$ ̈Ȧ$_{ɑ>}$A$_{ᴅ⊥}$$^{v×}$/

PROMISE /⌣G$_{>∧}$$^{×}$ ̈B̄$_{ɑ>}$B$_{<⊥}$$^{v×}$/

An adequate account of BSL phonology must indicate the kinds of limitations on sign structure which operate on these different classes of signs.

Phonological Constraints

There appear to be sign (morpheme) structure constraints which are determined by physical and/or perceptual factors. The interplay of productive and perceptual limitations can be seen clearly in relation to Class B1, double dez signs. The Symmetry Condition posited by Battison (1974, 1978) holds that when both hands are active they must behave in approximately the same ways.

In terms of the main parameters of sign formation, we can note firstly that both hands will adopt the same hand configuration. In the sign AGREE /ØÀ$_{>⊥}$,À$_{<⊥}$^{x}/ , both hands adopt the À dez, ie closed fist with raised thumb. Orientation will be either the same for both hands or complementary. In the sign BAKE /Ø5̈$_{b⊥}$ 5̈$_{b⊥}$$^{m.}$/ both hands have exactly the same orientation, palms facing down and fingers pointing forward. AGREE shows complementary rather than identical orientation in that although the fingers point in the same direction, one palm faces right and the other left. A similar type of patterning can be seen in the realisation of tab. Frequently the hands are held opposite each other in neutral space as in BAKE and AGREE. In COW /⌒Y$_{⊥∧}$ Y$_{⊥∧}$$^{x\hat{⊥}}$/ the hands are held at either side of the head. The sig parameter is realised either by identical movement as in BAKE or complementary movement as in AGREE. In all cases the same type of movement, eg movement in a straight line, rotating movement, nodding movement or crumbling movement, is produced by each hand. However, the movements of the two hands may be produced either simultaneously or in alternation. PARTY /ØY$_{>∧}$ Y$_{<∧}$^{ẅ}/ , WAIT /ØB̈$_{b⊥}$ B̈$_{b⊥}$^{v}/ , GIVE /ØB$_{a⊥}$ B$_{a⊥}$$^⊥$/ and AGREE /ØÀ$_{>⊥}$,À$_{<⊥}$^{x}/ all have simultaneous movements, while CYCLE /ØA$_{b⊥}$,A$_{b⊥}$$^{ë\sim}$/ , INFORMATION /◡G$_{T∧}$ G$_{T∧}$$^{I\sim·}$/, EXPLAIN /ØB$_{a>}$ B$_{a<}$$^{\dot{\ddot{⊥}}\sim}$/ and COMMUNICATION /◡C$_{>∧}$ C$_{<∧}$$^{I\sim}$/ all have alternating movement. Thus in the sign EXPLAIN while one hand is moving in towards the body, the other is moving outwards.

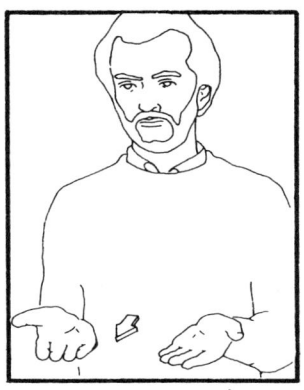

GIVE /ØB$_{a⊥}$ B$_{a⊥}$$^⊥$/

INFORMATION /◡G$_{T∧}$ G$_{T∧}$$^{I\sim·}$/

Double dez signs thus show remarkable symmetry in all aspects of their production. It is physically more demanding to produce completely different handshapes, movements, etc, when both hands are active. At least one Scottish sign, PORRIDGE /ØḆ̂$_{b>}$^{ẅ} Ḧ$_{b⊥}$$^{\dot{e}}$/ seems to break this constraint. Such examples are recognised as a rarity by native signers. Many double dez signs are produced outside the central point of focus, thus perceptually it is helpful to have the extra information supplied by symmetrical production.

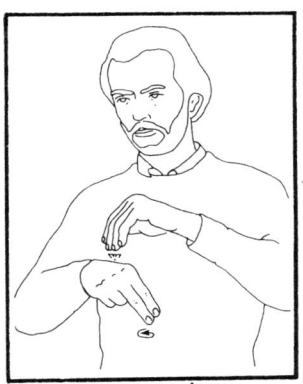

PORRIDGE /ØḆ̂$_{b>}$^{ẅ} Ḧ$_{b⊥}$$^{\dot{e}}$/

The second type of constraint posited by Battison refers to Classes B2 and B3, ie those signs in which one hand is the passive base on which the other active dez hand acts. In a sign like TRUE /B̄$_{a>}$ B$_{<⊥}$^{vx}/ the left hand acts as the base while the right hand performs the action. Because not all signers are right-hand dominant ("right-handed") it is probably more accurate to speak of the dominant hand and the non-dominant hand. This allows us to make general statements about sign structure which cover signs performed by both right-hand dominant and left-hand dominant signers. It should be noted that in actual performance the roles of the two hands may be more complex. A person whose dominant hand is occupied, perhaps holding something, may produce a one-handed sign with the non-dominant hand. However, this change-over will not bring about a change in meaning. Similarly, certain contexts encourage the omission of the activity of one hand in a two-handed sign, again without affecting meaning. More importantly the two hands may take on different grammatical roles when two lexical signs are produced simultaneously. This very important type of patterning is outside our present study.

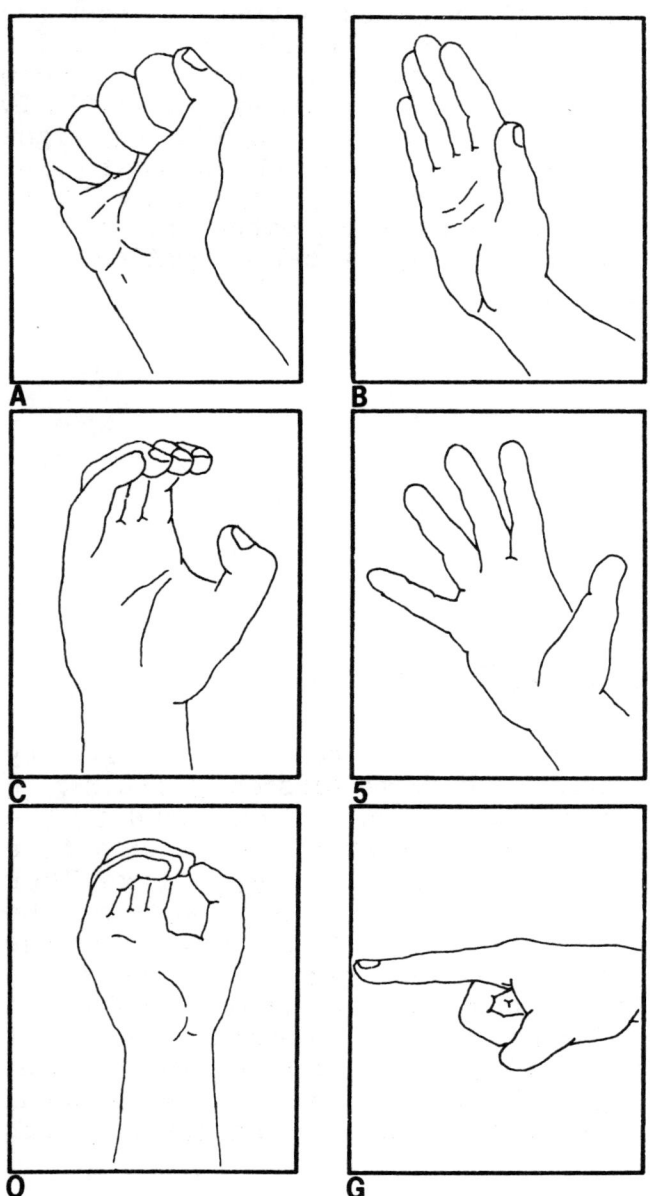

The Dominance Constraint holds that in two-handed single dez signs the non-dominant hand will either have the same handshape as the dominant hand (Class B2 signs) or, if the handshapes are different (Class B3 signs) the non-dominant hand must adopt one of a small subset of handshapes. In Class B3 signs, although the choice of handshape of the dominant hand is in theory as wide as the number of dez phonemes in the language, the choice of handshape for the non-dominant hand is highly restricted. Battison lists the members of this group for ASL as the handshapes A, S, B, 5, G, C and O, and suggests that these handshapes are particularly important in that they are "maximally distinct basic geometrical shapes". A and S (closed fist) are maximally compact solids; B is a simple flat surface; 5 involves maximal extension and spreading of all the digits; G is the single extension of the index finger; C is an arc and O is a full circle. These handshapes appear to constitute a special class of 'unmarked' handshapes in the language.

The marked/unmarked contrast has received considerable attention in recent linguistic theory, although it was first developed by the Prague school of linguistics in the 1930s. Two segments of a language can be distinguished by regarding one segment as unmarked for a particular feature and the other marked. An important assumption here is that the unmarked member represents the less complex and more expected option.

An example from spoken language may help to illustrate this phenomenon. Virtually all spoken languages seem to make use of at least three contrasting vowels, front unrounded [i], back unrounded [a], and back rounded [u]. Phonetically, these vowels are maximally opposed to one another. Some languages, such as Eskimo, have only these three choices in their vowel system. Jakobson (1968) has claimed that these three unmarked vowels are universally the first to appear in children's speech, hence the early appearance of such forms as /dada/, /mama/, /pipi/, /pupu/. This accords with Jakobson's more general claim that marked forms are the last to be learned by children, and, it seems, the first to be lost by patients suffering from aphasia.

The members of the class of unmarked handshapes in ASL certainly appear to meet with the criteria mentioned above. Evidence from studies of sign language acquisition (Boyes-Braem, 1973; McIntire, 1974, 1977) suggests that they are among the first handshapes to appear in children's sign production and all sign language studies so far make use of these handshapes. Even more important for our own study is that in both BSL and ASL they occur in a much wider range of contexts than other handshapes. The unmarked handshapes occur in signs where there is a change of handshape, eg HAVE /∅5ₐ⊥ ⌣#[ʌ]/ in which the 5 hand closes to an A, and FORGET /⌒O_Tʌ ˣḃ[5]/ in which the O hand opens to a 5. Signs belonging to Class C, ie compound signs, also make use of unmarked handshapes as realisations of one or both the dez elements in the sign. PROMISE /⌣G>ʌ ˣ⁄⁄B̄ₐ> B<⊥ᵛˣ/ uses the unmarked handshapes of G and B and REMEMBER /⌒G<ʌ ˣ⁄⁄Āₐ> A⊥ᵛˣ/ makes use of unmarked G and A. The realisation of the tab parameter in both these signs is the same as the final dez, eg B for PROMISE and A for REMEMBER. There is little doubt then that these handshapes constitute a particularly important class within BSL as well as ASL. However, it should be noted that the choice of handshapes for the non-dominant hand in Class B3 signs seems to be rather wider in BSL than ASL, eg F, V, X and other handshapes do occur as tab in these signs. But there are relatively few such examples, as compared with the large number of signs making use of the unmarked forms. A further difference between ASL and BSL is that the S handshape is not phonemic in BSL and therefore the separation of A and S as individual unmarked forms is unnecessary. Details of the role of these handshapes in BSL signs will be given in the relevant chapters on Tab and Dez.

Finger Spelling

The language of deaf people is often thought by the hearing community to consist of finger-spelling. However, finger-spelling is essentially a way of encoding spoken, or, more accurately, written language in a manual form. The items of the British manual alphabet have a direct relationship with the letters of the English alphabet. Because finger-spelled words are thus English, not BSL, they would seem to be quite outside this present study, but the situation is rather more complex than this. Signers may use finger-spelled items within BSL as borrowings from English, and may even adapt the finger-spelled words so that they take on the characteristics of BSL signs. It is therefore important here to make some observations on the form of finger-spelled items.

Unlike the majority of deaf communities in other parts of the world, Britain makes use of a <u>two-handed</u> finger-spelling system. The other countries using closely related two-handed systems have all had some political associations with Britain, eg Australia, India and other British Commonwealth countries, although two-handed systems unrelated to the British system are used elsewhere, eg Yugoslavia. A two-handed alphabet is

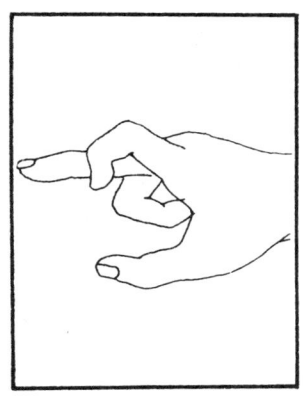
Portuguese R

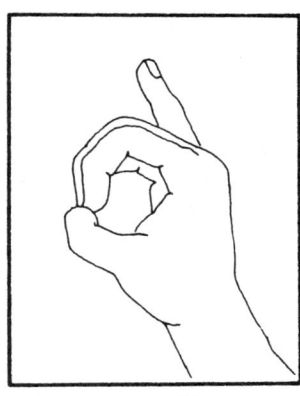
Japanese chi ち

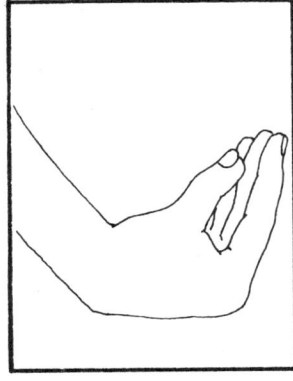
Greek O Ω

Korean ea ㅐ

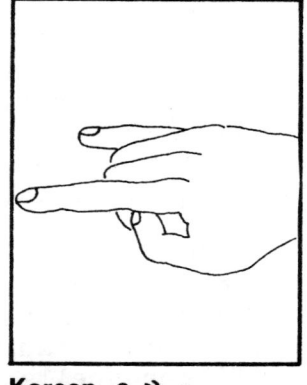 **Korean e** ㅔ 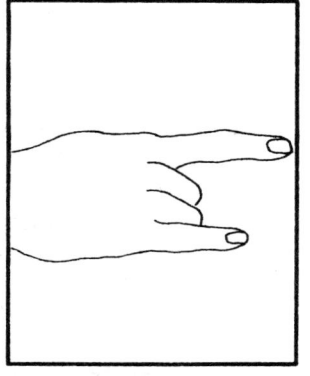 **Korean wo** ㅝ 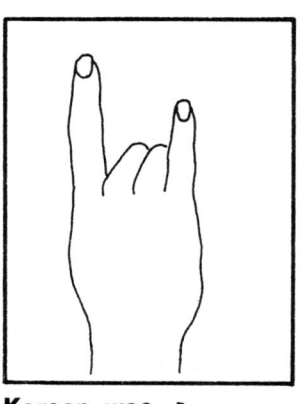 **Korean woe** ㅚ 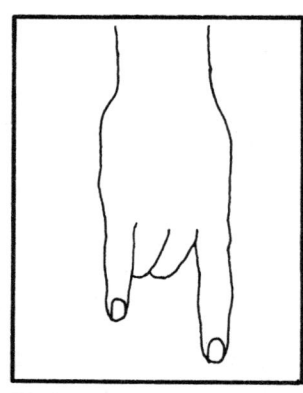 **Korean wee** ㅟ

 **Spanish** *h*  **Venezuelan** *h*

also used to represent the tonal language Thai: the right hand is used for the consonants and several of the vowels, while the left hand is used to represent the other vowels and, most importantly, to indicate the different tones required.

Most countries appear to make use of one-handed systems, although the choice of handshapes may vary considerably from country to country (see illustrations).

An examination of the alphabet charts presented by Carmel (1975) shows clearly that one-handed alphabets differ not only in the handshapes employed but in the orientation of the hand and in the execution of the individual letters. The *t* and *g* of the Greek alphabet have the same handshape, extended index finger and thumb, the two Greek letters are distinguished only by their orientation: in *g* the index finger points downward and in *t* the index finger points to the left. In the Korean alphabet the same handshape, involving extension of the index finger and the little finger from closed fist, is used for five letters: the differences are shown entirely by palm and finger orientation.

Individual letters of many alphabets demand specific types of movement, eg nine letters of the Russian manual alphabet require directional or circular movement. Positioning of the letters may also vary: Spanish *h* is articulated at the mouth and Venezuelan *h* under the chin.

These varying characteristics of the different hand alphabets can have a bearing on both the overall appearance of each system and the ways in which the system may be exploited in the native sign language. Battison (1979) describes American finger-spelling as 'very rigid, very strict and very complex visually'. Wikström and Bergman (1979) have demonstrated that Swedish finger-spelling, although one-handed, nevertheless constrasts sharply with its American counterpart. The numerous changes in orientation involved in the production of Swedish finger-spelled words give a rather more fluid appearance and these items may be more easily integrated into signed utterances.

The letters of the British two-handed alphabet also share many of the features of sign production. It is even possible to say which Sign Class each letter would fall into. However, it must be stressed that we are not thereby comparing like with like: the letters of the alphabet do not carry lexical meaning. The following comparison is between the form of the individual <u>letters</u> of finger-spelling and the formal properties of the <u>words</u> of BSL.

Only one letter of the British manual alphabet is produced by one hand, namely the letter *c* which is produced by the

British

dominant hand in neutral space (cf Class A1 signs). The items *b* and *w* share some of the features of Class B1, double dez signs, in that both hands perform the same type of motor activity. All the other letters are comparable to either Class B2 or Class B3 signs in that the non-dominant hand is passive. In the production of *f*, *h* and *x* both hands have the same handshape but the dominant hand performs the action. In all the other letters, eg *a*, *k*, *l*, *m*, the non-dominant and the dominant hands have different handshapes. Most of the letters of this group have either the flat palm B or the spread hand 5 as base: two exceptions are *y* which uses the B hand with prominent thumb and *q* which uses the F hand, ie index finger and thumb joined, other fingers spread.

The role of finger-spelling within BSL is somewhat complicated by variation factors. Differences in geographical origin, age and educational background can all influence the extent of finger-spelled usage. In the early part of this century several British schools used finger-spelling as the major medium of communication and therefore many older signers today make considerable use of rapid finger-spelling. The extent to which this finger-spelling is adapted and used within a BSL syntactic system is still under investigation. If we concentrate on the lexical level we can note considerable exploitation of the manual alphabet in the creation of BSL signs. Vocabulary borrowings from English can be modified in such a way that they take on the form and structure of BSL signs.

An intermediate class consists of items which are abbreviated finger-spelled forms. The manual letters are performed in the usual way although certain words may demand repetition of the initial letter. Typical abbreviations are *gf* for "grandfather", *y* articulated twice for "yellow" and *f* articulated twice for "father". Because these forms have common currency within the deaf community they can probably be seen as signs in their own right. It is noticeable that *m + f*, literally "mother father", is sometimes accompanied by the mouthing of the English word "parent": the finger-spelled form is in a sense a translation of the English word. Such forms can be clearly distinguished from one-off shortened forms. These occur when a signer decides to use either the initial letter or an abbreviation of the English word to avoid cumbersome repetition of the complete finger-spelling. Such abbreviations are only understood within the particular context and possibly only after the complete word has been spelled out at least once. This type of usage is idiosyncratic and the resulting forms cannot be regarded as BSL signs.

The most important group of borrowings consists of items which, while retaining some aspects of their alphabetic origins, have been adopted and modified to such an extent that they look like signs rather than English words. Battison (1978) has distinguished a number of phonological processes, such as assimilation and deletion which operate on finger-spelled words so that they eventually take on the features of ASL signs. Many ASL signers may not even be aware of the alphabetic origins of such signs. Knowledge of similar loan-signs in BSL is as yet very limited although there is some evidence for their existence. One of the BSL signs

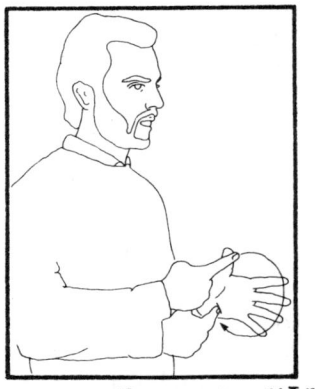

ABOUT /ᵃ5₍₎₁ G_T< ˣ⁺ᵀˣ /

for ABOUT /ᵃ5₍₎₁ G_T< ˣ⁺ᵀˣ / makes use of the 5 hand as the base of the sign: the dominant hand in the form of G (extended index finger) contacts the tip of the thumb of the base hand (*a* of the manual alphabet) then moves in a slight

American

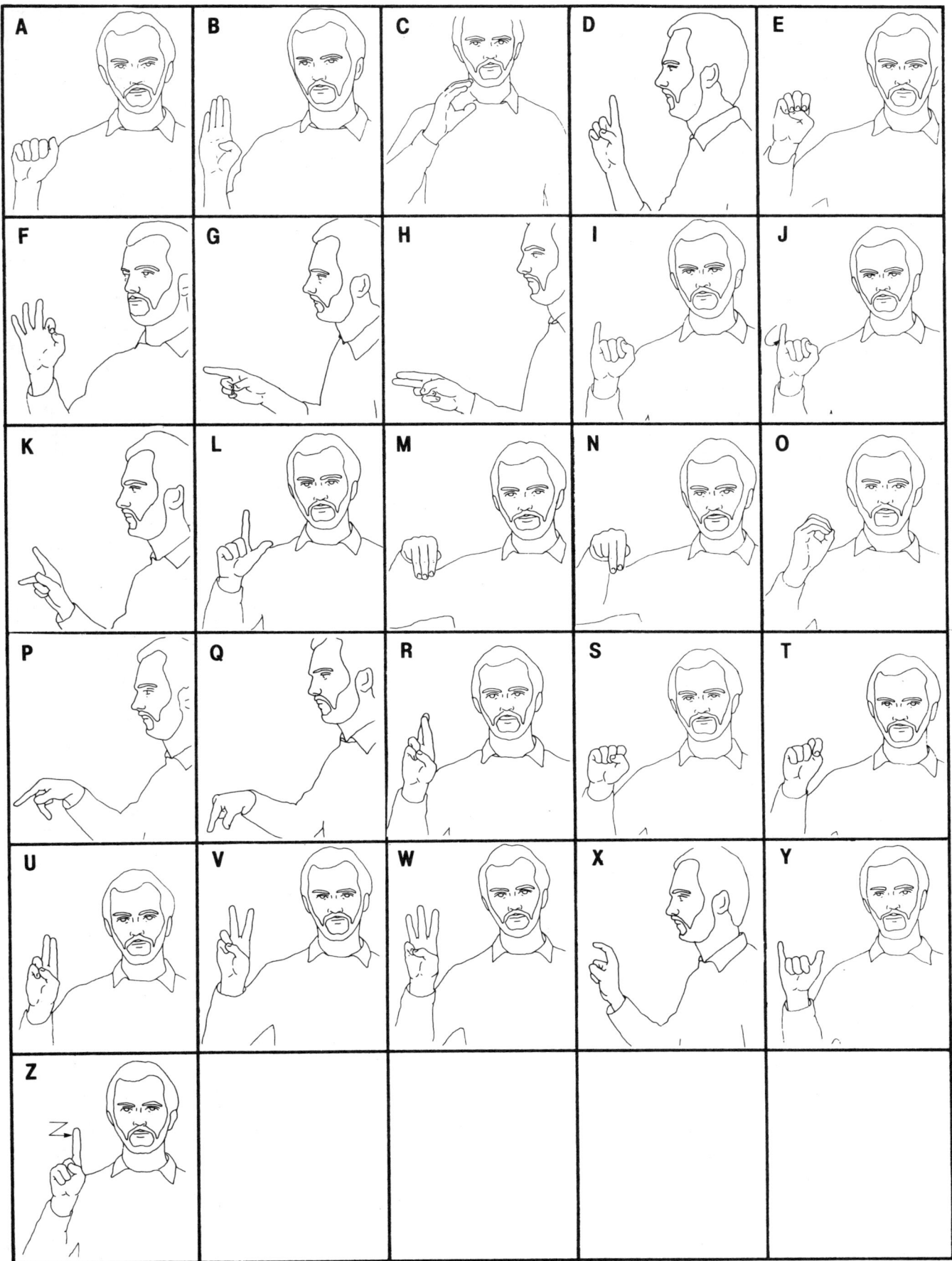

arc to contact the outer edge of the palm in the normal position of the letter t. There has thus been deletion of the medial letters of the finger-spelled word and the resulting form can be viewed as a sign of BSL. It is interesting to note that there are at least two other BSL signs translatable by English "about", eg /B̄ₐ﹥ₓG<⊥ ⁰ₓ̌/ and /∅5ᴅ⊥ ⁰̌/ hence, as Battison noted for ASL, the borrowings may not always indicate a vocabulary gap in the native sign language. One possible motivation for borrowing is to allow greater variation and the use of different signs for specialised purposes. A similar example, derived from one-handed Irish finger-spelling, can be seen in one of the signs for SHOP used by the Catholic deaf community. The hand changes from initial A handshape to fully open 5. Our informants point out that although the final handshape of the finger-spelled p only has three fingers raised, the move from a fully closed handshape to a fully open one is likely to occur over time. Once again the medial letters have been completely lost.

SHOP /∅A₅⊥∧ ⊥[5]·/

A particular type of borrowing can be seen in <u>initial dez signs</u> which have been noted in several languages. These signs use the handshape of the initial letter of the written word but the movements and locations may vary within the normal constraints of sign structure. ASL has many of these signs and their number seems to be increasing through explicit coinages for educational and technical purposes, eg RECORD /Āᴅ﹥ Rᴅ⊥ ˣ~ˣ/ and HORIZONTAL /∅H<⊥ ᐳ/.

Bergman (1977) reports similar examples for SSL and certainly in countries where one-handed alphabets are used, initialised signs are also found. Although the potential for initial dez signs based on the two-handed alphabet may be more limited, such signs do exist. Not unexpectedly, c, the only one-handed letter of the British manual alphabet, is particularly productive: examples include COMMITTEE /⌒C<∧ ⍵·/ in which the dominant hand, in the shape of c, performs a repeated twisting movement at the side of the forehead; COLLEGE /⌒C<∧ ⍵/ in which the hand shaped as the letter c, held at the forehead with palm towards the left, twists so that the palm faces towards the signer. RUBBER /B̄ₐ⊥ G̈ₜ< ᴵ·/ makes use of r in its normal position but with a rubbing movement on the palm; LEATHER /B̄ₐ⊥ Gₜ< ᴵ·/ uses the letter l with a stroking action; QUALIFICATION /∅Fᴅ﹥ ₒ G̈⊥∧ ˇ/ uses the letter q with a definite downward movement of both hands; NAME /⌒Hₜ∧ ˣ⍵/ uses the handshape of the manual letter n but the two fingers contact the forehead then twist outward away from the signer. Explicit 'educational' initial dez signs are becoming increasingly common. Examples include NOUN /B̄ₐ⊥ Hᴅ< ⁰ₓ̌/ in which the letter n is produced in the normal position for WORD /B̄ₐ⊥ Ḡᴅ⊥ ˣ/ using a short movement from the wrist to mid-palm of the non-dominant hand; VERB /B̄ₐ⊥ Vᴅ< ⁰ₓ̌/ produced in exactly the same way but using the handshape of the letter v; THE /∅B﹥∧ₓ Gᴅ< ⁰̌/ the manual t performed with a short downward movement.

LEATHER /B̄ₐ⊥ Gₜ< ᴵ·/   **NOUN** /B̄ₐ⊥ Hᴅ< ⁰ₓ̌/

Irish

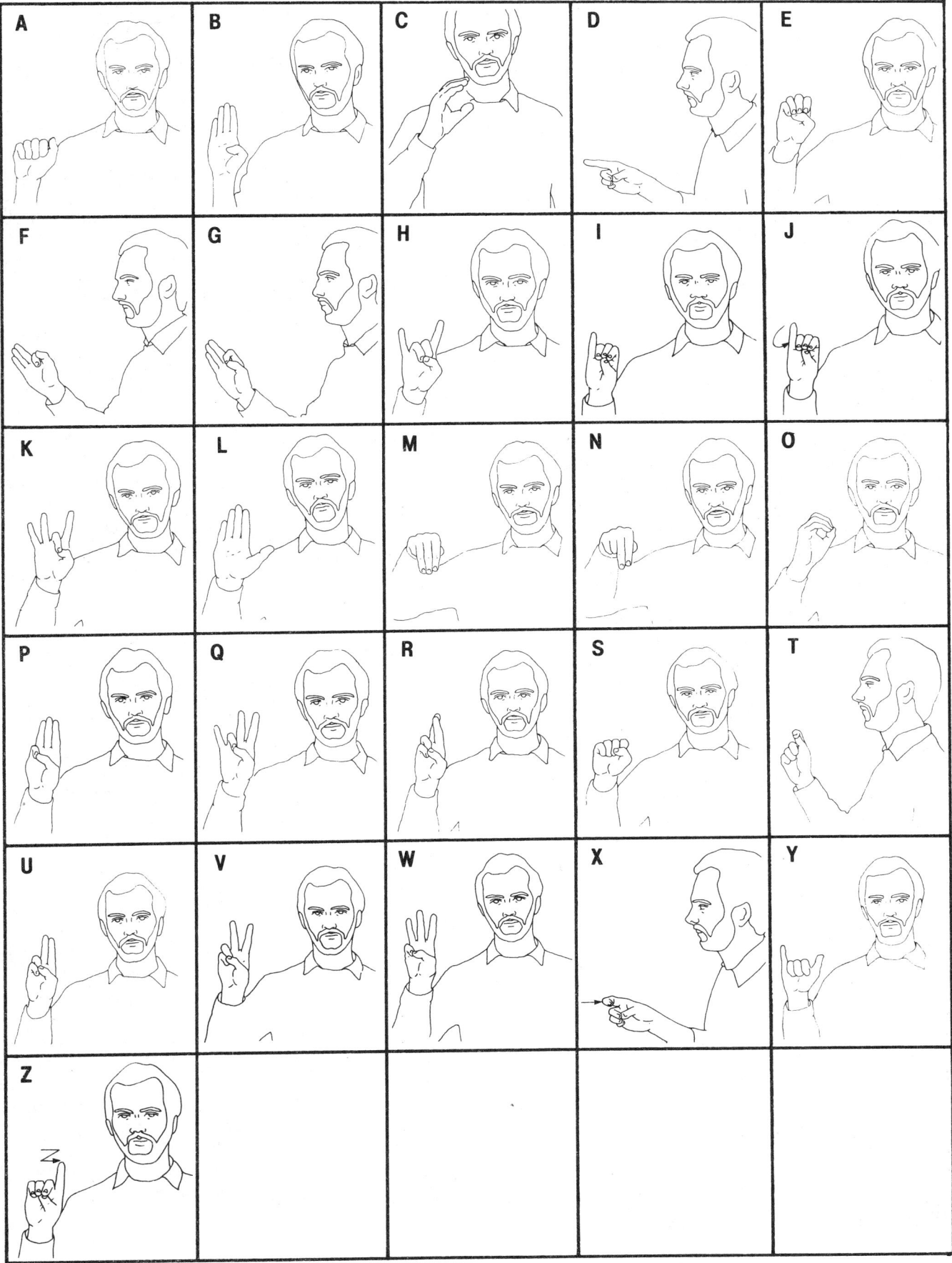

The account of sign structure which is presented in the following chapters includes examples of initial dez signs which are in common use within the deaf community. Examples of coinages which are known to originate outside the deaf community and which are not widely accepted or used by deaf people will be excluded. It is important to stress that all the signs presented here which derive from finger-spelled items can be described in terms of the formational parameters of BSL signs without reference to their alphabetic origins.

One further complicating factor is that a one-handed alphabet is also in use in certain parts of Britain. The Irish one-handed alphabet is used by some signers within Roman Catholic deaf communities in various regions, including the West of Scotland, North East and North West of England and London. While other members of Catholic deaf communities do not themselves use the one-handed alphabet, they may make use of signs which derive from that alphabet. One deaf informant from Glasgow used a number of signs including DAUGHTER /√Gd⊤>≠Gd⊤<~·/ and HELP /∅⊤⊤> ⊤⊤<×·/ which are initial dez signs, yet she herself did not know the Irish alphabet. Such examples are similar to those ASL signs which preserve a forgotten French borrowing: SEARCH FOR in ASL makes use of a C hand, probably because of its derivation from French "chercher" (Stokoe, 1978). Other examples of initial dez signs deriving from the Irish alphabet and in current use are HEAVEN /C⊤⊤> ⊄ ⊤⊤< ⸫/(Irish *h* is ⊤); FOR /F̄>⊥ˌ F<⊥ ˅×/ (Irish *f* is the same as the American *f* but the former has the thumb held across the index finger); GOAL /∅F⊥∧ ⚬̊/(Irish *g* is the same as American *f*) and WORD /⋃W<∧×·/. Further examples will be mentioned in the chapter on dez. Finally, it should be noted that the American one-handed alphabet has recently been used experimentally in some schools. Although there is fairly strong resistance to this practice within the deaf community there may be some limited influence on BSL vocabulary in future years. Some schools have made use of letters of the one-handed alphabet to represent English grammatical inflections, but these artificial adaptations are used only for the coding of manual English and are not part of BSL.

Iconicity

The analysis of sign structure so far presented may be somewhat at variance with the general approach taken by non-signers to the individual words of sign languages. Klima and Bellugi (1979, p9) suggest that:

> *"on viewing signs (particularly for objects that one can point to) the naive observer typically focuses on how their overall visual form is related to their meaning. The form of many signs appears to be strikingly appropriate for what it designates."*

So far we have looked at the formational properties of sign production as though they are entirely <u>arbitrary</u>, without any necessary link between form and meaning. However, this is to ignore one pervading aspect of all sign languages so far studied, namely <u>iconicity</u>.

One of the comments frequently made by critics of sign languages is that signs are merely 'pictorial gestures'. The implication here is that using gestures to provide a picture of what is being referred to is a rather unsatisfactory hit and miss substitute for 'real' language. Certainly such critics are

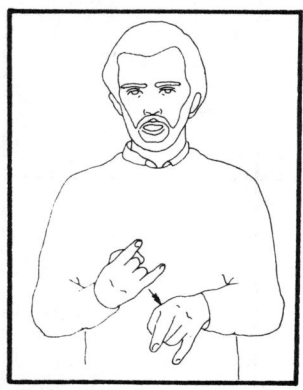
HELP /∅⊤⊤> ⊤⊤<×·/

FOR /F̄>⊥ˌ F<⊥ ˅×/

right to suggest that if we rely entirely on non-conventionalised gesture or mime to represent ideas, objects or persons, we will be very much dependent upon the individual's talent for such representation. The results will be completely idiosyncratic: one person's gestural representation of "shop" may be quite different from another person's. One individual may indicate the activity of exchanging money for goods, another a window display, another shelves packed with goods. Such mimed or gestured presentations are essentially unstable. They may vary from person to person and change according to how they are perceived and interpreted by the other participants in the communication. However, the words, the lexical items of BSL are stable. Signers can note errors made by sign language learners and correct these errors by demonstrating the typically accepted forms of the sign. The signs of BSL are gestures, but they are conventionalised gestures which conform to certain specific rules of patterning.

The distinction between mimetic gestures and conventional signs is an important one but it still leaves open the question of iconicity. Can we assume that the stable conventional signs of BSL are purely arbitrary and non-iconic? All the evidence suggests that the answer is "no". Even conventional signs can incorporate features which are particularly appropriate for what they represent. Rather than thinking of a simple contrast between arbitrary and iconic signs, we must recognise degrees and types of iconicity.

Some signs, such as MAN /⌣B̄₁₍ ˣ¥[ȃ]/ SLEEP /ʊG̣>⋏ G̣<⋏ #[ĜĜ]/ and WALK /∅B₀⊥,B₀⊥ ⸚~/ in BSL, are so obviously iconic that their meaning is easily apparent to a non-signer: these are categorised as <u>transparent</u> signs. Experiments conducted by American researchers (Klima and Bellugi, 1979) suggest that there are relatively few transparent signs in ASL. A larger group consists of items which Klima and Bellugi class as <u>translucent</u>: the meanings of such signs are not immediately apparent, but once non-signers know the meaning they can recognise some links between form and meaning. Examples from ASL include "the soft cheek of a girl" for GIRL and "placing a stamp" for LETTER. Similar descriptions would also be appropriate for the BSL signs GIRL /ƷG⊥⋏ ⸚/ and LETTER /⌣À<⋏ˣ//B̄ₐ> À₀⊥ᵛˣ/ although the structural properties of the signs are not identical in both languages. ASL uses the closed fist handshape À in the sign GIRL and contact is made with the thumb, whereas BSL uses the G handshape, and contact is made with the extended index finger.

The types of relation which may hold between the form of a sign and the idea, object or person to which it refers (the referent) are complex and varied. Although a full discussion of these types is outside the scope of this study, it may be useful to mention some of the more obvious classifications. Some signs are <u>deictic</u> in that the signer simply points to the referent. Deictic signs include the BSL pronouns and signs for parts of the body, eg NOSE /⌒G₁⋏ˣ/, MOUTH /⌣G₁⋏ˣ/, EAR /⊃G<⋏ˣ/.

MAN /⌣B̄₁₍ ˣ¥[ȃ]/   LETTER /⌣À<⋏ˣ//B̄ₐ> À₀⊥ᵛˣ/   NOSE /⌒G₁⋏ˣ/   EAR /⊃G<⋏ˣ/

As there is no attempt to incorporate the visual features of the nose, mouth or ear in the form of the sign, these signs form a special group.

HOUSE /ØB_{DΛ}×B_{DΛ} ÷ᵛ/

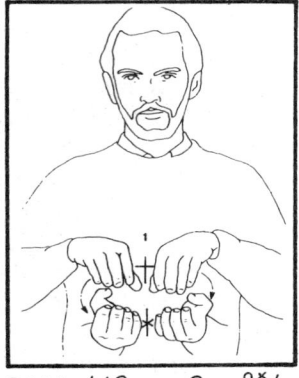

BALL /ØC_{DꞱ}ɪ×C_{DꞱ} ᵃˣ/

Some iconic signs show a <u>direct</u> link between form and meaning: the sign BALL /ØC_{DꞱ}ɪ×C_{DꞱ} ᵃˣ/ indicates the actual shape of a ball; HOUSE /ØB_{DΛ}×B_{DΛ} ÷ᵛ/ is produced by drawing the shape of a house in space. Of course, even here the shape is not necessarily a correct visual representation of any particular house; it is a stylised adaptation which employs handshapes already in use in BSL vocabulary.

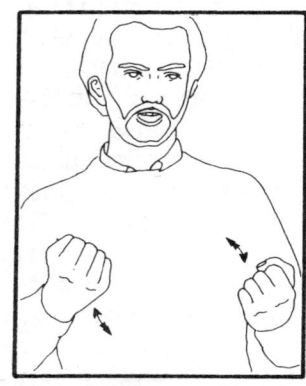

CAR /ØA_{T>} A_{T<} ~~·/

BIRD /ᴜG̈_{ꞱΛ} #[Ĝ]·/

In other signs there is an <u>indirect</u> relationship between the form and the referent. The steering wheel, or more accurately the driver's grasp of the steering wheel, is used as the base for the BSL sign CAR /ØA_{T>} A_{T<} ~~·/ BIRD /ᴜG̈_{ꞱΛ} #[Ĝ]·/ is signed by the thumb and index finger performing an opening and closing action at the side of the mouth. These signs use typical features of the referent to refer to the whole object;

'wheel' for 'car', 'beak' for 'bird'. It is important to note that the handshapes, positions and movements occurring in such signs are also used in other types of signs including non-iconic signs.

NICE /ᴜȦ_{T<} ˣ̌/

RIGHT /[ ]Ȧ_{T<} ˣ/

If we examine the major parameters of sign structure we can see different ways in which the links between form and meaning can be conventionalised within the language. The Ȧ dez (closed fist with prominent thumb) is sometimes referred to as the 'good' hand since this handshape occurs in meanings which appear to have good or pleasant connotations. A similar non-linguistic gesture also occurs in some hearing cultures, but it is important to note that the link between the handshape and the general meaning is culture specific, rather than universal. As used within the linguistic system of BSL, this handshape ocurs in NICE /ᴜȦ_{T<} ˣ̌/ and RIGHT /[ ]Ȧ_{T<} ˣ/ . However, other signs which make use of the same handshape do not have the same semantic connotations: obvious examples include CHEAT /ɜȦ_{<Λ} ˣ̌/ and DIFFICULT /B_{>Ʇ}ɪ×Ȧ_{DꞱ} ˢ̌/ .

CHEAT /ɜȦ_{<Λ} ˣ̌/

DIFFICULT /B_{>Ʇ}ɪ×Ȧ_{DꞱ} ˢ̌/

The so-called 'bad' hand, in which the little finger is extended from the closed fist (I dez) certainly appears in many BSL signs which have some semantic link with bad, for example SUSPICIOUS /⌒I̲ᴛ∧ ⁸⸝/ and ILL /[ ]Ï_a˃ Ï_a˂ ˣ/ .

SUSPICIOUS /⌒I̲ᴛ∧ ⁸⸝/

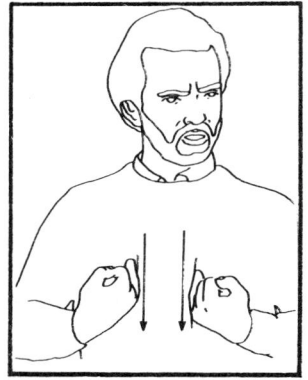
ILL /[ ]Ï_a˃ Ï_a˂ ˣ/

There seem to be very few examples of BSL signs in which this handshape is 'neutralised', except in LAST /I̲ᴛ˃ˏI̲˂⊥ ˆ⸝/, (both hands have the I dez), and in END /I̲ᴛ˃ B˂⊥ ᵛˣ/, (only the passive non-dominant hand has the I handshape).

Many other signs in BSL make use of handshapes which are iconically appropriate. The Y dez (thumb and little finger extended from the closed fist) is used to depict particular features of the referent in AEROPLANE /∅Υ_ᴅ⊥ ˆ/ , TEAPOT /∅Υ_ᴛ∧ ?/ and TELEPHONE /ᴈΥ_ᴛ˂ ˣ/ , but the same handshape is used in a non-iconic way in EMPLOYER /[ ]Υ_ᴅ˃ Υ_ᴅ˂ ˣ/ and PARTY /∅Υ˃∧ Υ˂∧ ω̂/ .

The importance of movement can also be seen in the difference between AEROPLANE and TEAPOT. AEROPLANE uses the Y handshape and an upward movement away from the signer's body to depict the flying action of the aeroplane, while in TEAPOT the Y hand is held with palm facing the body and the nodding action of the wrist depicts the pouring action. Thus realisations of the sig parameter can also have iconic significance.

The tab parameter appears to be particularly important in expressing links between form and meaning, but it is clear that many such links are indirect. Signs produced on the forehead frequently relate to thinking and knowledge presumably because of the location of the brain. The positioning of signs related to feelings on the chest may exploit the traditonal link between the heart and affection: such a link is, of course, culture specific. Signs related to the particular senses, eg sight, hearing and smell are located in the region of the appropriate sensory features, eyes, ears and nose. Sometimes slight distinctions in positioning are only important for conventional reasons, eg the sign DELICIOUS /⌒⌐ B_ᴛ˂ ⁸⸝/ is located in the stomach area.

Throughout the discussion of particular examples, reference will be made to iconic and non-iconic signs, although there will be no attempt to provide detailed accounts of the different types of iconicity. To ignore iconicity completely, would be to ignore an important difference between spoken and sign languages. However, because the iconic features of signs have been modified to fit the conventional patterning of the linguistic systems, it is still possible to describe sign structure in terms of the parameters already established. Certainly new signs frequently appear to exploit the visual possibilities in signing, and yet conform fairly quickly to existing patterns. Two sign creations by children may illustrate this point. One school child recently referred to one of British Rail's high-speed passenger trains by producing a sign located in front of the nose and using a B̿ hand, moving in a fast outward movement and

TELEPHONE /ᴈΥ_ᴛ˂ ˣ/

125 /⌒B̿˂∧ ≠[â]/

closing to a B̂ hand, /⌒B̄̂<∧ #[ê]/. This sign incorporated the special feature of such trains which have a wedge-shaped engine front section and travel up to 125 mph. Another creation in use in some schools is the sign for the American television phenomenon, "Wonder Woman". This sign has been noted in two forms: both exploit the action and movement used in the series where the main character places her outstretched hands in front of her, palms down and spins around to bring about her transformation. In one school the whole action is used, but in another school this action has been trimmed down so that the result is more like a typical BSL sign: the two B hands are placed palm down at one side of the body then moved in a quick action to the other side of the body /ØB_D> B_D> </. It is not suggested that these signs will necessarily become part of BSL vocabulary but simply that new signs can both exploit iconic possibilities and yet conform to the typical parameters of BSL production.

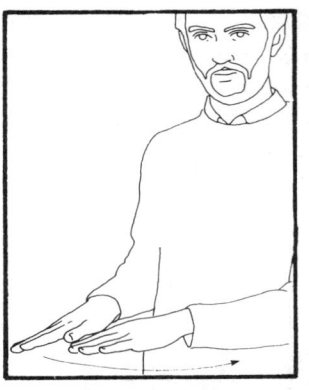
WONDER WOMAN

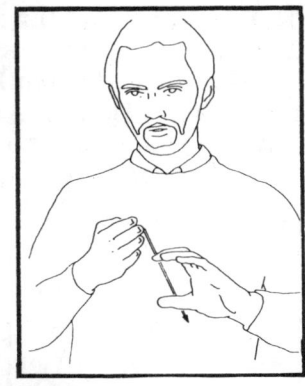
S.H.S.

The Sympathetic Hearing Scheme

More recent examples, noted during the preparation of this second edition of <u>Words in Hand</u> include signs for SHUTTLE (ie American space shuttle) /ØG>∧ ıx Y<∧ ^÷/ and SYMPATHETIC HEARING SCHEME /C̄>∧ B<⊥ ρ ˇ/. The latter is a scheme adopted by shops, businesses, airports and the like to inform deaf people that there are personnel available who can communicate with deaf people. The scheme uses the logo illustrated here, ie an ear with a discontinuous diagonal line and the sign used within the deaf community exploits the iconic elements of the logo while using handshapes already used in BSL. By combining iconic and arbitrary features in such ways, BSL is able to maintain itself as an efficient and productive system.

CHAPTER TWO

The Notation System

Glosses

There is a great danger that hearing researchers, analysing the nature of individual sign languages, will be misled by assumptions and preconceptions which are based on their knowledge of spoken languages. This danger is increased by the fact that spoken language glosses or literal word for word translations are frequently used in discussions of sign structure. Such glosses can be helpful but also distorting in that they leave out much of the essential information encoded within the signed utterance. The notions of 'spatiality' and 'simultaneity' suggest that such factors as where the sign occurs in space, its relation to other manual or non-manual signs occurring at the same time, and systematic changes in its base form, may all be relevant to an adequate interpretation of the signed utterance. No gloss which consists merely of English words in a particular order can possibly do justice to such complex and spatially-oriented patterning.

Stokoe Notation System

Since 1960 a more objective way of writing down the individual signs of ASL has been available. In Sign Language Structure (1960), William Stokoe provided a transcription method which was itself based upon his analysis of individual sign structure into the three major aspects of tab, dez and sig. The Stokoe Notation System (SNS) makes use of a set of symbols representing the significant positions, handshapes and movements of ASL and establishes conventions for using these symbols for writing ASL signs. The system is phonemic rather than phonetic in that no attempt is made to provide a method of describing all the fine, but linguistically non-significant, variations in the production of a single sign. As Stokoe has suggested (Stokoe, 1978, p83), a microanalytical examination of each sign's production may be useful but a clear distinction must be made between visible phenomena and significant linguistic contrasts. As in phonemic transcription systems for spoken language, the researcher presents an idealised version of the data: but the degree of idealisation and the level of abstraction are clearly recognised by those using the system.

Phonemic transcriptions of the English words "kit" /kit/ and "cot" /kɒt/ will ignore the phonetic difference in the point of contact between the tongue and the soft palate for the initial consonant: in the first example, contact will normally be on the forward part of the soft palate, in the second case contact will be further back. No explicit information is given as to the presence or absence of aspiration in the production of the stop consonants. It would be quite possible to provide such information, together with precise detail of variations in the production of these words in given instances. Additional symbols and diacritics can be added to produce a detailed phonetic transcription. While such phonetic transcriptions can be useful for specific purposes, it is important to recognise that linguistic contrasts may be obscured in the wealth of phonetic detail.

Supplementary diacritics and symbols can also allow the SNS to be used for the description of phonetic details. The system is particularly useful in allowing a quick and easy representation of changes in position, movement and direction of the 'base' forms of signs. As long as clear conventions are established and adhered to, the development and extension of the SNS for phonetic purposes should be quite feasible. However, the system as it exists is primarily a method for describing the individual manual signs of ASL in isolation. A full notation system for ASL utterances would necessarily include methods for transcribing the activities of the other articulators, including the eyes, mouth, face, shoulders and body. Ways of recording and notating signed utterances as opposed to individual signs are as yet in the early stages of development and none has acquired the universal status of the SNS.

Range of Notation Systems

Charlotte Baker at Gallaudet College, Washington DC, has made use of the Facial Action Coding System (FACS), developed by Paul Ekman and Wallace Friesen, for the analysis of facial expression in ASL. FACS is clearly phonetic in that the person coding the facial actions does not take the meaning of these movements into account. Moreover, the system of facial measurement is based on the anatomical analysis of facial action. The analysis is comprehensive in that the originators claim that it is capable of describing all possible visually distinguishable facial movements. It may be possible to use the FACS system as an aid to describing linguistic contrasts expressed through facial expression. Several other researchers including Bergman (1982), Vogt-Svendsen (1983), Lawson (1983) and the Edinburgh BSL Project (forthcoming) are developing categories and/or notation devices for non-manual behaviour. Our system uses the symbols of the SNS within a facial circle and thus exploits those similarities of movement which exist between manual and non-manual elements. One system which takes account of both manual and non-manual gesture is the Eshkol-Wachmann Movement Notation System which is used in A New Dictionary of Sign Language by Cohen, Namir and Schlesinger. The authors claim that with this system it is possible to provide a faithful reproduction and analysis of any sign and any bodily movement. As the system is primarily kinetic in that it is concerned with the physical properties of signing, it could be used as the basis for developing a linguistic description. However, the system is highly complex and if care is not taken such wealth of detail could confuse rather than clarify.

Transcribing BSL

As outlined in Coding British Sign Language, the first major issue which concerned researchers beginning the linguistic analysis of BSL was whether any of the existing transcription systems could be modified for use with BSL. The SNS seemed the most likely possibility, but it was not an automatic choice. As the SNS was developed specifically for the analysis of ASL, there was no guarantee that it would contain symbols appropriate to BSL sign structure. We cannot assume that the significant phonemes of the two languages are identical. In fact, as the following chapters will show, there are more similarities than differences and although BSL has phonemic contrasts which do not occur in ASL, and vice versa, the modifications have been relatively easy to make. A recognition that BSL and ASL make use of many of the same phonemes does not in any way imply that the signs of BSL and ASL are identical. The particular ways in which these aspects are combined and the links made between forms and meanings are noticeably different for each language.

Another reason for hesitating about the use of the SNS for transcribing BSL signs, is that the dez symbols are based on the letters of the American one-handed alphabet. Many of the handshapes which are significant in ASL are similar to the handshapes used in the manual alphabet, therefore it is quite easy for those familiar with this alphabet to memorise the names and the symbols for the handshapes. In Britian a two-handed alphabet is used and relatively few people are familiar with the American manual alphabet. However, the task of learning the one-handed alphabet, and through this the symbols for many of the significant handshapes of BSL, is a relatively easy one. As contact between various signing communities increases, at international conferences and the like, familiarity with different alphabets and different sign systems is increasing. We are already seeing borrowings into BSL of signs from several sign languages. As such contacts develop, the problem of using an alien alphabet as the source of notation symbols is likely to diminish. Moreover, there are considerable advantages in using a notation system which is accepted in other countries. Easy comparison between sign languages is allowed and reseachers in different parts of the world can have direct access to precise information about the structure of individual signs.

Transcription Conventions

In the chapters which follow detailed information on the significant contrasts and appropriate symbols within the tab, dez, ori and sig parameters will be presented. The rest of this chapter aims to provide some account of the conventions for notating signs. The conventions include the order in which the symbols are produced, the placing of subscripts and superscripts, and the use of special marks, or diacritics. It is hoped that the following sections will allow readers who are quite unfamiliar with the SNS to make some attempt at deciphering the transcriptions. The basic formula for sign transcription presented by Stokoe is:

$T\ D^s$ which can be read as $TAB\ DEZ^{sig}$

According to this formula, in transcribing any sign we first indicate the position of the sign, the tab: the second symbol indicates the handshape used and the third symbol, which is written as a superscript, indicates the types of movement produced. As signs are characterised by simultaneous production of the significant aspects, the order of the symbols is arbitrary but conventional. The major change made to the basic formula within this account is the addition of subscripts to represent palm and finger orientation. <u>A Dictionary of American Sign Language</u> (Stokoe, et al, revised edition 1976) provides information on orientation for many, though not all, ASL signs. Although Stokoe has suggested that "the dez as what acts is recognised both by its configuration and by its attitude (sometimes called orientation or direction)", he rejects the suggestion that orientation should be regarded as a separate parameter. However, as such orientation information is here regarded as essential for a descriptively adequate analysis of BSL signs, the original formula is revised to:

$T\ D_{o\ o}^{\ \ s}$ which can be read as:

$TAB\ DEZ_{palm\ ori\ finger\ ori}^{\ \ \ \ sig}$

The convention thus established is that information on the orientation of the palm will be given before information on finger orientation. This formula can be amended for two-handed signs. In double dez signs, where both hands are active, the formula is:

$T\ D_{o\ o}\ D_{o\ o}^{\ \ s}$ which can be read as:

$TAB\ DEZ_{ori\ ori}\ DEZ_{ori\ ori}^{\ \ \ \ sig}$

In hand tab signs, where the non-dominant hand acts as tab, the formula is:

$T_{o\ o}\ D_{o\ o}^{\ \ s}$ which can be read as:

$TAB_{ori\ ori}\ DEZ_{ori\ ori}^{\ \ \ \ sig}$

Although in this last example the non-dominant hand is acting as tab, information on the orientation of the hand is still essential.

Orientation

The chapter on orientation will provide full details on the choices of palm and finger ori which are available. At this stage it may be useful to mention several guidelines to the interpretation of ori symbols, given the wide range of handshapes and positions used within signs.

If the exact orientation of the palm is in doubt, a decision should be made by examining the position of the wrist. The convention here established is that wrist orientation always takes precedence and the palm ori symbol should always accord with the orientation of the wrist. In the majority of cases there is no problem in deciding on palm direction. However, in some signs a difficulty of interpretation arises. In a sign such as I, we have to decide whether the palm should be regarded as facing the right, facing the signer or at an angle facing both signer and right. In this case, palm ori is towards signer.

The orientation of the wrist should be seen as decisive in all similar cases. It may seem that the logical step would be to rename palm ori, wrist ori. But, in order to be consistent with accepted usage within sign language research, the original name has been retained.

The symbols for finger orientation may also cause some difficulty. If the finger ori is ∧:up, how does one interpret this for such differing handshapes as G:extended index finger, A:closed hand and F:thumb and index finger touching, other fingers extended? The basic rules are:

1. The direction of the four fingers takes precedence over the thumb.

2. In closed or bent handshapes, finger ori is the direction of the fingers when straightened.

Discussion and further clarification of these rules can be found in Chapter 5. While these conventions may seem somewhat complex, they do minimise the amount of special information required to interpret finger ori in particular handshapes. The following examples may clarify how the finger ori symbols are used. In the sign KNOW /∩À<∧ ˣ/ the finger ori for the right hand is given as pointing up (∧). The handshape is A with a prominent thumb, so in order to decide on finger ori, the fingers must be straightened. In the sign KING /∩̄5̈ᴅ< ᵛˣ/ the finger ori for the right hand is given as pointing to the left (<). The handshape is a bent 5, so in order to decide on finger ori the fingers must be straightened.

Sig Symbols

Where several sig symbols occur in one sign transcription, the exact positioning of the superscripts should

I /[ ]G̈T< ˣ/

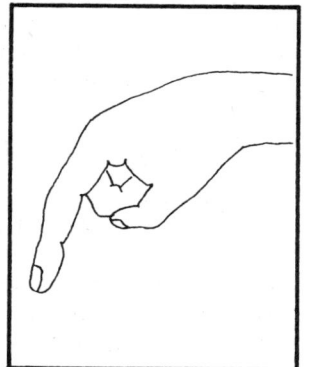

I (Signer's viewpoint)

KNOW /∩À<∧ ˣ/

KING /∩̄5̈ᴅ< ᵛˣ/

be carefully noted. If the symbols are positioned at the same level, one after the other, this suggests that the movements are made in sequence. In ELEPHANT /⌐C₍∧ ⌣ᵛ⌣/ the C hand, with palm to the left and fingers (when straightened) pointing up, is held at the nose. The first sig symbols (⌣) indicate that the hand moves from fingers pointing up to fingers pointing forward by the twisting of the wrist. The second sig symbol (ᵛ) indicates that the hand moves downward and the final sig symbols (⌣) indicate that the hand then turns outward. If the sig symbols are placed at two different levels, one above the other, this indicates that the movements take place simultaneously. In THANK YOU /⌒B_T∧ ⌄/ the B hand simultaneously moves away and down from the signer's mouth. As well as actual movements the sig symbols may indicate particular types of action, such as bending (η) or wriggling (ℛ); or interaction, such as approaching (⋈), separating (÷), entering (⊙) and grasping (ℤ). (cf Chapter 6).

the handshape is the G dez, ie closed fist with extended index finger	G
the G hand is held with palm facing the signer, so the palm ori is toward the signer	T
the G hand is held with index finger pointing up, so the finger ori is up	∧
the index finger touches a point just below the eye so there is actual contact which must be indicated by a symbol in sig position	×
after contact, the G hand moves outward, so a second aspect of sig is movement away from the signer	⊥

The basic formula can be amended and added to according to the type of sign and the complexity of movements and interactions involved. The easiest way to illustrate the varying kinds of

ELEPHANT /⌐C₍∧ ⌣ᵛ⌣/

THANK YOU /⌒B_T∧ ⌄/

SEE /⊔G_T∧ ×⊥/

Illustrative Examples

We can now look at a typical transcription of a BSL sign and note the order and choice of notation symbols. Details of the symbols can be found in the following chapters and a summary of these symbols is provided separately at the end of the book. The transcription for the BSL sign SEE /⊔G_T∧ ×⊥/, can be read as follows:

    the position is the eye tab   ⊔

transcription is to examine in more detail examples of the sign classes presented in Chapter 1. In examining these transcriptions, several general factors must be borne in mind. Firstly, it is assumed that in one-handed signs, the dominant hand will perform the sign. For right-handed signers the dominant hand will be the right hand, for left-handed signers, the left hand. For simplicity, the notation for right-hand dominant signers is given. In two-handed signs, in which one hand acts as tab

(Classes B2 and B3), the transcriptions are written as though it is the left hand which is tab, although for left-handed signers the right hand may act as tab. In double dez signs (Class B1) the first dez symbol indicates the left hand, the second dez symbol indicates the right hand.

YOUR /∅A⊥∧ ⊥/

HAVE /∅5ₐ⊥ #[A]/

CHEAT /3Ȧ<∧ ˇ/

FORGET /⌒O┬∧ ˣ□[5]/

The simplest type of signs are one-handed signs which do not involve contact (Class A1). Many of these signs occur in neutral space, indicated by the tab symbol ∅. YOUR /∅A⊥∧ ⊥/ is produced in neutral space: the A hand is held with palm away from signer and fingers pointing up; the hand moves outward away from signer. More complex Class A1 signs are those which involve changes of handshape: HAVE /∅5ₐ⊥ #[A]/ is produced in neutral space. The 5 hand is held with palm up and fingers pointing forward. The hand moves down and closes to an A hand. The symbol # indicates the closing action while the final handshape is shown in brackets.

Class A2 signs involve contact with the tab. CHEAT /3Ȧ<∧ ˇ/ is produced with contact between the thumb of the Ȧ hand and the signer's right cheek, with the palm pointing left and the fingers pointing upwards. The hand moves down the right cheek, thumb maintaining contact the whole time: this is shown in the transcription by the placing of the sig symbols one below the other. FORGET /⌒O┬∧ ˣ□[5]/ is a more complex sign involving change of handshape. The O hand with palm facing the signer and fingers pointing up touches the forehead. The hand moves away from signer (⊥) and opens (□) to a 5 hand ([5]).

In Class B signs the fact that two hands are involved almost inevitably means that there is a greater degree of complexity in structure and transcription. However, Class B1, double dez signs, show a symmetry which facilitates description. Double dez signs can be distinguished from B2 and B3 signs in which the non-dominant hand

AGREE /∅Ȧ>⊥ Ȧ<⊥ ˣ/

QUICK /Ḡ┬> G<⊥ ˇˣ∧̇/

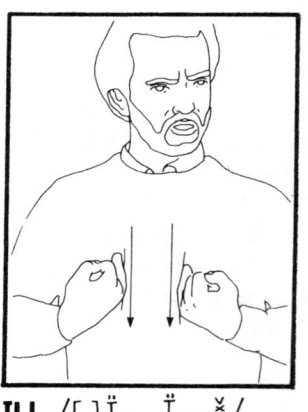

ILL /[ ]Ïₐ> Ïₐ< ˣ/

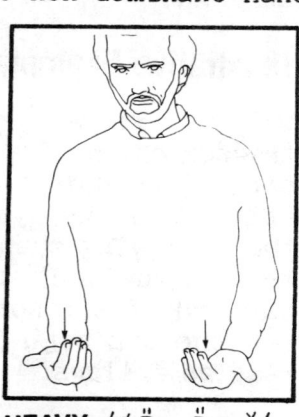

HEAVY /∅B̈ₐ⊥ B̈ₐ⊥ ˇ/

COW /⌒Y̧⊥⋏ Y⊥⋏ ˣ⇡/

COFFEE /Ā_T>ˣA_T< ᵉ⸝ₓ/

TRUE /B̄ₐ> B<⊥ ᵛˣ/

DIFFICULT /B>⊥ ıₓ Ȧᴅ⊥ ˣ⸝/

acts as tab: the former will have a separate tab symbol, for example, the neutral space symbol; the latter will have two symbols from the dez list, but the first of these will act as tab. In AGREE /⌀Ȧ>⊥ı Ȧ<⊥ ˣ/, a double dez sign, the tab symbol comes first, followed by a dez symbol and ori symbols to represent the activity of the left hand and a dez symbol and ori symbols to represent the activity of the right hand. The sig symbol indicates the movement of both hands. In QUICK /Ḡ_T> G<⊥ ˇˣ˄/ the first symbol, which can be recognised as a dez symbol, actually indicates that the non-dominant hand is acting as the tab, the place where the dominant hand acts. The choice of symbol will indicate the particular handshape adopted by the non-dominant hand as tab. As other tab symbols are quite different from hand tab symbols it is quite easy to recognise the specific type of two-handed sign which is being transcribed. If a tab symbol, such as [ ], ⌀, ⌒, occurs at the beginning of a transcription which also includes two dez symbols of the same size at the same level, then the example is a double dez sign, eg ILL /[ ]Ï_a> Ï_a< ˣ/ (B1); HEAVY /⌀B̈_a⊥ B̈_a⊥ ˇ/ (B1); COW /⌒Y⊥⋏ Y⊥⋏ ˣ⇡/ (B1). If no separate tab symbol occurs, then the first symbol must be taken as representing the shape of the non-dominant hand acting as tab, eg COFFEE /Ā_T>ˣA_T< ᵉ⸝ₓ/ (B2); TRUE /B̄ₐ> B<⊥ ᵛˣ/ (B2); DIFFICULT /B>⊥ıₓ Ȧᴅ⊥ ˣ⸝/ (B3).

Hand Arrangement

In two-handed signs there are various choices as to the exact relation of one hand to the other. Special diacritics indicate the possible relationships:

the hands may be held side by side, relatively close together	A ı A
one hand may be held above the other - here the left hand is held above the right	A̲ A
here the right hand is held above the left, ie the left hand is below the right	Ā A
one hand may be held behind the other	A ҩ A
one hand may be held in contact with the other	A ₓ A

In some signs the left hand is behind the right, and in others the right hand behind the left: the symbol ҩ is placed after the handshape which is behind. If the left hand is behind, as in MORE /B_T> ҩₓ B_T< ⊥/, the symbol ҩ comes after the left hand acting as tab. If the right hand comes behind the left, as in FOLLOW /⌀G_ᴅ⊥ ₓ G_ᴅ⊥ ҩ⊥/, then the symbol is placed after the right hand which is here represented by the second dez symbol.

To enable continuity to be maintained, those symbols which are specifically used for showing the relation of one hand to the other have been written as subscripts, ie at the same level as the orientation symbols. This indicates the close relationship between orientation, which shows the relationship between the hands to the body, and hand arrangement, which shows the relationship of one hand to the other. If the hand arrangement can be predicted from the realisations of the other parameters, then no symbol is used. The revised formulae would therefore be: (a) for double dez signs:

$$\text{TAB DEZ}_{\text{ori ori (ha)}} \, {}^{\text{DEZ}}\text{ori ori}^{\text{sig}}$$

and (b) for hand tab signs:

$$\text{TAB}_{\text{ori ori (ha)}} \, {}^{\text{Dez}}\text{ori ori}^{\text{sig}}$$

Apart from the diacritics previously mentioned the following symbols are also used to indicate the relation of one hand to the other: linking ($\mathcal{x}$), entering ($\odot$) and crossing ($+$). Examples of signs using the symbols and diacritics mentioned above are:

FOLLOW

FOLLOW /∅G⊐⊥×G⊐⊥ρ⊥/ Two G hands, palms facing down and fingers pointing away from the signer, held in neutral space. The right hand is held behind the left with the tip of the right index finger touching the back of the left hand. Both hands move forward in neutral space maintaining contact.

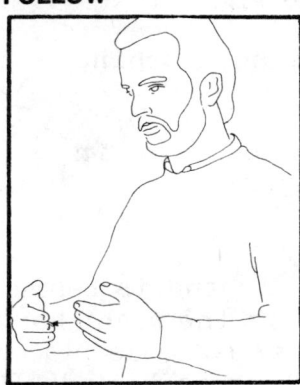

MORE

MORE /B⊤>ρ×B⊤<⊥/ Manual B tab is held with palm facing the signer and fingers pointing right. Right B hand, palm facing the signer and fingers pointing left. The left hand is held behind the right, touching. The right hand then moves away from the signer.

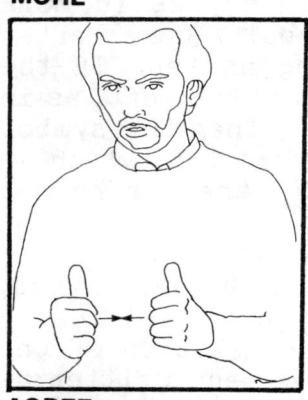

AGREE

AGREE /∅Ȧ>⊥₁Ȧ<⊥ˣ/ Two Ȧ hands: left hand, palm facing right and fingers pointing away from the signer; right hand, palm facing left and fingers pointing away from the signer. Hands held close together in neutral space. Hands come together and touch.

33

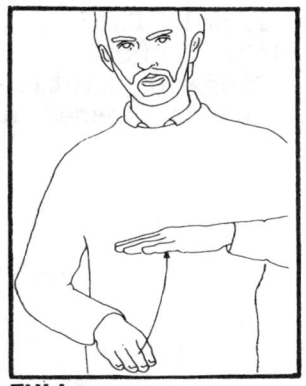
FULL

FULL /B̠ᵦ₌ Bᵦ₌ ^ˣ/

Manual tab B is held with palm facing down and fingers pointing right. Right B hand, palm facing down and fingers pointing away from the signer. Left hand held above right. Right hand moves up and makes contact with the fingers of the left hand.

UMBRELLA

UMBRELLA /Āᴛ>ₓAᴛ< ᵒˣ/

Manual tab A is held with palm facing the signer and fingers pointing right. Right A hand, palm facing the signer and fingers pointing left. Right hand held above left, touching. Right hand moves up in a short sharp movement.

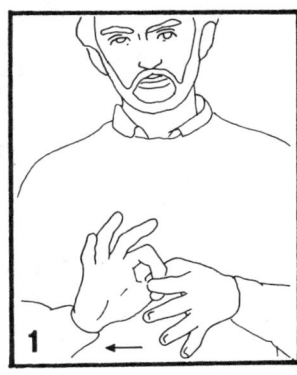 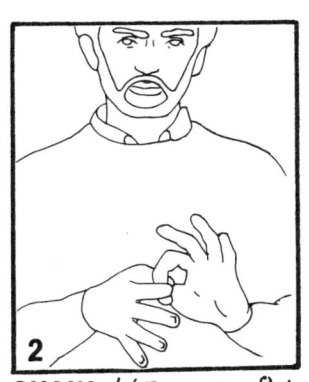

CHAIN

Two F hands: left hand, palm facing right and fingers pointing away from the signer; right hand, palm facing left and fingers pointing up. Hands are held in neutral space with index finger and thumb circles linking. Hands interchange to the right.

CHAIN /∅F>⊥ₓ F<∧ ᵒ/

EMPTY

EMPTY /Ō>⊥⊙G̈ᵦ₌ ˣ/

Manual tab O is held with palm facing right and fingers pointing away from the signer. Right G̈ hand, palm facing down and finger pointing away from the signer. Index finger of right hand is placed within circle of left hand. Index finger makes a circular motion, maintaining contact.

34

PRISON

PRISON /∅A_{α>}≠A_{bɪ}[∅]/ Two A hands: left hand, palm facing up and fingers pointing right; right hand, palm facing down and fingers pointing away from the signer. Hands crossed at wrists.

CHAPTER THREE

Tabulation

The Signing Space

All signs are produced in particular positions either on or in relation to the signer's body. In miming, a non-linguistic form of communication, there appear to be no restrictions as to where gestures can occur. In BSL, however, it is possible to specify the area in which the majority of signs are produced. This area is known as the signing space: it extends from the waist to just above the head and corresponds in width to the area from elbow to elbow when the arms are loosely bent. There are some signs which occur outside this area. These signs fall into quite distinct groups and will be discussed at the end of this chapter.

The Phonemes of Tab

The following account will illustrate the way in which the signing space is divided into significant sections expressing phonemic distinctions in the tab parameter. Minimal pairs of signs are used to demonstrate the necessity for the suggested distinctions. The number of separate tab phonemes is greater than the number posited for ASL by Stokoe. This may be due in part to differences in the criteria used to establish distinctions as well as the fact that, as separate languages, ASL and BSL may have quite different phonemic systems. Theoretical issues relating to the establishment of phonemic distinctions are discussed in Chapter 8.

Within the signing space used in BSL, there appear to be five obvious physical/spatial areas: the head (including the neck), the trunk, the arms, the hands and the area of space in front of the signer's body. Only one arm and one hand are mentioned because if one hand is serving as the tab, the place where the sign is articulated, then the other hand must be acting as dez. The major physical areas are further divided into specific locations, eg the head area has ten separate tabs, because signs have been found which differ only in terms of their exact position on or near the signer's head. Thus eye, ear, nose, mouth and forehead are all separate positions, ie tabs, for BSL signs.

Neutral Space ∅

Stokoe describes neutral space as "that place in front of the signer's body where the hands move naturally and easily." The area is not rigidly defined and will extend higher or lower, further to the left or right and nearer or further from the signer's body depending on the specific realisations of the other parameters. The realisation of the phonemes of the sign FAR /∅Ġ$_{<⊥}$ $^{⊥}$/ involves the hand moving outwards, elbow partially straightening, so that the final distance of the hand from the body is greater than in a sign such as COMPETITION /∅G̈$_{>⊥}$ G̈$_{<⊥}$ $^{×⫶}$/ .

Other factors may also affect the amount of space taken up by individual signs. However, these factors are related to the production of signs in context rather than to the citation forms of

36
Signing Space   Neutral Space

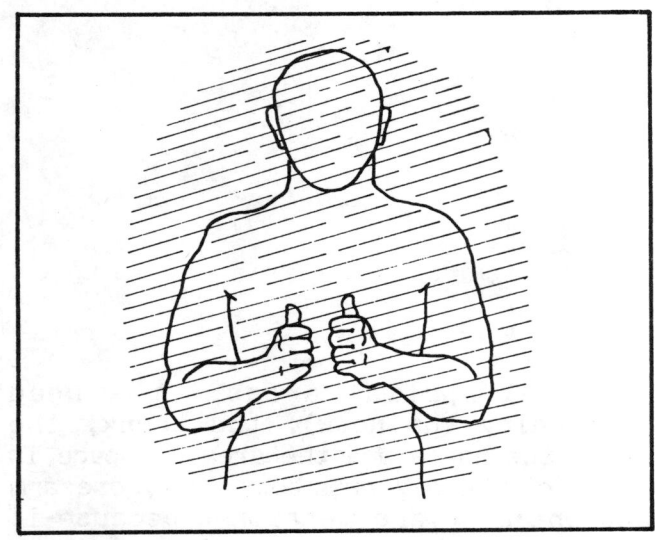 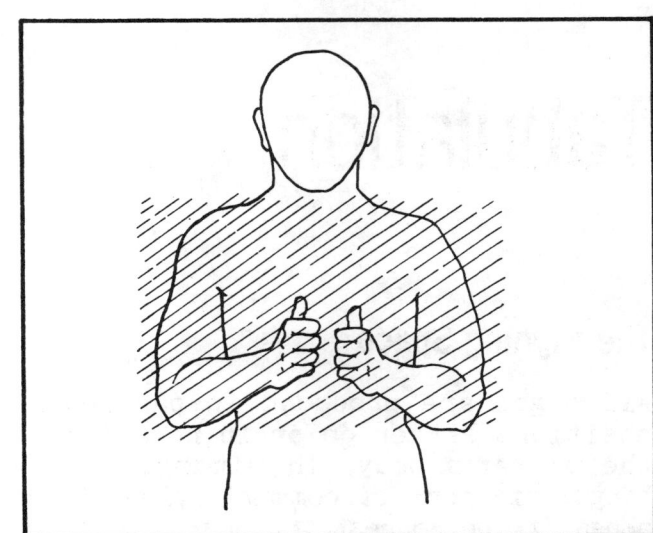
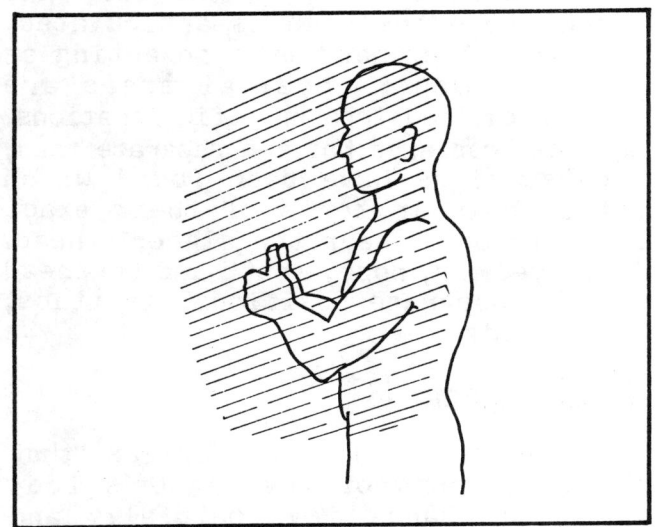 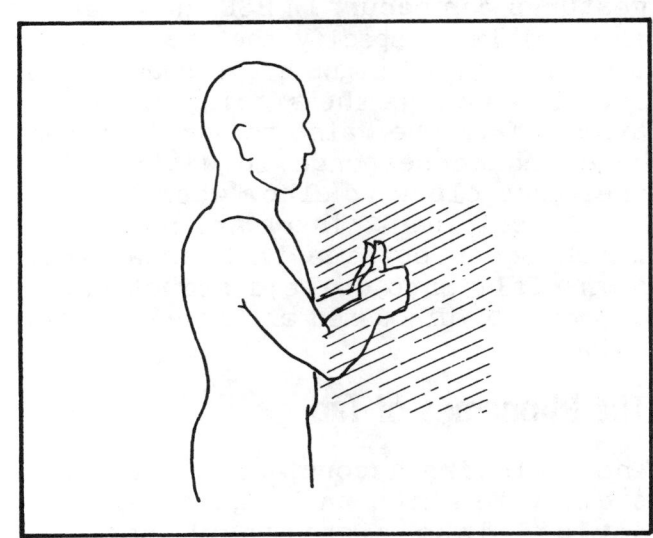
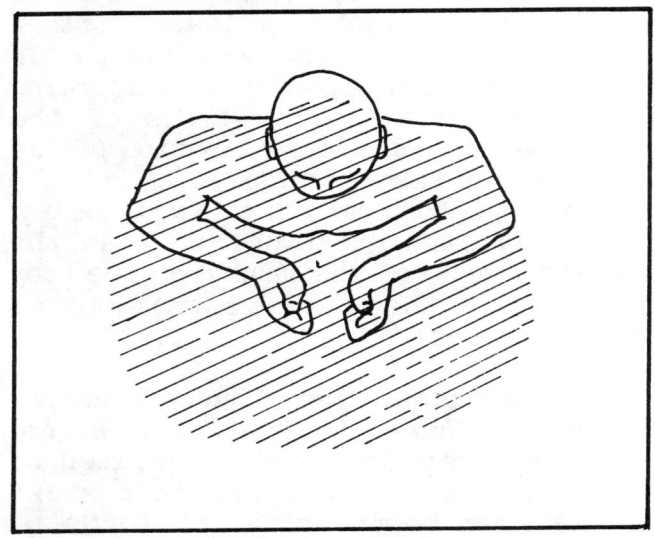 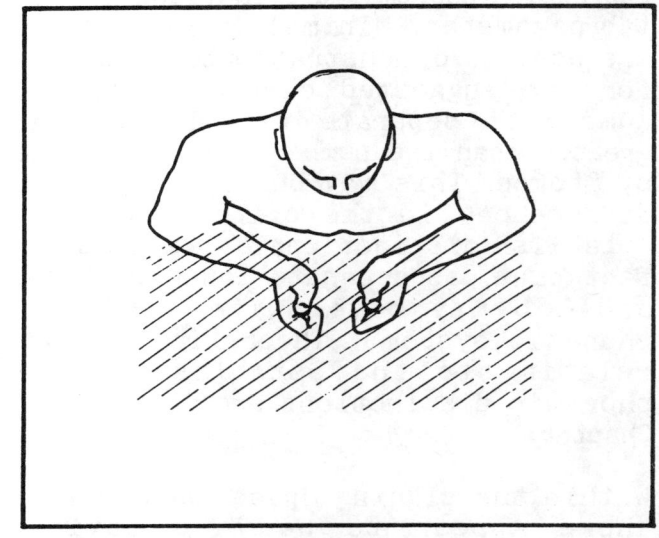

37

FAR /∅Ġ₍₎ ↑/

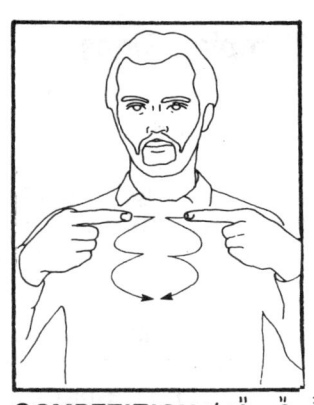
COMPETITION /∅G̈₍₎Ġ₍₎ ˣ⁺/

SEA /∅B₍₎,B₍₎ ≋/

STORMY SEA /∅B₍₎,B₍₎ ≋/

signs. Grammatical modulations, such as those expressing continuous aspect or plurality, may extend the space occupied by the sign articulation. It is possible in sign language to incorporate information within one sign which would be expressed in English by separate words or phrases. The sign SEA /∅B₍₎,B₍₎ ≋ / can be varied to indicate "calm sea" or "stormy sea": these variations will be indicated by changes in the size, frequency and intensity of the movements used. Thus although neutral space cannot be rigidly defined, in practice there are no real difficulties in using this categorisation.

It is a defining feature of the neutral space tab that no contact is involved other than contact between the hands. If a sign actually involves initial contact with a specific part of the body, then that part of the body is the tab. Signs which do not involve contact but demand close proximity with a specific part of the body also take their tab from that part of the body and are not considered as expressing neutral tab.

Signs occurring in neutral space include:

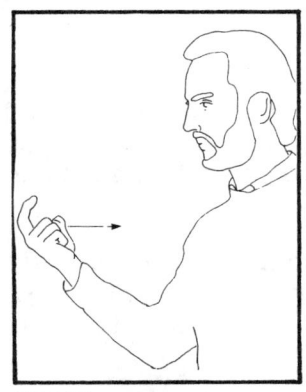
COME

REJECT /∅8̂₍₎ 8̌[5]/

COME /∅G̈₍₎ ᵀ/

Single Dez Signs

Right 8 hand, palm facing away from the signer and fingers pointing up, is held in neutral space. The hand nods downward opening to a 5 hand.

Right G̈ hand, palm facing signer's body and finger pointing up, placed in neutral space, moves towards the signer.

Double Dez Signs

WALK

LAZY /∅λ̈₍₎λ̈₍₎ ~/

WALK /∅B₍₎,B₍₎ ≋~/

Two λ̈ hands, palms pointing up and fingers pointing away from the signer, are held in neutral space. Hands move up and down in a repeated action.

Two B hands, palms facing down and fingers pointing away from the signer, are held side by side in neutral space. Hands move forward and down in short alternating movements.

38

HAVE

SAUSAGES /⌀H̄>∧, H̄<∧ ÷#[ΛΛ]·/

HAVE /⌀5α⊥ ⚹[A]/

Complex Signs

Two H̄ hands: left hand, palm facing right and fingers pointing up; right hand, palm facing left and fingers pointing up. Hands, held side by side in neutral space, separate, closing to Ĥ hands. The action is repeated.

Right 5 hand, palm facing up and fingers pointing away from the signer, is held in neutral space. Hand moves down and closes to an A hand.

Whole Face/Head ◯

Signs making use of the whole face do not normally involve contact but are articulated in front of, around or near the signer's face or head. Other tabs for specific points on the face normally involve contact. It is noticeable that the face and head have many clearly recognisable landmarks such as eyes, ears, nose, mouth, chin and forehead. This wealth of physical detail probably accounts for the greater number of separate tabs in this region. It is also relevant that many of these positions are associated with particular functions such as sight, speech and hearing. Signs related to these functions normally have specific tabs on the face or head. Signs occurring in the region of the head, but without touching the face or head, are said to have the whole face/head, ie ◯ as tab. Signs are normally positioned either in front of or to the side of the head. For non-contact signs, the signing space is primarily divided into whole head, approximately in front of and around the trunk region. The necessity for this distinction is shown by the minimal pair below.

EMBARRASS

LUCKY /◯B<∧ ?·/

EMBARRASS /◯5̄T∧ ?̊/

Single Dez Signs

Right B hand, palm facing left and fingers pointing up, is held at side of head. Hand moves to and fro in repeated nodding action.

Right 5 hand, palm facing signer's body and fingers pointing up, is held in front of face. Hand moves up and towards face in short movement.

Double Dez Signs

MISER

LIGHT /◯BT> ᵖ≠ BT< ÷̂/

MISER /◯B>∧ B<∧ ?·/

Two B hands: left hand, palm facing signer and fingers pointing right; right hand, palm facing signer and fingers pointing left. Hands held crossed in front of face, then move upwards and separate.

Two B hands: left hand, palm facing right and fingers pointing up; right hand, palm facing left and fingers pointing up. Hands held at sides of head. Hands move to and fro in repeated nodding action.

INCENSED

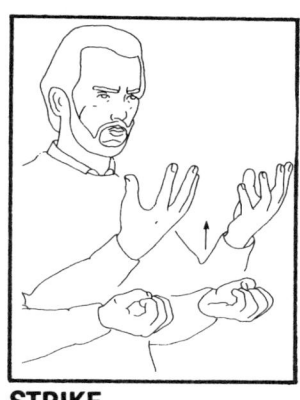
STRIKE

Minimal Pair

INCENSED /⌒O_{a⊥},O_{a⊥} â[5 5]/

Two O hands, palms facing up and fingers pointing away from the signer, are held side by side at lower part of the face. Hands move up and open to 5 hands.

STRIKE /∅O_{a⊥},O_{a⊥} â[5 5]/

Two O hands, palms facing up and fingers pointing away from the signer, are held side by side in neutral space. Hands move up and open to 5 hands.

Top of Head ⌒

Signs which have this tab include both contact and non-contact signs. The top of head tab, ⌒, is clearly distinguished from the whole face tab, ⌒, and from specific parts of the face which can occur as separate tabs. Many of the signs are iconic. Unless otherwise indicated, we can assume that if the two hands are active, and both come into contact with a particular part of the body, this contact will be ipsilateral, ie the right hand will contact the right-hand side of the tab, and the left hand will contact the left-hand side (see CROWN and TEDDY BEAR below). Contralateral contact, in which the hand contacts the opposite side of the tab, is found in a number of signs. Sometimes the information from the other parameters is sufficient to show that contact with the opposite side is required. For certain tabs, such as trunk, diacritics can be used to supply this extra, phonetic information.

QUEEN/KING

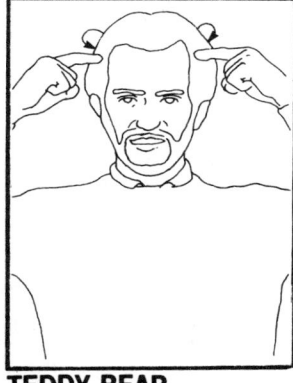
TEDDY BEAR

HALO /⌒G̈_{b<} ė/

QUEEN/KING /⌒5̈_{b<} ˇˣ/

CROWN /⌒C_{>⊥}C_{<⊥} ˇˣ/

TEDDY BEAR /⌒G̈_{b>}G̈_{b<} ˣ÷ˣ/

Single Dez Signs

Right G̈ hand, palm facing down and finger pointing left, makes a circular movement close to the top of the head.

Right 5̈ hand, palm facing down and fingers pointing to the left, is held above head. Hand moves down and touches top of head.

Double Dez Signs

Two C hands: left hand, palm facing right and fingers pointing away; right hand, palm facing left and fingers pointing away. Hands are held above head, then move down to contact head.

Two G̈ hands: left hand, palm facing down and finger pointing right; right hand, palm facing down and finger pointing left. Hands are held on top of head. Hands separate in a short movement and touch once more on the top of head.

40

RED INDIAN

GERMANY

Minimal Pair

RED INDIAN /⌒Ḡ<∧ˣ/

Right G hand, palm facing left and finger pointing up, touches the top of the head.

GERMANY /⌒G<∧ˣ/

Right G hand, palm facing left and finger pointing up, touches the forehead.

Upper Face/Forehead ⌒

This is the region extending from the browline to the hairline and from temple to temple.

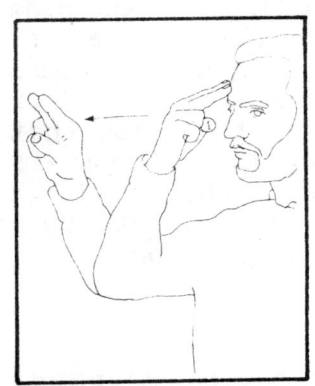
NAME

KNOW /⌒Ȧ<∧ˣ/

NAME /⌒H┬∧ ˣω̇/

Single Dez Signs

Right Ȧ hand, palm facing left and fingers pointing up. The tip of the raised thumb touches the right of the forehead.

Right H hand, palm facing the signer and fingers pointing up, touches right side of forehead then moves outward in a twisting action so that palm faces away from the signer.

Double Dez Signs

COW

RABBIT /⌒H⊥∧ H⊥∧ ˣω̇/

COW /⌒Y⊥∧ Y⊥∧ ˣω̇/

Two H hands, palms facing away from the signer and fingers pointing up, are placed on either side of the forehead. Fingers perform a repeated waving action.

Two Y hands, palms facing away from the signer and fingers pointing up, are placed on either side of the forehead. Hands move outwards and upwards.

The above examples are either directly iconic or have conventionalised associations. However, arbitrary signs do also occur in this region, such as:

KITCHEN /⌒G̈<∧ ᶻ/
Glasgow Area

Right G̈ hand, palm facing left and finger pointing up, jerks in a sideways movement at forehead.

PROSTITUTE

PROSTITUTE /⌒G̈₍ₐ ⦗/

Right G̈ hand, palm facing left and finger pointing up, makes circular movement at forehead.

UNDERSTAND

LOVELY

Minimal Pair

UNDERSTAND /⌒Ġ_T< ˀ'[G̈]/

Right Ġ hand, palm facing the signer and finger pointing left, is placed on the forehead. The index finger strokes the forehead and moves right to end in a final G̈ handshape.

LOVELY /ʊʃĠ_T< ˀ'[G̈]/

Right G hand, palm facing the signer and finger pointing left, is placed under the right eye. The index finger strokes under the eye and moves right to end in a final G̈ handshape.

Eye ʊʃ

In this analysis of BSL the eyes are seen as constituting a separate tab. Stokoe (1978) includes eyes as part of the mid-face tab, while Friedman regards the eyes as part of the upper face tab. However, within BSL, minimally contrasting pairs of signs can be found which demonstrate the need to separate the eye tab from other tabs occurring on the face. A minimal pair showing the distinction between eye tab and forehead tab, is given under upper face/forehead tab.

Single Dez Signs

SEE

LOOK /ʊʃV_<∧ ˣ⊥/

Right V hand, palm facing left and fingers pointing up, touches the face at the side of the right eye, then moves outwards.

SEE /ʊʃG_T∧ ˣ⊥/

Right G hand, palm facing the signer and finger pointing up, touches the face at the side of the right eye, then moves outwards.

42

CAREFUL

SHOW /⊐B_T> B_T< ⊥/

Double Dez Signs

Two B hands: left hand, palm facing the signer and fingers pointing right; right hand, palm facing the signer and fingers pointing left. Hands are placed just below the eyes, then move outwards and separate in a twisting action so that palms face upwards.

CAREFUL /⊐G̈_>∧ G̈_<∧ ×÷̊/

Two G̈ hands: left hand, palm facing right and finger pointing up; right hand, palm facing left and finger pointing up. Fingers touch face just below eyes. Hands move in a short separating movement then move towards each other in a continuing downward movement.

Minimal Pair

EYE /⊐V̈_T∧ ⌣/

Right V̈ hand, palm facing the signer and fingers pointing up, is held in front of right eye. Hand twists to the left.

EYE (as in glass eye)

CLOWN

CLOWN /⊔V̈_T∧ ⌣/

Right V̈ hand, palm facing the signer and fingers pointing up, is held in front of nose. Hand twists to the left.

Nose ⊔

Signs using the nose tab are mainly single dez signs, although a few double dez signs do occur. The following examples will show the range of contact points used in nose tab. Signs may be produced on the side, on the bridge, on the tip, in front of, or just beneath the nose.

POSH

OLD /⊔V̈_T∧ ˇ/

Right V̈ hand, palm facing the signer and fingers pointing up. Fingers are placed at either side of the nose and move downwards.

POSH /⊔H_<∧ ×·/

Right H hand, palm facing left and fingers pointing up, touches right side of nose twice.

PRETEND /⊔λ̈_T∧ ×⌣/

Right λ hand, palm facing the signer and finger pointing up, touches tip of nose then twists outwards.

SISTER

SISTER /⊔G̈<∧ ˣ·/

Right G̈ hand, palm facing left and finger pointing up, touches the centre of the nose twice.

MOUSE /⊔G̈>∧ G̈<∧ ˣω̈/

Two G̈ hands: left hand, palm facing right and finger pointing up; right hand, palm left and finger pointing up. Fingers touch each side of the nose and twist outwards, retaining contact.

Minimal Pair

HANDKERCHIEF /⊔B̿T< ⊥̇#[B̂]/

Right B̿ hand, palm facing the signer and fingers pointing left. Hand moves away and down from the front of the nose and closes to a B̂ hand.

THIRSTY /π B̿T< ⊥̇#[B̂]/

Right B̿ hand, palm facing the signer and fingers pointing left. Hand moves away and down from the throat and closes to a B̂ hand.

HANDKERCHIEF

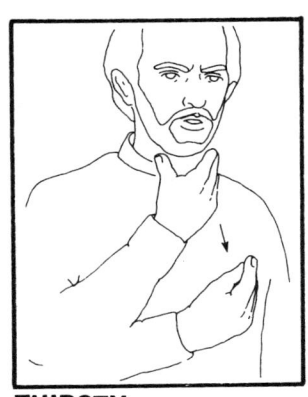
THIRSTY

Lower Face/Chin ⌣

As used here, the lower face tab does not include the mouth as this is regarded as a significantly different location for BSL signs. Most of the signs with chin tab appear to be single dez.

NUMBER

AFTERNOON /⌣HT∧ ˣω̈/

Right H hand, palm facing the signer and fingers pointing up. Fingers touch the chin then twist outwards.

NUMBER /⌣AT∧ ˣ·/

Right A hand, palm facing signer and fingers pointing up, touches chin twice.

MISTAKE

WATER /∪W₍ₐ ˣ˙/

Right W hand, palm facing left and fingers pointing up. Index finger contacts chin twice.

MISTAKE /∪5₍ₐ ˣ/

Right 5 hand, palm facing the signer and fingers pointing up. Fingers perform flickering action and touch chin.

Minimal Pair

HARD /∪G̈₍ₐ ˣ/

Right G̈ hand, palm facing left and finger pointing up, twists towards chin and touches chin sharply.

STEEL /∪G̈₍ₐ ˣ/

Right G̈ hand, palm facing left and finger pointing up, twists towards mouth and touches teeth sharply.

HARD

STEEL

Under Chin ∪

Although physically the areas constituting the lower face, under chin and neck tabs are very close together, it is useful to distinguish these as separate positions in BSL. The under chin area is very small, hence the absence of double dez signs using this tab.

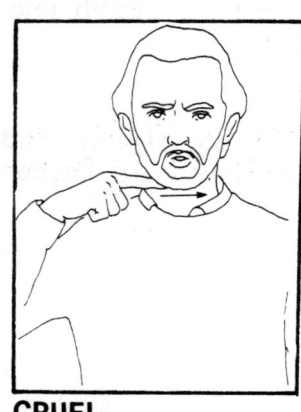
CRUEL

NOT /∪Ȧ₍ₐ ˣ/

Right Ȧ hand, palm facing left and fingers pointing up. The prominent thumb touches under the chin then moves away from the signer.

CRUEL /∪G₍< ˣ/

Right G hand, palm facing down and finger pointing left, is placed under chin. Hand moves to the left maintaining contact.

45

FRUIT

APPLE

Minimal Pair

FRUIT /⌒G̈₁< ω⊥/

Right G̈ hand, palm facing the signer and finger pointing left, is placed under chin. Hand twists in forward movement.

APPLE /⌒G̈₁< ω⊥/

Right G̈ hand, palm facing the signer and finger pointing left, is placed in front of mouth. Hand twists in forward movement.

Mouth and Lips

Both Stokoe (1972, 1978) and Friedman (1977) regard the mouth as a phonetic variant of lower face tab. Stokoe (1972) suggests that as signs which can have more specific descriptions, such as lips for "red" and chin for "beard", are actually made an inch or more from the face, "meaning, rather than accurate observation, is the governing consideration." Friedman's claim (1977) is similar to this in that all the signs made at the mouth have referents to do with the mouth or real or metaphoric functions of the mouth. While this is generally also true of BSL, there are minimal pairs which are distinguished only by positioning at the mouth or chin. This distinction is, therefore, regarded as phonemic. A minimal pair illustrating this distinction can be found under chin tab.

Single Dez Signs

Right F hand, palm facing left and fingers pointing away from the signer, is held in front of mouth. Hand nods upwards towards the signer.

Right G̈ hand, palm facing the signer and finger pointing up, is held touching the lower lip. Hand moves down and away.

Double Dez Signs

Two G hands: left hand, palm facing right and finger pointing up; right hand, palm facing left and finger pointing up. Fingers touch sides of mouth and then move away and to the left.

Two G hands, palms facing the signer and fingers pointing up, are held with index fingers touching either side of the mouth. Hands twist outward, moving down and away, separating at the same time.

RED

TEACHER

TEA /⌒F<⊥ ᵖ⁺/

RED /⌒G̈₁∧ ˣʸ/

REPORT /⌒G>∧ G<∧ ˣ⁺ˇ/

TEACHER /⌒G₁∧ G₁∧ ˣω⁺/

THANK YOU

SEEM

Minimal Pair

THANK YOU /⌒B$_{T\wedge}$ $\overset{..}{\div}$/

Right B hand, palm facing the signer and fingers pointing up. Fingertips are placed at the mouth and then hand moves away and down.

SEEM /⌒B$_{T\wedge}$ $\overset{..}{\div}$/

Right B hand, palm facing the signer and fingers pointing up. Fingertips are placed at the nose and then hand moves away and down.

Cheek ⊃

The cheek tab consists of the sides of the face, excluding those areas already specified as separate tabs. Both single dez and double dez signs make use of this tab.

BLACK

CHEAT /3Å$_{<\wedge}$ $\overset{x}{}$/

BLACK /3A$_{<\wedge}$ $\overset{x}{}$/

Single Dez Signs

Right Å hand, palm facing left and fingers pointing up. Tip of prominent thumb touches cheek and moves down maintaining contact.

Right A hand, palm facing the left and fingers pointing up, is placed on right cheek. Hand moves down maintaining contact.

Double Dez Signs

BLUSH

MEASLES /3$\ddot{5}_{T\wedge}$ $\ddot{5}_{T\wedge}$ $^{xvx\cdot}$/

BLUSH /3$\ddot{B}_{T\wedge}$ $\ddot{B}_{T\wedge}$ $\overset{\hat{}}{x}$/

Two $\ddot{5}$ hands, palms facing the signer and fingers pointing up, are held at cheeks. Hands contact cheeks and move down making contact again. The action is repeated.

Two $\ddot{B}$ hands, palms facing the signer and fingers pointing up, are placed on cheeks. Hands move up maintaining contact.

Minimal Pair

CHEEKY

LUCKY

CHEEKY /ᴐG̈⃛<∧ ˣ⁼/

Right G̈⃛ hand, palm facing left and finger pointing up, touches right cheek and shakes the cheek to and fro.

LUCKY /ᴐG̈⃛<∧ ˣ⁼/

Right G̈⃛ hand, palm facing left and finger pointing up, touches right earlobe and shakes the ear to and fro.

Ear ᴐ

Both Stokoe (1978) and Friedman (1977) treat the ear as part of the cheek/side-face tab. Friedman suggests that ear and cheek are not distinctive except that signs having to do with "ear" are made at the ear. However, signs such as CHERRY /ᴐV̈D< ⁼·/ and IGNORE /ᴐG<∧ ˣˢ˅<̣/ below, suggest that both iconic and non-iconic signs take ear as tab. It is clearly a significant location for BSL signs.

Single Dez Signs

CHERRY

DEAF /ᴐH<∧ ˣ/

Right H hand, palm facing left and fingers pointing up, touches right ear.

CHERRY /ᴐV̈D< ⁼·/

Right V̈ hand, palm facing down and fingers pointing left, is held beside right ear. The right hand moves to and fro twice in a short twisting action.

Double Dez Signs

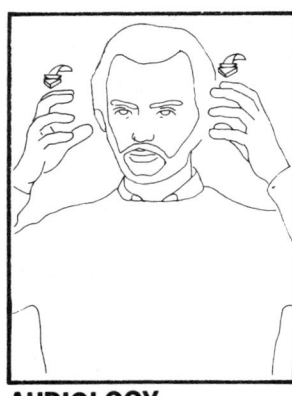
AUDIOLOGY

EAR-RINGS /ᴐF><∧ F<∧ ˣ/

Two F hands: left hand, palm facing right and fingers pointing up; right hand, palm facing left and fingers pointing up. Tips of thumbs and index fingers touch earlobes.

AUDIOLOGY /ᴐ5̈><∧ 5̈<∧ ⁼·/

Two 5̈ hands: left hand, palm facing right and fingers pointing up; right hand, palm facing left and fingers pointing up. Hands, held close to ears, twist away from the signer in a short movement. The action is repeated.

Minimal Pair

IGNORE /ʔG<∧ ˣ˃̥̊˅̌/

Right G hand, palm facing left and finger pointing up, touches ear. Hand moves in a short action to the right then a sharp downwards action to the left.

ORDER /⌣G<∧ ˣ˃̥̊˅̌/

Right G hand, palm facing left and finger pointing up, touches mouth. Hand moves in a short action to the right and then a sharp downwards action to the left.

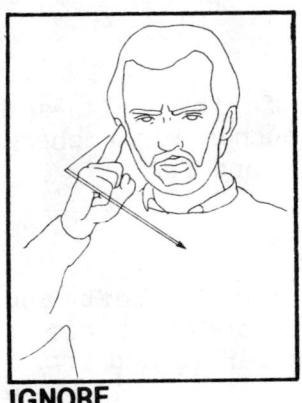
IGNORE

ORDER

Throat/Neck π

This tab is again a rather small area and relatively few signs exploit the neck tab. Most of these signs are single dez although some double dez signs also occur.

Single Dez Signs

DISAPPOINT /π V̈T∧ ˣ/

Right V̈ hand, palm facing the signer and fingers pointing up. Tips of index and middle fingers touch throat.

HANG /πA⊥< ˣ˄̂/

Right A hand, palm facing away from the signer and fingers pointing left, touches side of neck and then moves up and to the right.

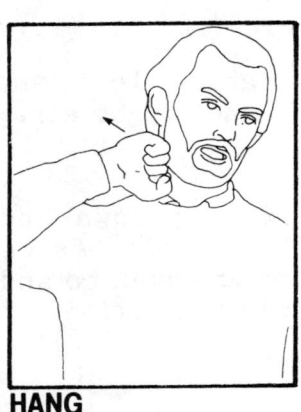
HANG

Double Dez Signs

MUMPS /π 5̈T∧, 5̈T∧ ˣ⊥/

Two 5̈ hands, palms facing the signer and fingers pointing up, are placed side by side at neck. Hands touch neck then move away from the signer.

BOW-TIE /π Ḧ̂T>, Ḧ̂T< ˣ⊟[vv]/ Two Ḧ̂ hands: left hand, palm facing the signer and fingers pointing right; right hand, palm facing the signer and fingers pointing left. Hands are held side by side at neck. Hands touch neck then separate, opening into V hands.

BOW-TIE

CRUEL   SWEET(noun)

Minimal Pair

CRUEL /π G$_{<∧}$ $\overset{x}{\underset{T}{⊙}}$/

Right G hand, palm facing left and finger pointing up. Index finger held touching right side of throat twists so that palm faces the signer.

SWEET(noun) /⊃ G$_{<∧}$ $\overset{x}{\underset{T}{⊙}}$/

Right G hand, palm facing left and finger pointing up. Index finger held touching right side of mouth, twists so that palm faces the signer.

Chest [ ]

In Stokoe (1978) the trunk region, from shoulders to waist, is given as one tab. Friedman (1977) suggests that there are four phonetic distinctions made in the trunk area, namely the chest, the shoulder, the stomach and the waist. For BSL it has been necessary to recognise three significantly contrasting tabs on the trunk region: the chest, the upper trunk/shoulders and the lower trunk, including waist and stomach. The chest is the central part of the trunk region and may be seen as the most neutral of the three distinctions. Signs produced in this area include single dez, double dez, iconic and non-iconic signs.

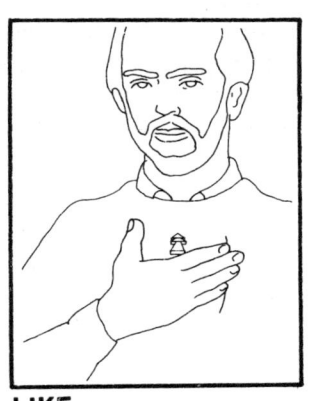
LIKE

LIFE /[ ] 8$_{T<}$ $\overset{\circ}{\underset{x}{∨}}$/

LIKE /[ ] B$_{T<}$ $\overset{x·}{}$/

Single Dez Signs

Right 8 hand, palm facing the signer and fingers pointing left. Middle finger touches chest and moves up and down in a short movement while maintaining contact with chest.

Right B hand, palm facing the signer and fingers pointing left. Palm touches chest twice.

Double Dez Signs

PATIENCE

FEAR /[ ] $\overline{\overline{5}}_{T>}$ $\overline{\overline{5}}_{T<}$ $^{x·}$/

PATIENCE /[ ] B$_{T>,}$ B$_{T<}$ $\overset{x~}{\underset{∨}{}}$/

Two 5 hands: left hand, palm facing the signer and fingers pointing right; right hand, palm facing the signer and fingers pointing left. Right hand is held above left hand. Hands touch the body twice.

Two B hands: left hand, palm facing the signer and fingers pointing right; right hand, palm facing the signer and fingers pointing left. Left hand, touching chest, is held behind right hand. Hands stroke chest in a repeated alternating downward action.

Upper Trunk ⌐ ⌐

The upper trunk tab includes the top and front of the shoulders and approximately the upper third of the chest region.

OFFICER

SOLDIER /⌐⌐B<∧ ˣ>ˣ/

OFFICER /⌐⌐V₀⊤ ˣ·/

RICH

READY /⌐⌐5ᵦ> 5ᵦ< ˣ·/

RICH /⌐⌐B̈ₐ> B̈ₐ< ˣ̌/

Single Dez Signs

Right B hand, palm facing left and fingers pointing up, makes contact with left shoulder and hand moves right to touch right shoulder.

Right V hand, palm facing down and fingers pointing towards the signer. Fingers touch the top of the left shoulder twice.

Double Dez Signs

Two 5 hands: left hand, palm facing down and fingers pointing right; right hand, palm facing down and fingers pointing left. Thumb tips contact upper trunk just below shoulders twice.

Two B̈ hands: left hand, palm facing up and fingers pointing right; right hand, palm facing up and fingers pointing left. Hands touch upper trunk just below shoulders. Hands move down while maintaining contact.

Lower Trunk ⌊ ⌋

The lower trunk tab includes the waist, the stomach and approximately the lower third of the region from waist to shoulders.

BUSINESS

OPERATION /⌊⌋Ȧᵦ⊥ ˣ̌/

BUSINESS /⌊⌋B̈ₐ⊥ ˣ·/

Single Dez Signs

Right Ȧ hand, palm facing down and fingers pointing away from the signer. Tip of thumb contacts lower trunk and moves to the right maintaining contact.

Right B̈ hand, palm facing up and fingers pointing away from the signer, contacts right side of waist twice.

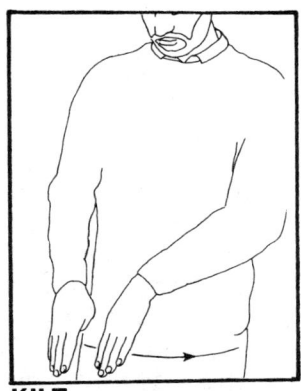
KILT

Double Dez Signs

PREGNANT /⌊⌋B_T>x B_T<ϙ ˣ⊥/ Two B hands: left hand, palm facing the signer and fingers pointing right; right hand, palm facing the signer and fingers pointing left. Left hand is held in front of right hand with fingers touching. Hands touch lower trunk and then move away from the signer.

KILT /⌊⌋B_Tv⸝B_Tv ˣ<ˣ/

Two B hands, palms facing the signer and fingers pointing down, are held side by side touching right side of lower trunk. Hands move left and touch left side of lower trunk.

The need to distinguish chest [ ], upper trunk ⌈ ⌉ and lower trunk ⌊ ⌋ as separate tabs for BSL signs can be shown by the following minimal pairs.

Chest/Lower Trunk

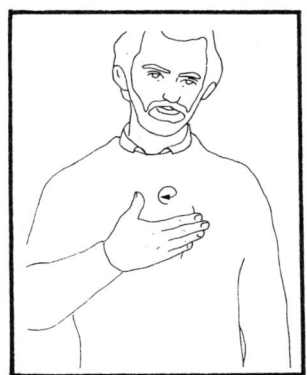
SORRY

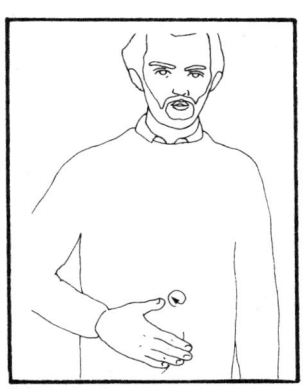
DELICIOUS

SORRY /[ ]B_T> ᶜ⁄ˣ/

Right B hand, palm facing the signer and fingers pointing left, makes a circular motion on the centre of the chest, maintaining contact.

DELICIOUS /⌊⌋B_T> ᶜ⁄ˣ/

Right B hand, palm facing the signer and fingers pointing left, makes a circular motion on the centre of the lower trunk, maintaining contact.

Upper Trunk/Lower Trunk

MEDICAL EXAMINATION

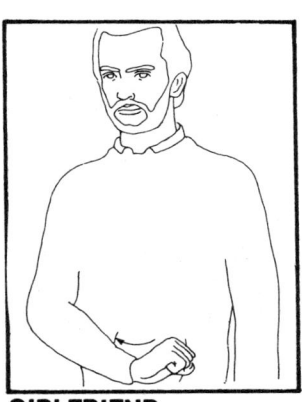
GIRLFRIEND

MEDICAL EXAMINATION /⌈⌉A_b< ˣ>ˣ/

Right A hand, palm facing down and fingers pointing left, contacts left side of upper trunk, then moves right to contact right upper trunk.

GIRLFRIEND /⌊⌋A_b< ˣ>ˣ/

Right A hand, palm facing down and fingers pointing left, contacts left side of lower trunk, then moves right to contact right lower trunk.

Diacritic Symbols

Because some signs are placed in particular parts of the trunk region for iconic reasons, it may be useful to have available a set of extra symbols, or diacritics, which can be used if more precise, detailed information is required on the positioning of individual signs within the whole trunk region. Thus it may be helpful to know that the sign is produced at the sides of the lower trunk, rather than the centre, or on top of the shoulders, rather than the front of the shoulders. Often this information can be gleaned from the realisations of the other parameters, particularly orientation. The following examples illustrate how diacritical marks can be used to give phonetic details should these be required for specific purposes. The diacritics are placed with reference to the side or sides of the body used as tab. The symbols are placed according to the signer's point of view, that is left or right according to the signer, not the viewer: right on the page means right to the signer in actual production.

The notation ˇ⏋ indicates the exact position on top of the left shoulder.

RESPONSIBILITY
/ˇ⏋B_DT x B_DT ˣ/

Two B hands, palms facing down and fingers pointing towards the signer. Left hand is held above right hand with fingers touching. Hands are held above left shoulder, then contact top of left shoulder.

The notation ⌈ˇ⌉ˇ indicates that each hand is placed on top of each of the shoulders.

GYM /⌈ˇ⌉ˇ B̈_b> B̈_D< ˣ·/

Two B̈ hands: left hand, palm facing down and fingers pointing right; right hand, palm facing down and fingers pointing left. Hands are held above shoulders, then contact the top of the shoulders twice.

The notation >⌈⏋ indicates that the exact position is the left side of the upper trunk, ie just below the left shoulder.

BIRTHDAY />⌈⏋A_T< ˣ·/
(Regional:Dundee)

Right A hand, palm facing the signer and fingers pointing left, touches the front of the left shoulder twice.

BIRTHDAY

**BIRTHDAY
(Regional: Glasgow)**
/⊃⌐ ⌐< A_T> A_T< ˣ⁾⁽ˣ/

The notation ⊃⌐ ⌐< indicates that the hands contact the upper trunk just below each shoulder.

Two A hands: left hand, palm facing the signer and fingers pointing right; right hand, palm facing the signer and fingers pointing left. Hands contact the upper trunk just below each shoulder, then move towards each other and contact centre of upper trunk.

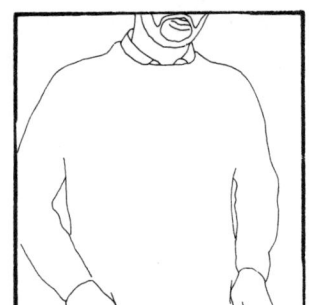
COURTING

COURTING /L ⌐< Ḃ_D⊥ ˣ/

The notation L ⌐< indicates that the hand contacts the right side of the lower trunk/waist.

Right Ḃ hand, palm facing down and fingers pointing away from the signer, contacts right side of lower trunk.

SKIRT

SKIRT /⊃L ⌐< B_Tv B_Tv ˣᵛ/

The notation ⊃L ⌐< indicates that the hands are placed on either side of the waist.

Two B hands, palms facing the signer and fingers pointing down. Hands are placed on either side of trunk, then move downwards.

LOUSY

LOUSY /⌐[Ḃ_T< ^ˣ/

By using the symbols [and] (ie the two separate halves of the original trunk symbol) it is possible to show that either the left side or the right side of the trunk is used as tab. 'Side', in this sense, refers to the area from under the arm to the waist. The placement of the diacritics > and < can show whether the precise point of contact is upper or lower trunk.

Right Ḃ hand, palm facing the signer and fingers pointing left, is held under left arm. Hand moves up and contacts body under arm.

SCOTLAND /]< √A<⊥ <ˣ·/ Right A hand, with prominent elbow, palm facing left and fingers pointing away from the signer. The arm moves to the left so that the elbow makes contact with right side of body. The action is repeated.

SCOTLAND

The Arm Area

Stokoe (1978) provides separate tab symbols for the upper and lower arm as well as for the ventral (supinated) wrist and the dorsal (pronated) wrist. Friedman (1977) also distinguishes elbow as a separate tab. In this analysis of BSL, five tabs are given for the arm region. Minimal pairs exist which show the need to distinguish elbow and lower arm as well as dorsal and ventral wrist. However, very few signs occur in some of these areas, particularly on the ventral wrist. Therefore, this account accords with Friedman's suggestion that some of these tabs should be considered as marginal locations. A further problem arises in distinguishing upper and lower arm. It is difficult to find minimal pairs distinguished only by location on upper as opposed to lower arm. This is partly because physically the arm is usually bent at the elbow, which means that even if a sign on the lower arm has exactly the same handshape and movement as one on the upper arm, the orientation is likely to be different. Here the distinction between upper and lower arm has been retained because it is descriptively important.

Upper Arm ⌒

The outside of the arm (dorsal) is used rather more than the inside (ventral). Iconic factors usually account for the choice of ventral or dorsal.

STRONG /⌒G_D< ˣ⊥ˣ/ₐ/ Right G hand, palm facing down and finger pointing left. Index finger touches inner side of left upper arm. Hand moves away and down while palm twists upwards and then contacts arm again.

SERGEANT /⌒W_T< ˅ˣ/ Right W hand, palm facing the signer and fingers pointing left, is placed on the outer side of left upper arm. Hand moves down and up, maintaining contact.

SERGEANT

Lower Arm ✓

The symbol used for the lower arm tab is different from that used by Stokoe as the elbow is here distinguished as a separate tab. In this account, ✓ is used for elbow; ✓ is used for lower arm.

GREEN

BEFORE /✓B₍ₗ ˣ˂ˣ/

GREEN /✓B₀ₗ ˣ/

Most of the examples using lower arm tab make use of the outer surface of the arm. Therefore it is assumed that, unless otherwise stated, the arm is held so that the inner surface is facing down as in GREEN below.

Right B hand, palm facing left and fingers pointing away from the signer, placed on the outer side of lower arm. Hand moves to the left and contacts arm again.

Right B hand, palm facing down and fingers pointing away from the signer, is placed at the outer side of lower arm. Hand moves to the left maintaining contact.

Elbow ✓

The elbow can be distinguished as a separate location, although very few signs make use of this tab.

LAZY

BISCUIT /✓5̈ₐ< ^ˣ·/

LAZY /✓B̈ₐ< ^ˣ·/

Right 5̈ hand, palm facing up and fingers pointing left, is held under left elbow. Hand moves up and contacts elbow twice.

Right B̈ hand, palm facing up and fingers pointing left, is held under left elbow. Hand moves up and contacts elbow twice.

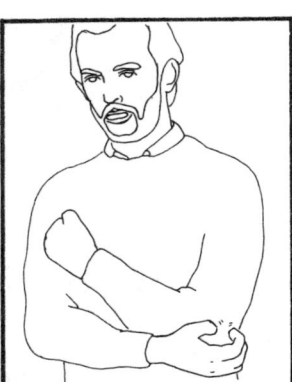
POOR

ITCH

Minimal Pair

POOR /✓5̈ₐ< ˣ/

Right 5̈ hand, palm facing up and fingers pointing left, contacts left elbow. Fingers perform flexing movement, maintaining contact.

ITCH /✓5̈ₐ< ˣ/

Right 5̈ hand, palm facing up and fingers pointing left, contacts the outer side of left lower arm. Fingers perform flexing movement, maintaining contact.

Wrist : pronated ɒ

In signs using pronated wrist, the arm is held so that the wrist faces down, ie pronated. The signs are thus located on the outer surface of the wrist.

COUSIN

APPRENTICE /ɒCɒ⊥ ᶦ/ Right C hand, palm facing down and fingers pointing away from the signer, grasps left wrist and holds.

COUSIN /ɒB̿ɒ⊥ ˣ⩯[B̂]·/ Right B̿ hand, palm facing down and fingers pointing away from the signer, contacts the pronated wrist, fingers on the outer edge and the thumb on the inner edge. The hand moves up closing to a B̂ hand. The action is repeated.

Wrist: supinated ɑ

This is probably the most questionable tab on the arm area, in that, although it has been possible to find one minimal pair distinguished by wrist orientation, very few signs using ɑ tab have yet been found.

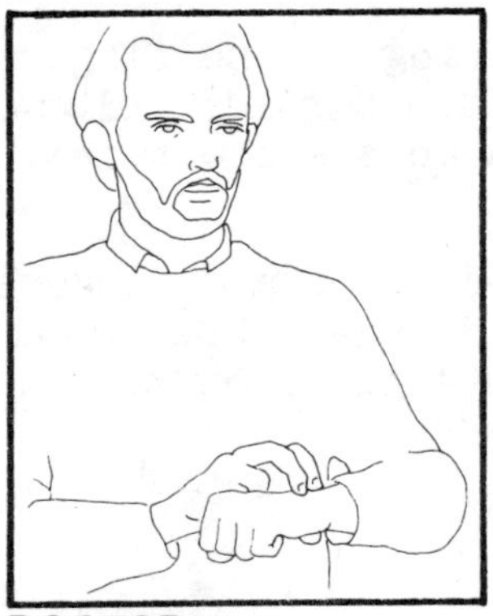

DOCTOR

PULSE

Minimal Pair

DOCTOR /ɒH̿ɒ< ᶦ/

Right H̿ hand, palm facing down and fingers pointing left, contacts pronated wrist so that fingers touch outer side and thumb contacts inner side.

PULSE /ɑH̿ɒ< ᶦ/

Right H̿ hand, palm facing down and fingers pointing left, contacts supinated wrist so that fingers touch the inner side and thumb contacts the outer side.

Manual Tabs

The following sections will deal with Class B2 and Class B3 signs, ie those in which the non-dominant hand acts as tab, while the other hand takes on the role of dez. As indicated in Chapter 1 (see pages 9 - 10), in Class B2 signs both handshapes will be the same, even though one hand is acting as dez. In Class B3 signs, the handshapes of the tab and dez are different. Wherever possible, examples will be given of both types, symmetrical and asymmetrical, for each of the hand tabs mentioned.

One complicating factor here concerns what should be regarded as the 'same' handshape. In Chapter 4 several of the A handshapes are said to be phonemic, while others are merely allophonic variants. If the handshape of the tab is A and the handshape of the dez is Ȧ, should we regard these as belonging to Class B2 or Class B3 signs? It seems that if the more marked variety of the particular handshape is used for tab, this is often for phonetic reasons, eg relating to point of contact. In BECAUSE /B̄$_{>⊥}$B$_{▷<}$$^{x⊕x}_{\widehat{?}}$/ the B̈ hand must be used for tab as the dez contacts the tab both on the index finger edge and on the inside of the thumb. Indeed, it could be argued that the hand tabs can be grouped together as one location or tab, with the specific variants, Ä, B̈, 5̈, etc, conditioned by other formational aspects of the sign. Therefore, in this account, regardless of whether or not the closely related handshapes constituting the A set, the B set, etc, are phonemically distinct when realising dez, they will be treated as belonging to the same handshape family when realising tab. A sign will be classed as symmetrical B2, if both hands have hand configurations belonging to the same handshape group. Realisations such as BB̈, AÄ, 55̈ will all be regarded as symmetrical signs. The secondary importance of the tab handshape, as compared with the dez, can be seen in signs which allow variation in the choice of tab realisation. NEVER can be produced either as /B̄$_{T>}$$_{?}B_{T<}$$^{\lor}_{≷}$/ or /Ā$_{T>}$$_{?}B_{T<}$$^{\lor}_{≷}$/ without any change of meaning. Although the tab choice may be partly conditioned by the preceding sign, in this case B and A occur in free variation as realisations of tab.

One further problem should be noted here, namely that of indicating the exact position on the manual tab which is contacted by the active dez. In the majority of cases, such information is either already implicit through the realisation of the other parameters, or is unnecessary as the precise place of contact is unimportant. However, the problem does occur in signs such as MARRY /5̈$_{▷>}$F$_{▷⊥}$$^{≷}$/ and THROUGH /5$_{T∧}B_{<⊥}$$^{♀}$/. In MARRY the information provided by the transcription just given, is insufficient to show that the place of contact is the fourth finger, while the transcription for THROUGH does not indicate that the hand moves in between the index finger and middle finger. Even in these cases such information is primarily phonetic in that there are no minimal pairs distinguished only by

contact on the fourth finger as opposed to contact on the index finger. It has been decided to use diacritics to show place of contact on tab within the phonemic transcription for a limited number of cases where descriptive adequacy seems to demand further clarity.

The system developed by Lilian Lawson for place of contact on tab, involved numbering each of the fingers and the spaces between the fingers. Since the development of the original labelling system, Margaret Carter (Carter and Maddix, 1980), in association with the Bristol Sign Language Research Group, has worked on a method of labelling point of contact for both tab and dez realisations. (On point of contact for dez see Chapter 7.) Some adaptations have been made to allow for consistency between the two systems. The thumb and fingers are labelled as in the British finger-spelling system, so the lower case letters a, e, i, o, u, are used, while the spaces in between are simply numbered. These additional symbols are then written as superscripts before the tab. The transcription of MARRY thus becomes /^{o}5̈$_{▷>}$F$_{▷⊥}$$^{≷}$/ and THROUGH becomes /^{2}5$_{T∧}$B$_{<⊥}$$^{♀}$/.

The hand tabs normally make use of the small group of unmarked handshapes illustrated on page 12. Nevertheless, it is clear that in BSL a number of other handshapes are also used, although there are very few signs exploiting these extra handshapes compared to the numerous signs using unmarked forms. Examples of all types will be presented here, beginning with the unmarked set.

A Tab
Class B2 Signs

BEST

KEEP /Ā₀> A▽⊥ ˣ˙/ — Manual tab A is held with palm facing up and fingers pointing right. Right A hand, palm facing down and fingers pointing away from the signer, is held above left hand, then moves down to contact left hand. The action is repeated.

BEST /Ā>⊥ Ȧ▽⊥ ᵖ ⁺/ₓ/ — Manual tab A is held with palm facing right and fingers pointing away from the signer. Right Ȧ hand, palm facing down and fingers pointing away from the signer, is held slightly behind left hand, then hand moves forward so that right thumb brushes sharply along left thumb.

Class B3 Signs

IRELAND

INTERVIEW /Ȧ>⊥ ᵖ F<⊥ ˣ˙/ — Manual tab Ȧ is held with palm facing right and fingers pointing away from the signer. Right F hand, palm facing left and fingers pointing away from the signer, is held in front of left hand. Right finger and thumb move towards the signer and touch tip of left thumb. The action is repeated.

IRELAND /Ā▽> V̈▽⊥ ˣ˙/ — Manual tab A is held with palm facing down and fingers pointing right. Right V̈ hand, palm facing down and fingers pointing away from the signer, is held above left hand. Fingers contact back of left hand twice.

B Tab
Class B2 Signs

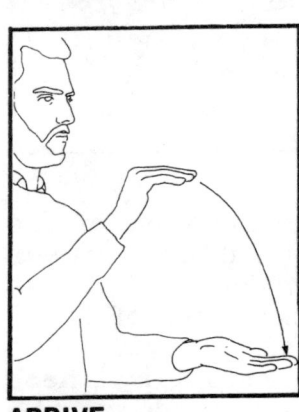
ARRIVE

EXPLAIN /B̄₀> B▽⊥ ᵖ/ₓ/ — Manual tab B is held with palm facing up and fingers pointing right. Right B hand, palm facing down and fingers pointing away from the signer. Left hand is held below right. Right hand makes circular movement on palm of left hand.

ARRIVE /B̄₀⊥ B̈▽⊥ ᵖ ⊥ˣ/V̈/ — Manual tab B is held with palm facing up and fingers pointing away from the signer. Right B̈ hand, palm facing down and fingers pointing away from the signer, is held above and behind left hand. Right hand moves away and down and contacts left hand so that fingertips touch fingertips.

Class B3 Signs

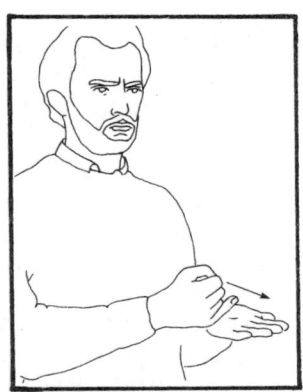

OBJECT

CAKE /B̄~D>~ 5̈~bL~ ˣ·/   Manual tab B is held with palm facing down and fingers pointing right. Right 5 hand, palm facing down and fingers pointing away from the signer. Left hand is held below right hand. Tips of right fingers and thumb contact the back of left hand twice.

OBJECT /B̄~aL~ I~T<~ ˣ/ **(verb)**   Manual tab B is held with palm facing up and fingers pointing away. Right I hand, palm facing towards the signer and finger pointing left. Left hand is held below right hand. Outer edge of little finger of right hand moves along palm and fingers of left hand, maintaining contact.

C Tab
Class B2 Signs

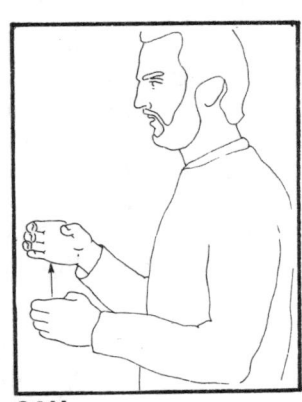

CAN

COACH /C~>∧x~C~<∧~ ᵀ/   Manual tab C is held with palm facing right and fingers pointing up. Right C hand, palm facing left and fingers pointing up, is held behind and contacting left hand. Right hand moves towards the signer.

CAN /C̄~>⊥x~C~<⊥~ ∧/ **(noun)**   Manual tab C is held with palm facing right and fingers pointing away from the signer. Right C hand, palm facing left and fingers pointing away from the signer, is held on top of left hand, then right hand moves up.

Class B3 Signs

PARTICIPATE

DROWN /C~>⊥o~B̄~aL~ ˇ[B̂]/   Manual tab C is held with palm facing right and fingers pointing away from the signer. Right B̄ hand, palm facing up and fingers pointing away from the signer, is held inside left hand, then drawn down closing to a B̂ hand.

PARTICIPATE /C~>⊥¡~ Ḃ~bL~ °/   Manual tab C is held with palm facing right and fingers pointing away from the signer. Right Ḃ hand, palm facing down and fingers pointing away from the signer. Hands are held side by side. Right hand moves to enter C hand.

60

5 Tab
Class B2 Signs

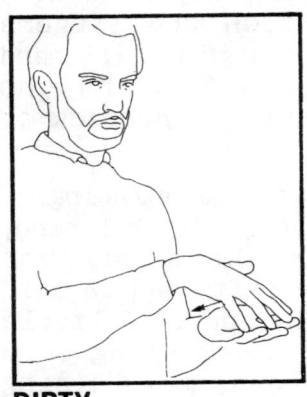
DIRTY

LANGUAGE /5₇> 5₇< ᵩ ˣ̌/ — Manual tab 5 is held with palm facing the signer and fingers pointing right. Right 5 hand, palm facing the signer and fingers pointing left, is held behind left hand. Right hand moves right touching palm and fingers of left hand.

DIRTY /5ₐ⊥ 5ᵦ⊥ ˣ̇·/ — Manual tab 5 is held with palm facing up and fingers pointing away from the signer. Right 5 hand, palm facing down and fingers pointing away from the signer, is held above left hand. Right fingers move across left palm twice, maintaining contact.

Class B3 Signs

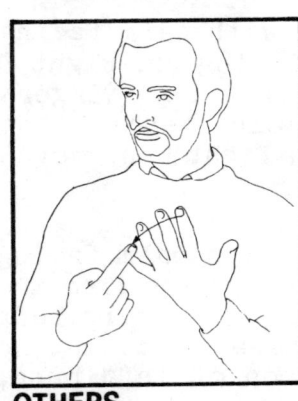
OTHERS

BETWEEN /²³5̄₇∧ B<⊥ ᵛˣ∿ˣ/ — Manual tab 5 is held with palm facing the signer and fingers pointing up. Right B hand, palm facing left and fingers pointing away from the signer, is held above left hand and then moves down into the gap between the index and middle fingers, then up and down into the gap between the middle and third fingers.

OTHERS /5₇∧ ᵩ G₇< ˣ̌/ — Manual tab 5 is held with palm facing the signer and fingers pointing up. Right G hand, palm facing the signer and finger pointing left, is held in front of left hand. Right hand is drawn across, contacting left hand.

G Tab
Class B2 Signs

ENGLAND

TRY /G_D⊥ ı G_b⊥ ˣ̇/ — Manual tab G is held with palm facing down and finger pointing away from the signer. Right G hand, palm facing down and finger pointing away from the signer. Hands are held side by side. Right hand moves forward so that right index finger brushes along side of index finger of left hand.

ENGLAND /Ḡ₇> G_D⊥ ᵒ̌ˣ̇/ — Manual tab G is held with palm facing the signer and finger pointing right. Right G hand, palm facing down and finger pointing away from the signer. Right index finger, held above left, moves right and left along left index finger, maintaining contact, in a short repeated action.

Class B3 Signs

IMPROVE

BERRY /G₇>ₓ Ĥ<∧ ˣ̃/ — Manual tab G is held with palm facing the signer and finger pointing right. Right Ĥ hand, palm facing left and fingers pointing up. Fingers and thumb of right hand contact tip of left index finger. Right hand twists forward holding contact.

IMPROVE /G>∧ ıₓ F<∧ ˣ̂/ — Manual tab G is held with palm facing right and finger pointing up. Right F hand, palm facing left and fingers pointing up. Hands are held side by side. Tips of thumb and index fingers of right hand move up left index finger, maintaining contact.

O Tab
Class B2 Signs

POLE

MICROSCOPE /Ō>⊥ₓ O<⊥ ˣ̆·/ — Manual tab O is held with palm facing right and fingers pointing away from the signer. Right O hand, palm facing left and fingers pointing away from the signer. Left hand is held on top of right. Right hand performs nodding action twice.

POLE /Ō₇>ₓ O₇< ^/ — Manual tab O is held with palm facing the signer and fingers pointing right. Right O hand, palm facing the signer and fingers pointing left, is held on top of left hand, then moves up.

Class B3 Signs

POISON

EGG /Ō>⊥ ı Hₐ⊥ ˣ̌/ — Manual tab O is held with palm facing right and fingers pointing away from the signer. Right H hand, palm facing up and fingers pointing away from the signer, is held by the side of, and slightly above, the left hand. Right hand moves left brushing over the top of left hand.

POISON /Ō>⊥ ₒ Ï♭⊥ ˣ̌ᵉ/ — Manual tab O is held with palm facing right and fingers pointing away from the signer. Right Ï hand, palm facing down and finger pointing away from the signer. Little finger of right hand is placed within circle of left O hand. Little finger makes circular motion, maintaining contact.

Minor Manual Tabs

Several handshapes are used as tabs relatively infrequently. The following examples illustrate the possibility of using the marked handshapes E, F, H, I, G, V, G̈, ʊ, ʎ, ⋏, as tabs.

E Tab

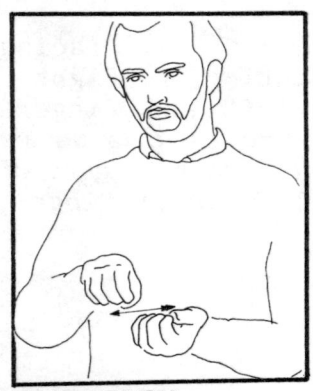

NAIL BRUSH /Ē₀⊥ E_D⊥ $\overset{\circ}{\hat{x}}$·/   Manual tab E is held with palm facing up and fingers pointing away from the signer. Right E hand, palm facing down and fingers pointing away from the signer, is held above left hand, then moves left and right in a short repeated movement, maintaining contact.

NAIL BRUSH

F Tab

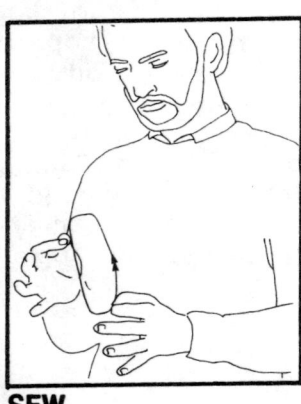

SEW /F̱>⊥ ı F<⊥ $\overset{\hat{\wedge}}{x}$·/   Manual tab F is held with palm facing right and fingers pointing away from the signer. Right F hand, palm facing left and fingers pointing away from the signer. Hands are held side by side with right hand slightly below left hand. Right hand moves up so that the right index finger and thumb circle makes contact with the left-hand circle, twice.

SEW

H Tab

KNIFE /H̄_T> H<⊥ $\overset{I·}{x}$/   Manual tab H is held with palm facing the signer and fingers pointing right. Right H hand, palm facing left and fingers pointing away from the signer. Left hand is held below right. Right hand moves to and fro so that fingers of right hand move backwards and forwards on top of fingers of left hand twice.

KNIFE

I Tab

END

END /Ī_T, B_<⊥ ˅ˣ/

Manual tab I is held with palm facing the signer and finger pointing right. Right B hand, palm facing left and fingers pointing away from the signer, is held above left hand. Right hand moves down to contact little finger of left hand.

G Tab

THEN

THEN /Ġ_T, G_<⊥ ॰ ⁽ˣᵖˣ⁾/

Manual tab Ġ is held with palm facing the signer and finger pointing right. Right G hand, palm facing left and finger pointing away from the signer, is held behind left hand. Right hand moves left so that index finger contacts thumb, then twists downwards to the right to contact left index finger.

V Tab

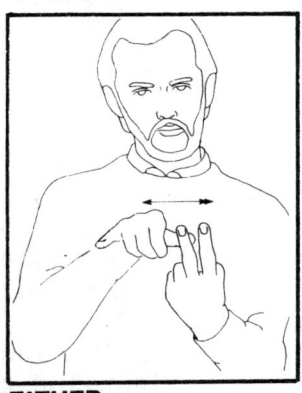
EITHER

EITHER /V_T∧ Y_b⊥ ॰ ᶻ/

Manual tab V is held with palm facing the signer and fingers pointing up. Right Y hand, palm facing down and fingers pointing away from the signer, is held behind left. Right hand moves from side to side.

G Tab

DEPEND

DEPEND /Ḡ_α, G̈_b⊥ ˅ˣ/

Manual tab G̈ is held with palm facing up and finger pointing right. Right G̈ hand, palm facing down and finger pointing away from the signer, is held above left hand, then moves down so that index fingers make contact.

64

ȣ Tab

CENTRE

CENTRE /ȣ_{a>} B_{bꞱ}^{×·}/ Manual tab ȣ is held with palm facing up and fingers pointing right. Right B hand, palm facing down and fingers pointing away from the signer. Left hand is held below right hand. Right palm contacts left middle finger twice.

Ɥ Tab

GOAL

GOAL /Ɥ_{>∧} G_{T<}^{<∘}/ Manual tab Ɥ is held with palm facing right and fingers pointing up. Right G hand, palm facing the signer and finger pointing left, moves to the left in a sharp movement so that index finger enters Ɥ hand.

λ Tab

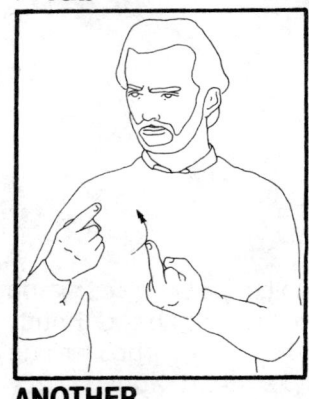
ANOTHER

ANOTHER /λ̈_{aꞱ ₁ ₚ} G_{T<}^{x̂·}/ Manual tab λ̈ is held with palm facing up and fingers pointing away from the signer. Right G hand, palm facing the signer and finger pointing left. Hands are held side by side with left hand slightly behind right hand. Right index finger brushes back of left middle finger twice.

Atypical Signing Space

The majority of BSL signs are articulated within the tab areas specified above. However, there are some signs which have citation forms making use of tabs outside the typical signing space. In practice, these signs may be moved either nearer to or within the typical signing space, although at present there is insufficient evidence to indicate how often and in what circumstances this happens.

All the signs so far noted in atypical signing space are either deictic or iconic. The deictic signs involve indicating the parts of the body concerned. Usually a pointing action involving the G hand with appropriate orientation is used. The signs for "knee", "heel" and "thigh" are all deictic signs of this type. Virtually all other signs occurring outside the typical signing space are iconic.

Relatively few signs occur above the top of the head. The following signs are here given whole head tab, but it could be argued that their citation forms are articulated several inches above the normal limits of this area.

HEAVEN

CEILING /⊂B̈<∧ ⊥/

Right B̈ hand, palm facing left and fingers pointing up, is held above the head. Hand moves forward away from the signer.

HEAVEN /⊂B̈>∧ ⨯ B̈<∧ ÷/

Two B̈ hands: left hand, palm facing right and fingers pointing up; right hand, palm facing left and fingers pointing up. Hands are placed side by side and touching in the area above the head. The hands separate to the left and right.

STAR

STAR /⊂Ĥ⊥∧ □[v̇]/

Right Ĥ hand, palm facing away from the signer and fingers pointing up, is held at right side, above head. Fingers open to a V hand.

Although the first two signs are above the head, the top of the head tab would be inappropriate as this implies either contact or close proximity to the top of the head.

Rather more signs occur below the waist area, and thus below the typical signing space, than occur above the head area. All such signs appear to be iconic and a major sub-category consists of sexual signs. As in spoken language, these signs form a rather special grouping in that there appear to be different vocabularies of signs used depending upon the linguistic and situational contexts in which they are used. The spoken words used for sexual meanings within the context of a medical discussion or a lecture on genetics will be very different from those used either within an intimate relationship or within totally male company. In both sign and spoken languages, sexual signs are not always easily studied by the outsider, yet the insider may be familiar with only some groups of signs. Typical sexual signs occurring in the area below the waist region are VAGINA /⊔Ġ₎ᵥᵢₓĠ₍ᵥ ˣ/ and PENIS /⊔(Ḡₐ₎ ₍ₓḠₐ₍ ˇ)/. Woodward (1979) in his work on American sexual signs suggests that these are often moved from the region below the waist, to waist level, thus losing some of their explicit iconicity and conforming to the more typical patterns of ASL signs. We have noted examples of this in BSL as well. For example MASTURBATE /⊔O_T< ~·/ and CONDOM /⊔(G_bɪɪₓF_<ɪ ˣ)/ can be signed above or below the waist. Sufficient signs do occur below the waist to make it useful to distinguish the following extra tab areas. The first of these, labelled the hip region, includes the whole lower body area from waist to thighs.

Hip Region

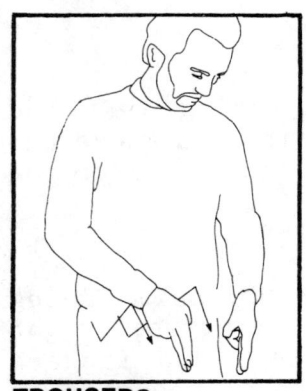

TROUSERS

TROUSERS /⊔H₎ᵥᵢH₍ᵥ ˅^˅/
ˣ<ˣ

Two H hands: left hand, palm facing right and fingers pointing down; right hand, palm facing left and fingers pointing down. Hands, placed side by side on right hip, move downward maintaining contact. Hands then move up and left and perform the same action on left hip.

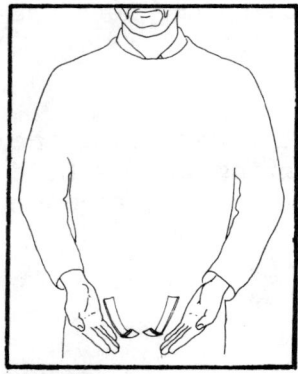

BIRTH

BIRTH /⊔B₎ᵥB₍ᵥ ˘/

Two B hands: left hand, palm facing right and fingers pointing down; right hand, palm facing left and fingers pointing down. Hands, held at either side of hip region, move down and twist so that palms face up.

Minimal Pair

BRA /[ ]Ḡ_Tᵥᵢ Ḡ_Tᵥ ÷/

Two Ḡ hands, palms facing the signer and fingers pointing down, are placed side by side on chest then separate.

PANTS /⊔Ḡ_Tᵥᵢ Ḡ_Tᵥ ÷/

Two Ḡ hands, palms facing the signer and fingers pointing down, are placed side by side on hip then separate.

BRA   **PANTS**

A further example, problematic in several respects, occurs on the back of the hip region: this is the iconic sign SQUIRREL /ʜC♭﹥ ˣâ/ . The only other example so far noted that demands back of body contact, is SAILOR /└⌐B⊥﹥ˣB┬﹤ ˣᴼˣ/ which involves contact on the front and back of lower trunk. Both are difficult to transcribe, although orientation can help to clarify the articulations involved.

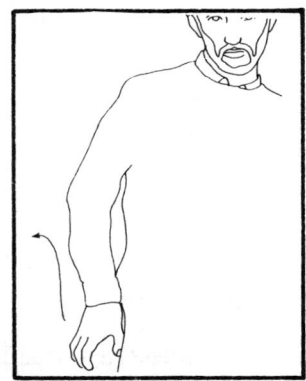

SQUIRREL /ʜC♭﹥ ˣâ/

Right C hand, palm facing down and fingers pointing right, is placed on back of lower right hip region. Hand moves up and twists upwards.

SAILOR /└⌐B⊥﹥ˣB┬﹤ ˣᴼˣ/

Left B hand, palm facing away from the signer and fingers pointing right, is held on back of lower trunk. Right B hand, palm facing the signer and fingers pointing left, is held on front of lower trunk. Hands exchange positions: left hand contacting front of body and right hand contacting back of body. The action is repeated.

Upper and Lower Leg Tabs ↓↑

Two other minor tab regions, upper leg and lower leg, can be distinguished for signs made on the leg, although there are very few signs exploiting these tabs.

DOG /↓B﹤ᵥ ˣ·/

Right B hand, palm facing left and fingers pointing down, is placed on right upper leg. Hand touches leg twice.

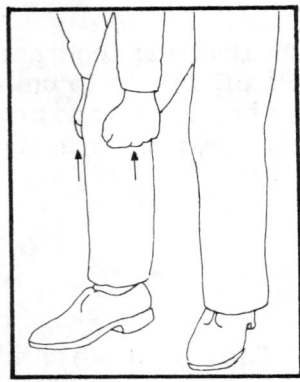

BOOT /ᶦA>ᵥ A<ᵥ ˆˣ/

Two A hands: left hand, palm facing right and fingers pointing down; right hand, palm facing left and fingers pointing down. Hands, placed on either side of right lower leg, move upward maintaining contact.

BOOT

Articulatory and Perceptual Constraints

Friedman (1977) suggests that the basic constraints on place of articulation are not language specific, but rather articulatory and perceptual: the place of articulation must be easily available to the signer and clearly visible to the addressee. Despite the exceptions mentioned above, significant tab realisations do not normally include positions on the back of the signer's body, probably because they would be both awkward to produce and difficult to see. However, it remains an open question as to whether such positions can occur phonemically on a regular basis. It is interesting to note that behind the signer positions have been found in gesture systems used by non-deaf linguistic communities. The Australian Aboriginal Community, the Worora, described by Love in 1941, used a set of gestures to accompany and clarify spoken words expressing family relationships. Several of these involved contact on the back of the body. According to Love these gestures were in daily use and were seen as helpful for communication at a distance. This suggests that despite their location these gestures were easily perceivable. While these examples indicate that we should approach the notion of universal perceptual constraints with some caution, evidence from sign languages within deaf communities does point to the likely importance of perceptual factors in limiting the signing space.

The creative opposition characterised by Martinet (1960) as the "permanent conflict between Man's communicative needs and his tendency to reduce to a minimum his mental and physical activity" affects sign languages as well as spoken languages. Historical changes in sign language, for example, those reported by Frishberg (1975) for ASL, indicate that adaptations coincide with the demands of both the perceptual and productive systems. New signs are rationalised into the system by losing some of their iconic aspects and becoming more arbitrary, thus exploiting the existing phonemic distinctions. The explicit iconicity may aid initial understanding but the principle of least effort ensures that new additions to the phonemic inventory are avoided if possible.

The perceptual visual constraints on sign structure have received considerable attention recently, although as yet there is surprisingly little in the way of detailed research. Siple (1978, p9) has suggested that one aspect of the visual perception system, visual acuity, may constrain the structure of individual signs:

> *"Visual acuity is at its best at the center of focus and rapidly drops off as the distance from that point increases. This means that a receiver could pick up finer discriminations between signs made near the point of focus than between others made farther away."*

Siple has suggested that visual acuity may determine not only where signs are produced but the structure of signs which are likely to occur in given areas. Signs which occur in the outer area below the neck, are often two-handed and because of the symmetrical patterning in double dez signs (see Chapter 1) the same information is presented twice; the decrease in visual acuity may be compensated for by an increase in redundancy.

Double Contact Signs

Both articulatory and perceptual factors may also affect the patterning of signs which involve more than one contact or more than one tab specification. Battison (1973) suggests that ASL signs involving double contact have both contacts within the same major area unless they are compound signs. Double contact signs in BSL include the following:

FRIDAY /⌒H<ʌ ˣ>ˣ/

Right H hand, palm facing left and fingers pointing up, is held touching left side of mouth. Hand moves to the right so that fingers touch right side of mouth.

HOSPITAL

HOSPITAL /∧G_T< ˣᶻ/

Right G hand, palm facing the signer and fingers pointing left. Index finger, placed on upper arm moves down, maintaining contact, then touches arm again making a movement to the right (tracing cross on arm).

SOLDIER /⌐ ⌐B<ʌ ˣ>ˣ/

Right B hand, palm facing left and fingers pointing up, makes contact with left shoulder. Hand moves right to touch right shoulder.

PLAN /B̄ₐ⊥ V̈ᵦ< ˣωˣ·/
(verb)

Manual tab B is held with palm facing up and fingers pointing away from the signer. Right V hand, palm facing down and fingers pointing left. Fingers of right hand touch left palm, twist to the right then touch palm again. The action is repeated.

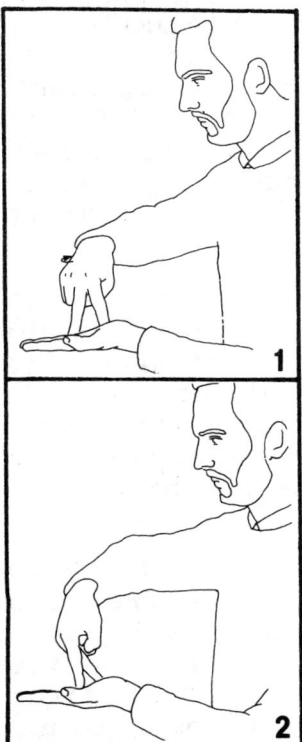

PLAN

Compound Signs

In compound signs involving double contact, the hand(s) generally move from one major area to another. However, Friedman and Battison (1973) suggest that in ASL not all possible sequences of locations are used. Typical sequences are:

head ⟶ trunk

head ⟶ arm

hand ⟶ head

Unused sequences include:

trunk ⟶ head/arm/hand

arm ⟶ head/trunk/hand

hand ⟶ trunk/arm

If the head is the first place of contact then there is greater freedom of choice as to the second place of contact. As yet, the sequences most frequently used in BSL have not been computed, but present estimations suggest that the majority of double contact compound signs have head/face as the first place of contact. Within this group, the most common specific tab is the mouth. In rare instances the head is the second place of contact. The transcription of such signs may give the impression that there is a definite break between the two parts of the sign. However, this is not normally the case.

DECIDE

LEARN

CONFESS
/∪G_{T∧}^{×⌄}∥[]Ï_{α>₁}Ï_{α<}^{×}/

Right G hand, palm facing the signer and finger pointing up, is held with index finger touching mouth. Right hand moves down and away from signer. Two Ï hands: left hand, palm facing up and fingers pointing right; right hand, palm facing up and fingers pointing left, contact left side of chest.

DECIDE
/⌒G_{<∧}^{×}∥B̂_{α>}G_{<⊥}^{⌄×}/

Right G hand, palm facing left and finger pointing up, is held touching the forehead. Manual tab B is held with palm facing up and fingers pointing right. Right G hand, palm facing left and finger pointing away from the signer, moves down so that index finger makes contact with left palm in a sharp movement.

KISS
/∪B̂_{⊥∧}^{×}∥B̂_{T∧}B̂_{⊥∧}^{⊥×}/

Right B̂ hand, palm facing away from the signer and fingers pointing up, is placed at mouth. Manual tab B̂ is held with palm facing the signer and fingers pointing up. Right hand moves away from the signer and contacts left hand.

LEARN
/B̄_{α⊥}×B̿_{b⊥}^{∧}∥⌒B̂_{⊥∧}^{×}/

Manual tab B is held with palm facing up and fingers pointing away from the signer. Right B̿ hand, palm facing down and fingers pointing away from the signer, is held above left palm. Right hand moves up to forehead closing to a B̂ hand, and is held with palm facing away from the signer and fingers pointing up. Hand contacts forehead.

Simultaneous Double Tab Signs

A further category of double tab signs has also been noted in BSL. This category is neither double contact nor compound, but involves the simultaneous use of two tabs. Examples so far noted make use of a specific body tab and a hand tab. It is difficult to transcribe such signs using present notation conventions. However, in the examples below the use of bracketing ( ) allows us to treat these signs as manual tab signs which can then be placed on various regions of the body. In FOCUS the section in curved brackets ( ) is a manual tab sign which is then placed on a body tab, in this case the eye ⊓. If contact is involved between hand and body this can be shown by placing the contact symbol x outside the curved brackets.

FOCUS /⊓(O$_{>\wedge}$?x O$_{<\wedge}$ $\overset{x}{\underset{<}{\check{\eta}}}$)/ Manual tab O is held at right eye with palm facing right and fingers pointing up. Right O hand, palm facing left and fingers pointing up, is held touching the front of the left hand. Right hand nods to the left, the action is repeated.

FOCUS

PUBLICISE /∪(A$_{>\wedge}$?x A$_{<\wedge}$^{I})/ Manual tab A is held at mouth with palm facing right and finger pointing up. Right A hand, palm facing left and fingers pointing up, is held touching the front of the left hand. Right hand moves to and fro.

PUBLICISE

72
Notes

Designation

The Handshape Parameter

The significant handshapes of BSL are those which can bring about a change of meaning. Relatively small changes in the shape of the hand may be significant, while other comparable differences may be merely phonetic and non-significant.

Clearly there are numerous possible handshapes which are not exploited within BSL but may exist in other sign languages. While the bent index finger is significant in BSL, the bent little finger does not occur phonemically. Even a feature such as thumb extension which is clearly significant in some handshapes, may be (phonemically) non-significant in others. Thus, while the difference between closed fist with extended thumb and closed fist without extended thumb is significant in BSL, the difference between flat hand with extended thumb and flat hand without extended thumb is non-significant and merely phonetic. In the following sections, the phonemic dez realisations of BSL will be described, together with the main phonetic (allophonic) variants.

It should be noted that this section includes a number of changes from the first edition. Most of these changes relate to the labelling of the handshapes. Originally, we tried to avoid making changes to Stokoe's notation system as it was clearly important to have a system which could be used and understood by researchers in different countries. However, those learning the transcription system have brought to our attention a number of inconsistencies which have caused them difficulty. Some of these inconsistencies were linked to our addition of extra diacritics to the original system. We have now tried to rationalise the use of these marks to the extent that it has seemed appropriate to change the names of some of the handshapes.

As noted in Chapter 2, the labels used for the handshapes are largely based on the American finger-spelling alphabet. While this link has been retained overall, in individual handshapes we have been prepared to change from the finger-spelling label if this move appears to provide more consistency for the learner. The phoneme originally labelled X involves extension of the index finger (as in the handshape G) and the bending of this finger. However, in other handshapes, such as H, V, 5 and W, the bending of the fingers is shown by the addition of the diacritic ¨ , ie Ḧ, V̈, 5̈, Ẅ. Therefore, in order to retain this consistency we have relabelled X so that it now becomes G̈. A similar change, exploiting the use of the diacritic ˙ for prominent thumb, involves the relabelling of L so that it becomes Ġ. To clarify such changes and the use of diacritics within this section, the main symbols are presented and illustrated on the following pages.

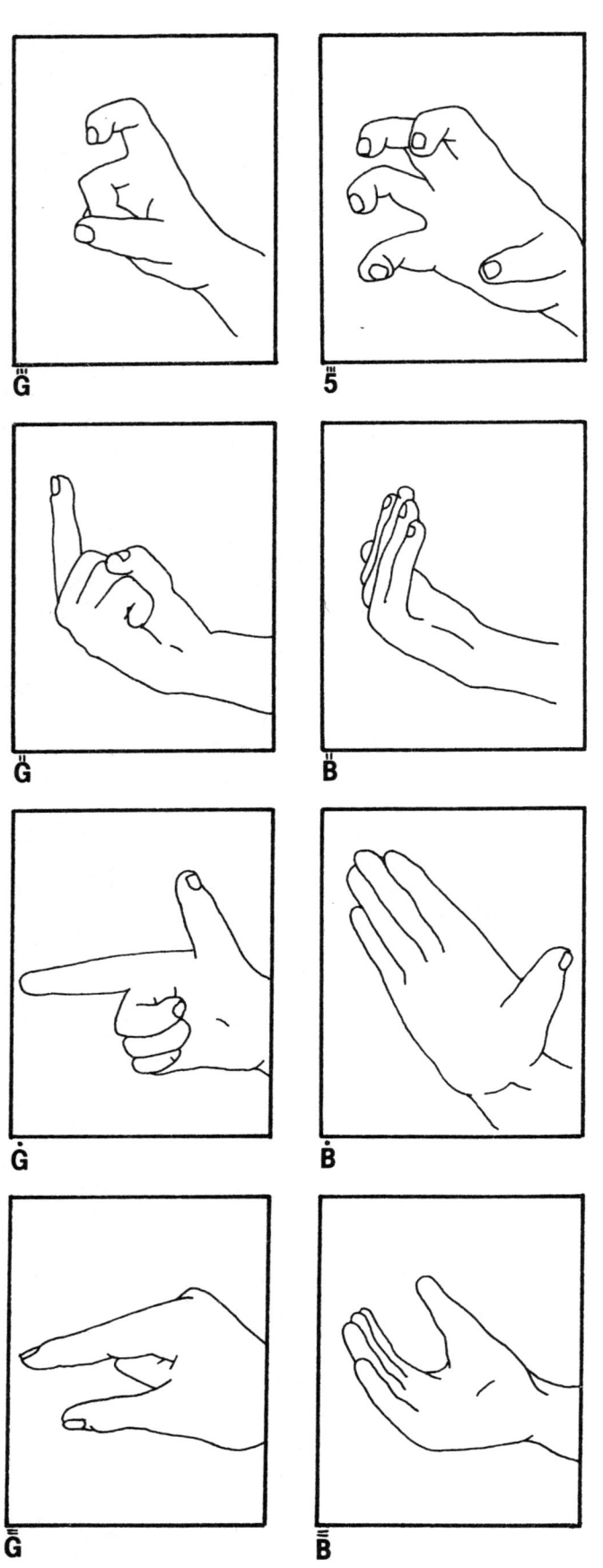

$'''$ as in $\ddot{\ddot{G}}$, $\ddot{\ddot{H}}$, $\ddot{\ddot{V}}$, $\ddot{\ddot{W}}$, $\ddot{\ddot{5}}$, $\ddot{\ddot{E}}$

interpreted as 'bending of the finger(s)'.

$''$ as in $\ddot{B}$, $\ddot{G}$, $\ddot{H}$, $\ddot{I}$, $\ddot{V}$, $\ddot{W}$, $\ddot{\lambda}$

interpreted as 'bending at the knuckles'.

$'$ as in $\dot{A}$, $\dot{B}$, $\dot{G}$, $\dot{H}$, $\dot{V}$, $\dot{\curlyvee}$

interpreted as 'prominent thumb', ie extension of the thumb so that it is at right angles to the index finger.

$=$ as in $\bar{\bar{B}}$, $\bar{\bar{G}}$, $\bar{\bar{H}}$

interpreted as 'thumb and index finger parallel', ie the thumb is extended but held parallel, rather than at right angles, to the index finger. The gap between finger and thumb may vary.

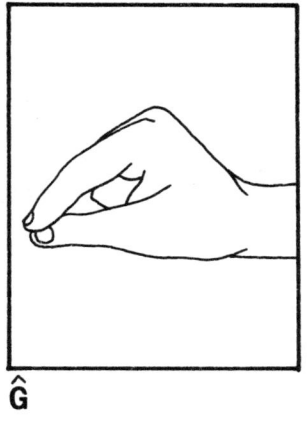
Ĝ

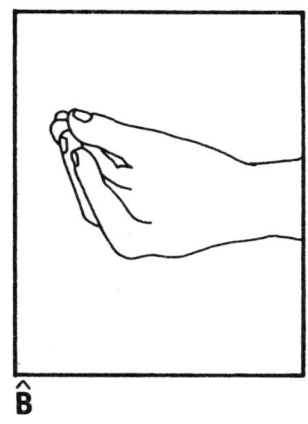
B̂

^ as in B̂, Ĝ, Ĥ, ◌̂, ◌̂, Â,

interpreted as 'thumb and finger(s) touching'. In all cases except Â the contact is between thumb tip and fingertip(s).

In some cases two sets of diacritics are added to the dez label: this may appear complex at first, but once the basic rationale has been understood, reading these symbols becomes relatively easy.

The marks are used in such a way that if one reads the diacritics in order, from lowest to highest, the physical configuration should be apparent, as in the following examples.

In G̈

- G tells us that the index finger is extended
- = tells us that the thumb is held parallel
- ''' tells us that both finger and thumb are bent.

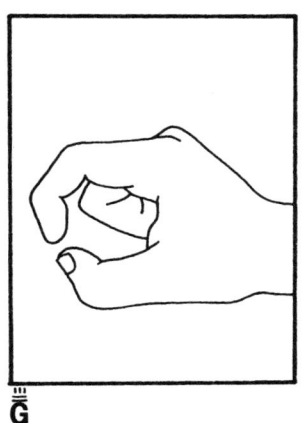
G̈

In G̈

- G tells us that the index finger is extended
- ''' tells us that the index finger is bent
- · tells us that the thumb is prominent.

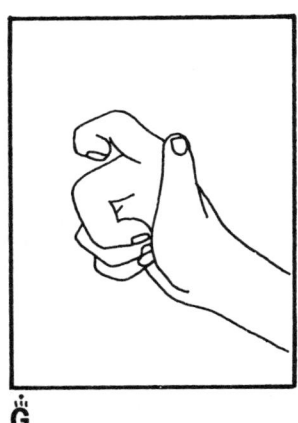
G̈

In this last example the thumb is not bent because the 'thumb prominent' diacritic is placed above the diacritic for 'bent'. A set of illustrations showing the main handshapes of BSL with their new labels can be found in the pull-out section at the end of the book.

There is some difficulty in deciding on the appropriate ordering of BSL handshapes: so far no fully acceptable convention for ordering has been established. In <u>Words in Hand 1</u>, we aimed to present the unmarked handshapes first, but this did not work out in practice as it also seemed sensible to place related handshapes together. Therefore, Ȧ, Â and A_s were all shown before B. Of course, attempting to order the handshapes in relation to aspects of their physical formation is also a dubious practice - after all, the letters of English do not occur in an order related to their shape. However, again keeping in mind the needs of those learning the system, we have decided to group handshapes on the basis of such features as closed, open, bent, etc. We stress that because each handshape is, in fact, a complex of such features, the result cannot be totally satisfactory. As the feature 'bent' is inherent in Group 1 and Group 2 and possible in all other groups, it is somewhat artificial to give this title to any single group. In most cases we have tried to place handshapes within a group by pinpointing that central feature which, even in modified versions of the handshape, is not lost. Thus, although B is often referred to as "the flat hand", it may be modified by having bending at the knuckles so that the hand is no longer fully flat. One feature which does remain constant in all the handshapes labelled B, eg Ḃ, B̈, B̿, B̂, B̤, is the fact that the fingers are held close together, rather than apart. This then is seen as the central feature of the B handshape. The groups of BSL handshapes established on this basis are presented below.

BSL HANDSHAPES

Group 1   Fully Closed

          A Ȧ Â A_s

Group 2   Curved or Bent

          C O E Ë Ë̈

Group 3   Fingers Together

          B Ḃ B̈ B̿ B̂ B̤

Group 4   Fingers Spread

          5 5̈ F F_(RC) ȣ ȣ̂

Group 5   Finger(s) Extended from Closed Fist

          G Ġ G̈ G⃛ Ḡ Ĝ G̿ G̈̇ Ĝ̇ G_d

          H Ḣ Ḧ H⃛ H̄ Ĥ H̿

          V V̇ V̈ V⃛ V̿

          R W Ẅ W⃛ W_m I Ï Y ʯ ʯ̇

          ʯ̂ 人 人̇

The status of each of these handshapes is discussed in the appropriate section. Thus some of these handshapes can be regarded as separate phonemes of BSL, others can be regarded as allophones of one phoneme. The use of diacritics does not imply any particular status.

Group 1: Fully Closed A Dez

The closed fist dez, A, is one of the unmarked handshapes and is used in all the classes of signs described in Chapter 1, including complex and compound signs. There are several variations in the formation of A which can be regarded as phonetic: some of these can be predicted by the phonetic context. The basic variable is the positioning of the thumb. It can be held across the edge of the fingers, or across the dorsal side of the closed fingers, as in American finger-spelled A_s (see page 17).

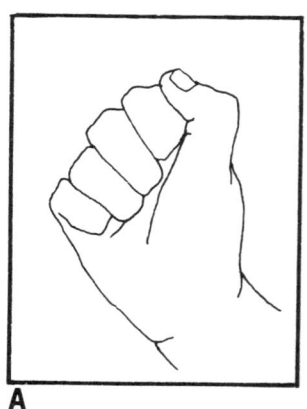
A

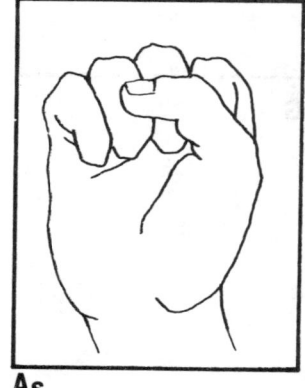
A_s

WILL

BREAK

NUMBER

AUNT

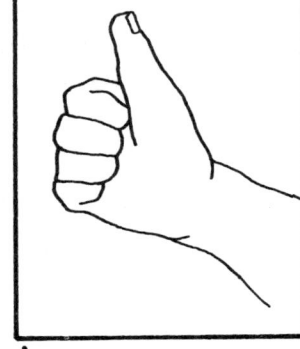
Ȧ

ROCK /⌒A$_{<∧}$ ẙ/
(eg Blackpool Rock)

WILL /3A$_{⊥<}$ ẋ̃/

CRASH /ØA$_{T>}$ A$_{T<}$ ⁺ẋ/

BREAK /ØA$_{⊅⊥}$ ₁ₓ A$_{⊅⊥}$ ä̇/

Single Dez Signs

Right A hand, palm facing left and fingers pointing up, is held at mouth. Hand twists so that palm faces the signer.

Right A hand, palm facing away from the signer and fingers pointing left, is held against side of right cheek. Hand twists, holding contact.

Double Dez Signs

Two A hands: left hand, palm facing the signer and fingers pointing right; right hand, palm facing the signer and fingers pointing left. Hands, held in neutral space, come together in sharp action.

Two A hands, palms facing down and fingers pointing away from the signer, are held side by side and touching in neutral space. Hands move apart in twisting action.

Minimal Pair

NUMBER /⌒A$_{T∧}$ ˣ˙/

Right A hand, palm facing the signer and fingers pointing up, is held at chin. Hand contacts the chin twice.

AUNT /⌒Ḧ$_{T∧}$ ˣ˙/

Right Ḧ hand, palm facing the signer and fingers pointing up, is held at chin. Fingers contact the chin twice.

Ȧ Dez

The Ȧ dez is closely related to A: both handshapes make use of the closed fist but in Ȧ the thumb is extended. This handshape is significantly distinct from A.

CLEVER

FRIEND

RIGHT

YOUR

NEXT /ø$\dot{A}_{b\perp}$ $\overset{\omega}{>}$/

CLEVER /∩$\dot{A}_{<\wedge}$ $\overset{\dot{x}}{}$/

KIND /[ ]$\dot{A}_{\top>}$, $\dot{A}_{\top<}$ $^{x\perp}$/

FRIEND /ø$\dot{A}_{>\perp}$, $\dot{A}_{<\perp}$ $^{x\cdot}$/

Single Dez Signs

Right $\dot{A}$ hand, palm facing down and fingers pointing away from the signer, is held in neutral space. Hand twists to the right.

Right $\dot{A}$ hand, palm facing left and fingers pointing up, is held with thumb touching left side of forehead. Thumb moves to the right maintaining contact.

Double Dez Signs

Two $\dot{A}$ hands: left hand, palm facing the signer and fingers pointing right; right hand, palm facing the signer and fingers pointing left. Hands, held side by side on chest, move away from the signer.

Two $\dot{A}$ hands: left hand, palm facing right and fingers pointing away from the signer; right hand, palm facing left and fingers pointing away from the signer. Hands are held side by side in neutral space, then come together, touching twice.

Minimal Pair

RIGHT /ø$\dot{A}_{\perp\wedge}$ $^{\perp}$/
(You are right)

Right $\dot{A}$ hand, palm facing away from the signer and fingers pointing up, is held in neutral space. Hand moves away from the signer.

YOUR /øA$_{\perp\wedge}$ $^{\perp}$/
(2nd person singular)

Right A hand, palm facing away from the signer and fingers pointing up, is held in neutral space. Hand moves away from the signer.

79

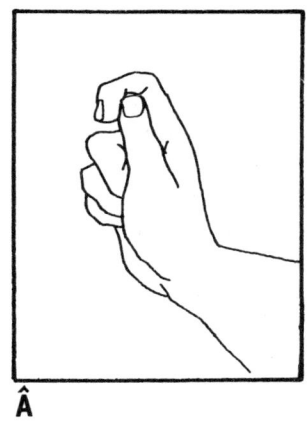
Â

Â Dez

The Â dez has the index finger extended from the closed fist and bent at both joints. The thumb is also extended and touches the middle of the two joints of the bent index finger.

Single Dez Signs

BUY

KEY /∅Âᵦ⊥ ᵚ/ — Right Â hand, palm facing down and fingers pointing away from the signer, is held in neutral space. Hand twists to the right.

BUY /B̄ₐ₎ Âᵦ⊥ ᵛˣ/ — Manual tab B is held with palm facing up and fingers pointing right. Right Â hand, palm facing down and fingers pointing away from the signer, is held above left hand, then moves down onto left palm.

Double Dez Signs

CONTROL

XYLOPHONE /∅Â₎⊥,Â₍⊥ ᵚ~/ — Two Â hands: left hand, palm facing right and fingers pointing away from the signer; right hand, palm facing left and fingers pointing away from the signer. Hands, held side by side in neutral space, move up and down in an alternating action while moving to the right.

CONTROL /∅Â₎⊥,Â₍⊥ ᴵ~/ — Two Â hands: left hand, palm facing right and fingers pointing away from the signer; right hand, palm facing left and fingers pointing away from the signer. Hands, held side by side in neutral space, move to and fro alternately.

SELL

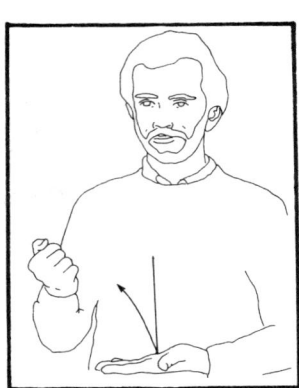
PRINT

Minimal Pair

SELL /B̄ₐ₌ Âᵦ⊥ ᵛˣᵃ⁄ᴧ/

Manual tab B is held with palm facing up and fingers pointing right. Right Â hand, palm facing down and fingers pointing away from the signer, is held above left hand. Right hand moves down to make contact with the left-hand palm, then twists upward.

PRINT /B̄ₐ₌ Aᵦ⊥ ᵛˣᵃ⁄ᴧ/

Manual tab B is held with palm facing up and fingers pointing right. Right A hand, palm facing down and fingers pointing away from the signer, is held above left hand. Right hand moves down to make contact with the left-hand palm, then twists upward.

A rather specialised group of Â signs can be found within the Catholic deaf community in Britain. Irish Sign Language (ISL) appears to use a number of initial dez signs derived from the one-handed Irish manual alphabet, (see page 19). It is interesting to note that while such derived signs are in common use among Catholic deaf communities in Britain, many individuals using these signs may be quite unfamiliar with the one-handed alphabet. It is likely that the original Irish signs have undergone different modifications in different parts of Britain. Â is the same as the letter *t* of the Irish alphabet, hence the minimal pair:

TEA

COFFEE

TEA /Āₜ₌ₓ Âₜ₍ ᵉ⁄ₓ/

Manual tab A is held with palm facing the signer and fingers pointing right. Right Â hand, palm facing the signer and fingers pointing left, is placed on top of left hand and makes an anti-clockwise circular motion.

COFFEE /Āₜ₌ₓ Aₜ₍ ᵉ⁄ₓ/

Manual tab A is held with palm facing the signer and fingers pointing right. Right A hand, palm facing the signer and fingers pointing left, is placed on top of left hand and makes an anti-clockwise circular motion.

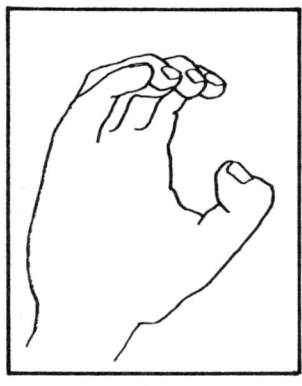
C

Group 2: Curved or Bent
C Dez

The essential features of this handshape are that the fingers and thumb are bent into a curve resembling the letter *c* of the Irish, American and British manual alphabets. This could be regarded as a bent form of B but because it is clearly one of the unmarked handshapes of the language, it is more appropriate to give the handshape a separate name. It is also used in initial dez signs relating to English words beginning with 'C'.

Single Dez Signs

COFFEE /⊃C<∧ ω̇/

Right C hand, palm facing left and fingers pointing up, is held at right side of mouth. Hand twists in a short repeated action.

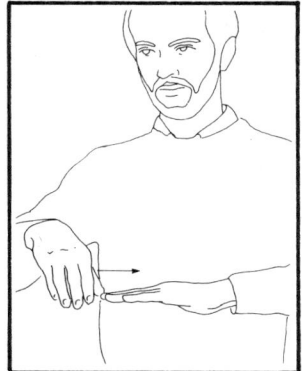
SHOE

SHOE /B⊃>⊥ C⊐⊥ ˂/

Manual tab B is held with palm facing down and fingers pointing right. Right C hand, palm facing down and fingers pointing away from the signer. Hands are held side by side. Right hand moves to the left over left hand.

Double Dez Signs

GROUP

BRICK /∅C>⊥ ₁ₓC<⊥ ÷/

Two C hands: left hand, palm facing right and fingers pointing away from the signer; right hand, palm facing left and fingers pointing away from the signer. Hands, held side by side and touching in neutral space, separate to the right and left.

GROUP /∅C>⊥ ₁C<⊥ ᐣˣ/

Two C hands: left hand, palm facing right and fingers pointing away from the signer; right hand, palm facing left and fingers pointing away from the signer. Hands, held side by side in neutral space, move together and touch.

Minimal Pair

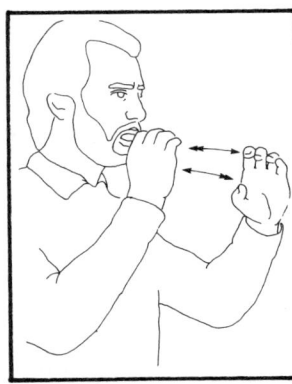
COMMUNICATION

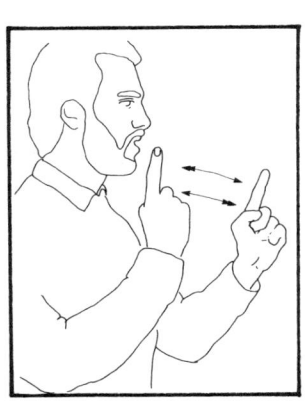
CONVERSATION

COMMUNICATION /⊃C>∧ C<∧ ᴵ~/

Two C hands: left hand, palm facing right and fingers pointing up; right hand, palm facing left and fingers pointing up. Hands, held in front of the mouth, move to and fro alternately.

CONVERSATION /⊃G>∧ G<∧ ᴵ~/

Two G hands: left hand, palm facing right and fingers pointing up; right hand, palm facing left and fingers pointing up. Hands, held in front of the mouth, move to and fro alternately.

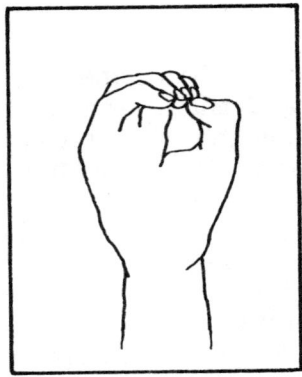
O

EAT

SAID

O Dez

This is the handshape in which all the fingers are bent and together. The thumb is bent and touching the fingertips. Again, despite its formational similarity to C, it is more appropriate to give this handshape a separate label as it is unmarked in the sense discussed in Chapter 1. However, it does not seem to occur in as wide a range of signs as A, B and 5.

Single Dez Signs

LIGHT /⌒O⊐⊥ ^{□[5]}/
(noun)

Right O hand, palm facing down and fingers pointing away from the signer, is held at the side of the face. Hand opens to a 5 hand.

EAT /⌒O⊤∧ ^{T×}/

Right O hand, palm facing the signer and fingers pointing up, is held at mouth. Hand contacts mouth.

Double Dez Signs

PRACTISE /∅O>⊥ ı× O<⊥ ^{I·}/

Two O hands: left hand, palm facing right and fingers pointing away from the signer; right hand, palm facing left and fingers pointing away from the signer. Hands, held side by side and touching in neutral space, move repeatedly to and fro, maintaining contact.

SAID /∅O>⊥ ı O<⊥ ^{×·}/
(Regional: Glasgow)

Two O hands: left hand, palm facing right and fingers pointing away from the signer; right hand, palm facing left and fingers pointing away from the signer. Hands are held side by side in neutral space, then contact each other in repeated action.

Minimal Pair

NIL /∅O<∧ ^{°⊥}/

Right O hand, palm facing left and fingers pointing up, is held in neutral space. Hand moves forward in a short sharp movement.

SUPERB /∅F<∧ ^{°⊥}/

Right F hand, palm facing left and fingers pointing up, is held in neutral space. Hand moves forward in a short sharp movement.

NIL · SUPERB

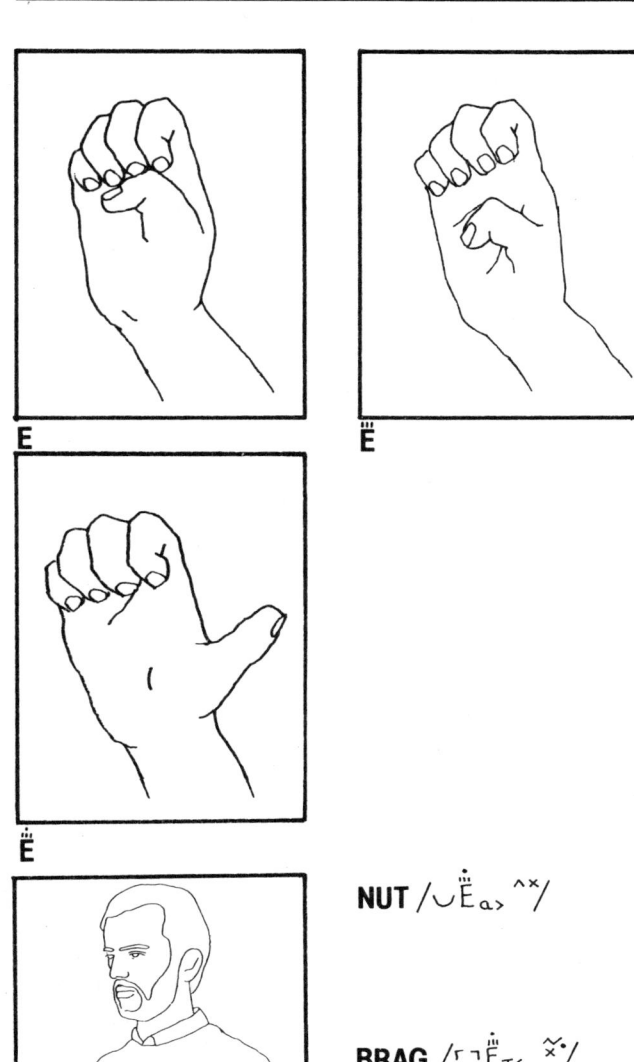

E Dez

The contracted hand configuration E is the same as the letter *e* of the American manual alphabet. The handshape involves bending at mid finger joints and thus has some similarity with A. The realisations of E which are used most frequently in BSL are the so-called bent E, Ë, and bent E with a prominent thumb, Ë. The handshape Ë has the fingers bent but held at a distance from the bent thumb, while in Ë the thumb is held straight. Ë could be regarded as a closed variant of 5̈ but minimal pairs show that this distinction is phonemic. The E dez is used infrequently in BSL.

Single Dez Signs

NUT /∪Ëₐ> ^×/

Right Ë hand, palm facing up and fingers pointing right, is held below chin. Hand moves up so that heel of palm contacts chin, pressing upwards.

BRAG /⌐⌐Ëт< ˜×˙/

Right Ë hand, palm facing the signer and fingers pointing left, is placed on upper trunk. Hand moves up and down in a repeated action, maintaining contact.

Double Dez Signs

ESKIMO /⊃Ë>⊥ᵢË<⊥ ⁝⊃ᶜ×/

Two Ë hands: left hand, palm facing right and fingers pointing away from the signer; right hand, palm facing left and fingers pointing away from the signer. Hands, held side by side at forehead, separate moving down each side of the face and finally come towards each other and contact.

HIPPOPOTAMUS /∅Ēₐ⊥ Eᴅ⊥ ×÷/

Two E hands: left hand, palm facing up and fingers pointing away from the signer; right hand, palm facing down and fingers pointing away from the signer. Right hand is held above left in neutral space. Hands contact and separate.

HIPPOPOTAMUS

KEEN

EXCITING

Minimal Pair

KEEN /[ ]Ë_{T>} Ë_{T<} ˣ˜·/

Two Ë hands: left hand, palm facing the signer and fingers pointing right; right hand, palm facing the signer and fingers pointing left. Hands, placed on chest, move up and down alternately in a repeated action, maintaining contact.

EXCITING /[ ]5̈_{T>} 5̈_{T<} ˣ˜·/

Two 5̈ hands: left hand, palm facing the signer and fingers pointing right; right hand, palm facing the signer and fingers pointing left. Hands, placed on chest, move up and down alternately in a repeated action, maintaining contact.

Group 3: Fingers Together

B Dez

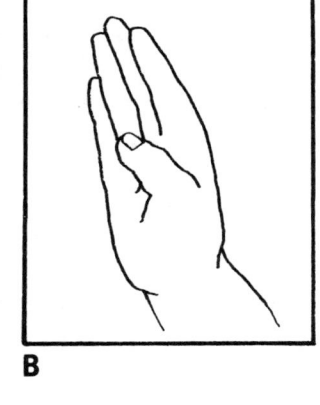

B

Like A, the B dez is one of the unmarked handshapes in BSL. It has a high frequency of occurrence. The essential features of the handshape are that the fingers are together and the hand is flat. The exact position of the thumb is unimportant: it may be held loosely at the side or across the palm without bringing about a change of meaning. Even the full extension of the thumb appears to be phonetically conditioned rather than phonemically significant (see page 85).

Single Dez Signs

DANGER

FISH /∅B_{<⊥} ᵑ·/

Right B hand, palm facing left and fingers pointing away from the signer, is held in neutral space. Hand moves forward, simultaneously performing a repeated side to side waving action.

DANGER /⌒B_{<∧} ᵀˣ/

Right B hand, palm facing left and fingers pointing up, is held in front of right forehead. Hand moves towards the body and touches forehead sharply.

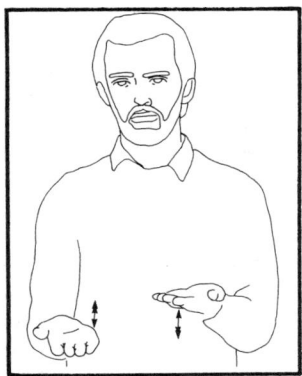
COMPARE

Double Dez Signs

WITHOUT /∅B₀⊥,B₀⊥ ᵃ/

Two B hands, palms facing down and fingers pointing away from the signer, are held side by side in neutral space. The hands simultaneously move towards the signer and twist upwards.

COMPARE /∅Bₐ⊥ Bₐ⊥ ~~˙/

Two B hands, palms facing up and fingers pointing away from the signer, are held in neutral space. Hands move up and down alternately in repeated action.

TRUE

LAW

Minimal Pair

TRUE /B̄ₐ﹥ B﹤⊥ ᵛˣ/

Manual tab B is held with palm facing up and fingers pointing right. Right B hand, palm facing left and fingers pointing away from the signer, is held above left hand. Right hand moves down to touch left palm.

LAW /B̄ₐ﹥ G﹤⊥ ᵛˣ/

Manual tab B is held with palm facing up and fingers pointing right. Right G hand, palm facing left and fingers pointing away from the signer, is held above left hand. Right hand moves down so that right index finger touches palm of left hand.

Ḃ

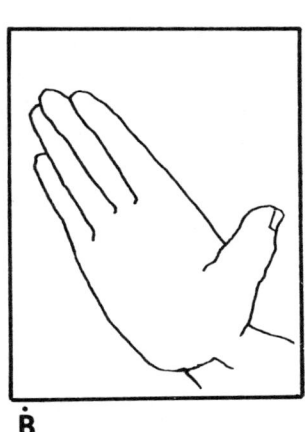
Ḃ

The B in which the prominent thumb is extended from the flat hand, Ḃ, was originally thought to be phonemic. However, it has not been possible to find minimal pairs to support this claim. Nevertheless, this variant is required in certain phonetic contexts, especially when thumb contact is used, or when a waving action is involved. In the latter case this may simply be to avoid the thumb getting in the way of the moving fingers. To clarify examples like those given below, the diacritic ˙ will be used to indicate that a prominent thumb is necessary.

COURTING

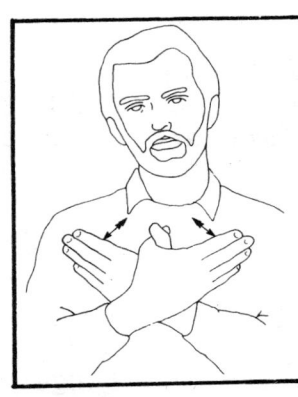
BUTTERFLY

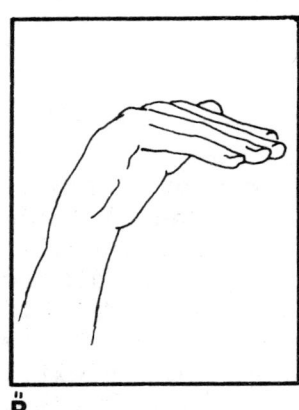
B̈

HOME

ITALY /⌣Ḃ_T∧ ᵐ·/

COURTING /⌐⌙<Ḃ_b⊥ ˣ/

PREPARE /⌐⌐Ḃ_D>Ḃ_D< ˆˣ·/

BUTTERFLY /∅Ḃ_T>ₓḂ_T< ᵐ·/

NUISANCE /B̄_D>B̈_b⊥ ᵛˣ·/

HOME /∅B̈_⊥∧ ᵖ/

Single Dez Signs

Right Ḃ hand, palm facing the signer and fingers pointing up, is held so that fingertips are parallel with mouth. Hand makes a repeated downward waving action at the knuckles.

Right Ḃ hand, palm facing down and fingers pointing away from the signer, contacts lower side of right trunk. (Contact is made so that inner surface of thumb and fingers are in contact with the body.)

Double Dez Signs

Two Ḃ hands: left hand, palm facing down and fingers pointing right; right hand, palm facing down and fingers pointing left. Hands are held with thumbs touching either side of upper trunk. Thumbs stroke upwards twice.

Two Ḃ hands: left hand, palm facing the signer and fingers pointing right; right hand, palm facing the signer and fingers pointing left. Hands are held with thumbs interlinking in neutral space, then wave to and fro at knuckles in repeated action.

B̈

This handshape, normally labelled bent B, B̈, has all the fingers together and straight but the hand is bent at the major knuckles. The exact positioning of the thumb may vary. The original diacritic for bending ‴ has been changed to show that the bending is at the knuckles. B̈ is phonemically distinct from B.

Single Dez Signs

Manual tab B is held with palm facing down and fingers pointing right. Right B̈ hand, palm facing down and fingers pointing away from the signer, is held above left hand. Right hand moves down and touches back of left hand twice.

Right B̈ hand, palm facing away from the signer and fingers pointing up, is held in neutral space, then hand nods away from the signer.

WITHDRAW

VISIT

UNDER

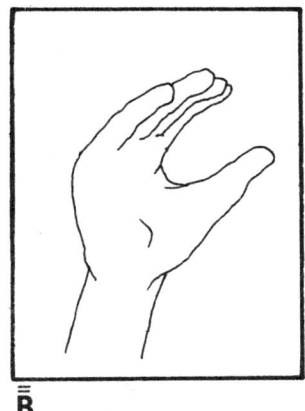
B̿

Double Dez Signs

WELCOME /∅ B̈ₐ⊥ B̈ₐ⊥ ᵐ·ᵀ/

Two B̈ hands, palms facing up and fingers pointing away from the signer, are held in neutral space. Hands wave towards the signer in repeated action.

WITHDRAW /∅ B̈ᵦ⊥ B̈ᵦ⊥ ᵀ/

Two B̈ hands, palms facing down and fingers pointing away from the signer, are held side by side in neutral space. Hands move towards the body.

Minimal Pair

VISIT / B̈ᵦ﹥ B̈ᵦ⊥ ₚ ⊥/

Manual tab B̈ is held with palm facing down and fingers pointing right. Right B̈ hand, palm facing down and fingers pointing away from the signer, is held under and behind the left hand. Right hand moves away from the signer.

UNDER / Bᵦ﹥ Bᵦ⊥ ₚ ⊥/

Manual tab B is held with palm facing down and fingers pointing right. Right B hand, palm facing down and fingers pointing away from the signer, is held under and behind the left hand. Right hand moves away from the signer.

B̿

This handshape also involves bending at the major knuckles, but in this case the thumb and fingers are held parallel. The width of the gap between fingers and thumb may vary. Originally the handshape was described as a bent B with a prominent thumb, Ḇ̈, but this was a less than accurate description of the actual configuration. As the parallel positioning of thumb and fingers occurs with other handshapes, eg G and H, it was decided to create a new diacritic to show this feature and to allow consistency across the system.

In <u>Words in Hand 1</u>, B̿ (then labelled Ḇ̈) was regarded as a phonetic variant of B̈, occurring primarily in signs that involve a closing or both closing and opening action. While the examples below will clearly illustrate its use in such signs, further research has shown that B̿ must now be regarded as phonemic in that it contrasts significantly with handshapes such as G̿ and H̿. The signs below also illustrate the possible variation in distance between index finger and thumb. A sign such as USE begins with thumb and fingers held quite close to each other, while in PHOTO the gap is larger. While the gap between thumb and index finger can be relatively wide in $\bar{\bar{B}}$, once the angle of the thumb changes from parallel to right angles, then the handshape is labelled $\ddot{B}$ rather than $\bar{\bar{B}}$. The closed counterpart to B, ie $\hat{B}$, occurring as the final handshape in the signs below, is also a separate phoneme in BSL and is illustrated in the next section.

PHOTO

USE /⌣$\bar{\bar{B}}_{T\wedge}$ ⊥̌# [$\hat{B}$]/

PHOTO /⌒$\bar{\bar{B}}_{T\wedge}$ ↓# [$\hat{B}$]/

Single Dez Signs

Right $\bar{\bar{B}}$ hand, palm facing the signer's body and fingers pointing up, is held grasping chin. Hand moves down closing to a $\hat{B}$ hand.

Right $\bar{\bar{B}}$ hand, palm facing the signer and fingers pointing up, is held in front of face. Hand moves away and down closing to a $\hat{B}$ hand.

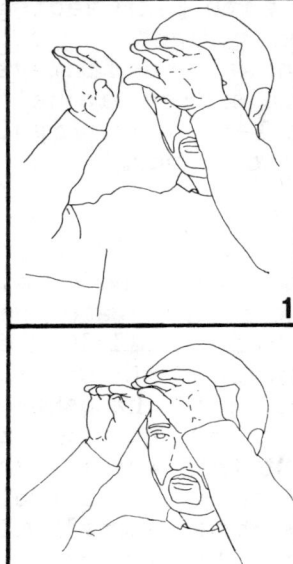
LEARN 1
          2

FINISH /∅$\bar{\bar{B}}_{\perp\wedge}$ $\bar{\bar{B}}_{\perp\wedge}$ #[$\hat{B}\hat{B}$]/

LEARN /⌒$\bar{\bar{B}}_{\perp\wedge}$ $\bar{\bar{B}}_{\perp\wedge}$ ⊤#[$\hat{B}\hat{B}$]/

Double Dez Signs

Two $\bar{\bar{B}}$ hands, palms facing away from the signer and fingers pointing up, are held in neutral space. Hands close to $\hat{B}$ hands.

Two $\bar{\bar{B}}$ hands, palms facing away from the signer and fingers pointing up, are held in front of the forehead. Hands move towards the forehead, closing to $\hat{B}$ hands.

SPEAK

DUCK

Minimal Pair

SPEAK /⌣$\bar{\bar{B}}_{\perp\wedge}$ #[$\hat{B}$]·/

Right $\bar{\bar{B}}$ hand, palm facing away from the signer and fingers pointing up, is held at mouth. Hand closes to a $\hat{B}$ hand. The action is repeated.

DUCK /⌣$\bar{\bar{H}}_{\perp\wedge}$ #[$\hat{H}$]·/

Right $\bar{\bar{H}}$ hand, palm facing away from the signer and fingers pointing up, is held at the mouth. Hand closes to an $\hat{H}$ hand. The action is repeated.

89

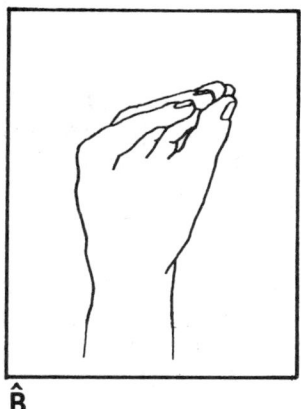
B̂

B̂

The closed counterpart to B̿, in which the thumb and fingers are held parallel and touching, occurs frequently in the types of sign mentioned above, where a closing action or opening action is involved. However, it also occurs in other signs in which such actions are not involved. Originally this handshape was labelled Ô and was thus seen as a flattened form of O. Despite the close physical similarity between Ô and B̂, we have now decided to place B̂ in the B group. This allows a certain consistency across the system in that all the parallel handshapes can be seen to have closed counterparts, for example, G̿:Ĝ; H̿:Ĥ; B̿:B̂.

Single Dez Signs

FLOUR

SEVERAL /∅B̂ₐ⊥ ⌇/

Right B̂ hand, palm facing up and fingers pointing away from the signer, is held in neutral space. Hand moves to the right and simultaneously the fingers perform a crumbling action.

FLOUR /∅B̂ᴅ⊥ ⌇/

Right B̂ hand, palm facing down and fingers pointing away from the signer, is held in neutral space. Fingers perform a crumbling action.

Double Dez Signs

EDUCATION

FINGER SPELLING /∅B̂>⊥ ıx B̂<⊥ ⁑/

Two B̂ hands: left hand, palm facing right and fingers pointing away from the signer; right hand, palm facing left and fingers pointing away from the signer. Hands, held side by side and touching in neutral space, move to the right with fingers flickering, maintaining contact.

EDUCATION /∩B̂⊥∧ B̂⊥∧ ⁰ᵢ/

Two B̂ hands, palms facing away from the signer and fingers pointing up, are held in front of the face. Hands move to and fro in a short repeated action.

SEND

THROW

Minimal Pair

SEND /∅B̂⊥∧ ᵇ[5]/

Right B̂ hand, palm facing away from the signer and fingers pointing up, is held in neutral space. Hand moves away from the signer opening to a 5 hand.

THROW /∅O⊥∧ ᵇ[5]/

Right O hand, palm facing away from the signer and fingers pointing up, is held in neutral space. Hand moves away from the signer opening to a 5 hand.

5

Group 4 : Fingers Spread
5 Dez

The 5 hand is similar to B in that the hand is flat. However, in the case of 5, the fingers are held apart, while in B they are close together. This unmarked handshape occurs frequently in BSL and is used in all categories of signs.

AGE /⊔5ᴛ∧ ˣ/

SORE /∅5ᴛ< ˣ·/

Single Dez Signs

Right 5 hand, palm facing the signer and fingers pointing up, is held in front of the nose. The fingers flicker.

Right 5 hand, palm facing the signer and fingers pointing left, is held in neutral space. Hand nods repeatedly in a short action.

SORE

Double Dez Signs

RAIN /∅5ᵇ⊥ ₁ 5ᵇ⊥ ˣ·/

CLOTHES /[ ]5ᴛ> 5ᴛ< ˣ·/

CLOTHES

Two 5 hands, palms facing down and fingers pointing away from the signer, are held side by side in neutral space. Hands move down and left. The action is repeated.

Two 5 hands: left hand, palm facing the signer and fingers pointing right; right hand, palm facing the signer and fingers pointing left. Hands, held against chest, move down maintaining contact. The action is repeated.

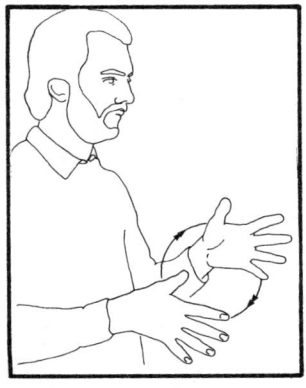
SIGN

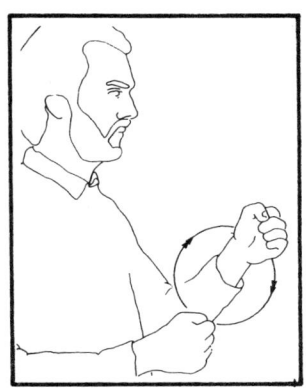
RUN

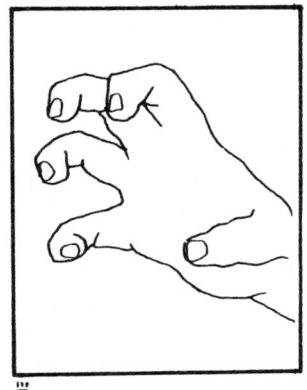
5̈

TRANSISTOR

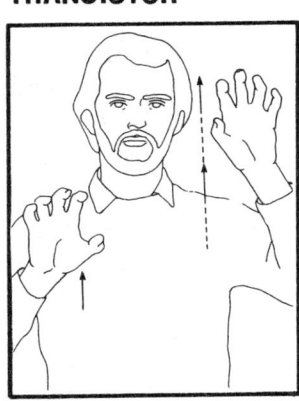
CLIMB

Minimal Pair

SIGN /∅5$_{>⊥}$,5$_{<⊥}$ $^{e}_{\check{x}}$~/

Two 5 hands: left hand, palm facing right and fingers pointing away from the signer; right hand, palm facing left and fingers pointing away from the signer. Hands, held side by side in neutral space, move alternately in a forward circular action.

RUN /∅A$_{>⊥}$,A$_{<⊥}$ $^{e}_{\check{x}}$~/

Two A hands: left hand, palm facing right and fingers pointing away from the signer; right hand, palm facing left and fingers pointing away from the signer. Hands, held side by side in neutral space, move alternately in a forward circular action.

5̈ Dez

The bent 5 hand, 5̈, in which the fingers are spread and bent, is significantly different from the 5 dez.

Single Dez Signs

JEALOUS /[]5̈$_{T<}$ $^{\hat{x}}_{\check{x}}$/

Right 5̈ hand, palm facing the signer and fingers pointing left, is held on chest. Hand moves up and to the right, maintaining contact.

TRANSISTOR /ᵓ5̈$_{<∧}$ $^{\dot{\omega}}$/

Right 5̈ hand, palm facing left and fingers pointing up, is placed next to the ear. Hand twists in a short repeated action.

Double Dez Signs

ANXIOUS /⌊⌋5̈$_{T>}$,5̈$_{T<}$ $^{e}_{\check{x}}$/

Two 5̈ hands: left hand, palm facing the signer and fingers pointing right; right hand, palm facing the signer and fingers pointing left. Hands contact lower trunk, with right hand above left hand, and make circular movements while maintaining contact.

CLIMB /∅5̈$_{⊥∧}$,5̈$_{⊥∧}$ $^{\hat{~}}$/

Two 5̈ hands, palms facing away from the signer and fingers pointing up, are held in neutral space. Hands move up alternately.

THIEVE

DIRTY

Minimal Pair

THIEVE /5̄ₐ⊥ 5̈_b⊥ ˣ⋅/

Manual tab 5 is held with palm facing up and fingers pointing away from the signer. Right 5 hand, palm facing down and fingers pointing away, is held above left hand. Right fingers move across left palm twice, maintaining contact.

DIRTY /5̄ₐ⊥ 5_b⊥ ˣ⋅/

Manual tab 5 is held with palm facing up and fingers pointing away from the signer. Right 5 hand, palm facing down and fingers pointing away, is held above left hand. Right fingers move across left palm twice, maintaining contact.

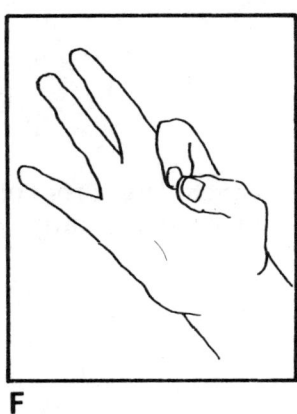
F

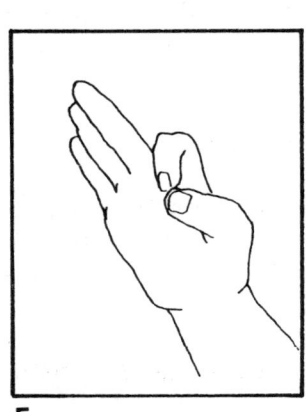
F

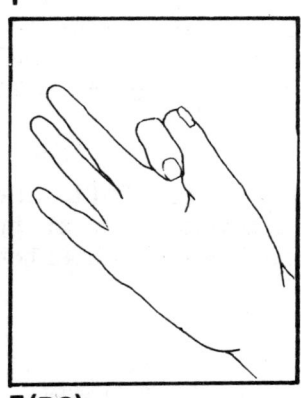
F(RC)

F Dez

In this handshape, the index finger and thumb are joined in a circle. The other fingers are extended and, most typically, spread. Although the fingers can be held close together, this is a much less frequent variant. This is the same as the old letter *q* of the British manual alphabet, and some derived signs still show links with this letter. Within the Catholic deaf community a slightly different variant, in which the thumb contacts the middle of the bent index finger, may be used in signs deriving from the Irish finger-spelled *f*. The more typical BSL configuration is the same as the Irish finger-spelled *g*, hence the use of such closely similar signs as FOOTBALL /∅F_RC<⊥ ~°~/ and GOAL /∅F⊥∧ °~/.

Single Dez Signs

ASK

TEMPT /⌐⌐F_T< ˣ⁺/

Right F hand, palm facing the signer and fingers pointing left, is held touching the upper trunk. Hand moves away and right.

ASK /∪F<∧ ⊥/

Right F hand, palm facing left and fingers pointing up, is held with finger/thumb circle at mouth. Hand moves away from the signer.

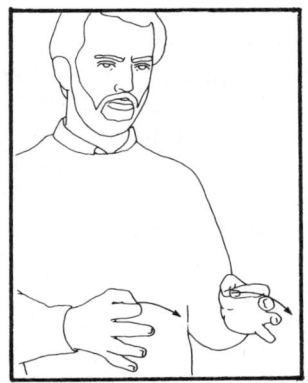
DELAY

INTERVIEW

GOAL

TEA

DRINK

Double Dez Signs

INSTEAD /∅F₀⊥ F₀⊥ ⊤/

Two F hands, palms facing down and fingers pointing away from the signer, are held in neutral space. Hands cross.

DELAY /∅F>⊥ ₁ F<⊥ ⊥/

Two F hands: left hand, palm facing right and fingers pointing away from the signer; right hand, palm facing left and fingers pointing away from the signer. Hands, held side by side in neutral space, move away from the signer.

Derived Signs

QUESTION /∅F<∧ ⟲ⁱ˙/

Right F hand, palm facing left and fingers pointing up, is held in neutral space. Hand makes a clockwise circular motion then moves away in a short sharp movement.

INTERVIEW /Ȧ>⊥ ₚ F<⊥ ᵗ˙ˣ/

Manual tab Ȧ is held with palm facing right and fingers pointing away from the signer. Right F hand, palm facing left and fingers pointing away from the signer, is held in front of left hand. Right finger and thumb move towards the signer and touch tip of left thumb. The action is repeated.

FOOTBALL /∅F_RC<⊥ ⟲̃°/

Right F hand, (with thumb and index finger crossed) palm facing left and fingers pointing away from the signer, is held in neutral space. Hand twists up and down in short movement.

GOAL /∅F⊥∧ ⟲̃°/

Right F hand, palm facing away from the signer and fingers pointing up, is held in neutral space. Hand twists right and left in short movement.

Minimal Pair

TEA /∪F<⊥ ᵖ⁄ᵗ/

Right F hand, palm facing left and fingers pointing away from the signer, is held in front of mouth. Hand nods towards the signer.

DRINK /∪C<⊥ ᵖ⁄ᵗ/

Right C hand, palm facing left and fingers pointing away from the signer, is held in front of mouth. Hand nods towards the signer.

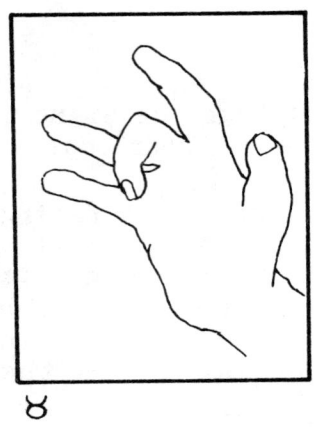
ȣ

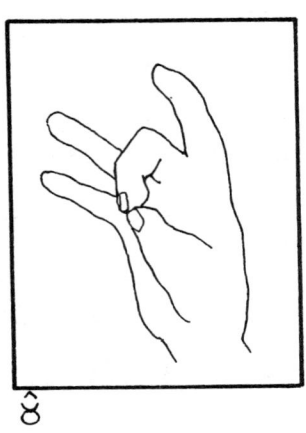
ȣ̂

ȣ Dez

The essential features of the ȣ dez are that the fingers are spread and the middle finger is extended at an angle to the rest of the fingers. Friedman (1977) comments that for ASL, this handshape is associated with verbs of feeling. This is also partially true of BSL, but other meanings are expressed by the use of this handshape. Examples of both types are given below. Some signs use the closed variant ȣ̂, usually where an opening or closing action is involved.

Single Dez Signs

LIVE

THEATRE /B̄_D> ȣ_DꞱ ⁿĕ̃ˣᵒ/

Manual tab B is held with palm facing down and fingers pointing right. Right ȣ hand, palm facing down and fingers pointing away from the signer, is held above left hand. Middle finger is placed on top of left hand and right hand twists from side to side in a short repeated action, holding contact.

LIVE /[ ] ȣ_T< ˣ̂·/

Right ȣ hand, palm facing the signer and fingers pointing left, is held with middle finger touching chest. Hand moves up and down maintaining contact. The action is repeated.

Double Dez Signs

LEFT   1

THRILL /[ ] ȣ_T>, ȣ_T< ˣ̂ ˣ̌ ~/

Two ȣ hands: left hand, palm facing the signer and fingers pointing right; right hand, palm facing the signer and fingers pointing left. Middle finger of each hand touches either side of chest. Hands move up alternately, maintaining contact, then move away and down.

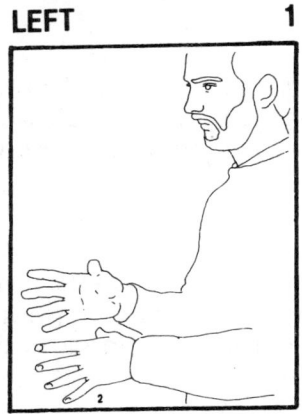
LEFT   2

LEFT /∅ ȣ̂_>Ʇx ȣ̂_<Ʇ ǡ[55]/

Two ȣ̂ hands: left hand, palm facing right and fingers pointing away from the signer; right hand, palm facing left and fingers pointing away from the signer. Right hand is held on top of left hand in neutral space. Hands move away from the signer and open to 5 hands.

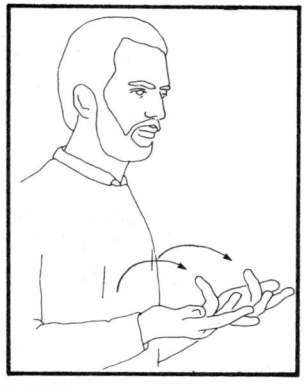
FEEL

ANGRY

Minimal Pair

FEEL /[ ]ö_T> ö_T< ˣᵃ/

Two ö hands: left hand, palm facing the signer and fingers pointing right; right hand, palm facing the signer and fingers pointing left. Middle finger of each hand touches either side of chest. Hands move up, maintaining contact, then twist so that palms face up.

ANGRY /[ ]5_T> 5_T< ˣᵃ/

Two 5 hands: left hand, palm facing the signer and fingers pointing right; right hand, palm facing the signer and fingers pointing left. Fingers of each hand touch either side of chest. Hands move up, maintaining contact, then twist so that palms face up.

Group 5: Finger(s) Extended from Closed Fist

G Dez

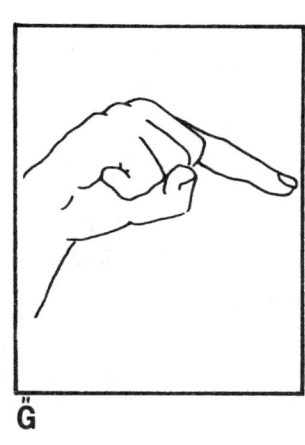
G   G̈

The G configuration is the first of a series of handshapes involving extension of one or more of the fingers from the closed fist. G makes use of the extended index finger and is one of the most frequently occurring handshapes in BSL. The most common form of G has the finger extended, without bending at the knuckles. However, in some cases, physical factors may encourage the use of bending at the knuckles. The sign MYSELF /[ ]G̈_α< ˣ/ (see page 99), is rather awkward to perform with a fully straight hand. It has therefore been thought useful to label this variant, with bending at the knuckles, G̈. However, it is stressed that the use of G or G̈ normally depends on what is most comfortable for a particular individual. These two variants are thus in free variation. A similar choice is available for most of the handshapes involving finger extension, particularly H, V, I and λ. In the following examples, THINK makes use of the bent variant.

THINK

MEET

CONSIDER

DREAM

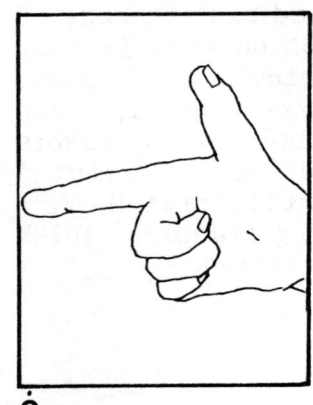
Ġ

BUT /ØG⊥∧ ṗ/

THINK /⌒G̈ₜ∧ ˣ/

CANNOT /ØG♭⊥ ᵢ G♭⊥ ᵀ/

MEET /ØG＞∧ ᵢ G＜∧ ᵓᶜˣ/

CONSIDER /⌒Gₜ∧ ↺/

DREAM /⌒Bₜ∧ ↺/

Single Dez Signs

Right G hand, palm facing away from the signer and finger pointing up, is held in neutral space. Hand nods sharply to the right.

Right G̈ hand, palm facing the signer and finger pointing up, is held at right side of forehead. Index finger contacts forehead.

Double Dez Signs

Two G hands, palms facing down and fingers pointing away from the signer, are held side by side in neutral space. Hands simultaneously move towards the signer and twist upwards.

Two G hands: left hand, palm facing right and finger pointing up; right hand, palm facing left and finger pointing up. Hands, held side by side in neutral space, move towards each other and touch.

Minimal Pair

CONSIDER /⌒Gₜ∧ ↺/

Right G hand, palm facing the signer and finger pointing up, makes an anti-clockwise circular motion at the right side of the forehead.

DREAM /⌒Bₜ∧ ↺/

Right B hand, palm facing the signer and fingers pointing up, makes an anti-clockwise circular motion at the right side of the forehead.

Ġ Dez

The Ġ handshape has both the index finger and the thumb extended. This is the same as the letter *l* of the American manual alphabet, hence the use of the label L in <u>Words in Hand 1</u>. As explained above, this handshape is now referred to as G with a prominent thumb, Ġ.

Single Dez Signs

SWISH (i.e. Smart)

LOVELY /⌣Ġ₁< ˟'[Ġ̈]/

SWISH /[ ]Ġ₁< ˆ˙/
(i.e. Smart)

Right Ġ hand, palm facing the signer and fingers pointing left, is held with index finger touching the mouth. Hand moves right and closes to a Ġ̈ hand.

Right Ġ hand, palm facing the signer and fingers pointing left, is held so that the closed fingers contact the body. Hand moves upward, maintaining contact, in repeated action.

Double Dez Signs

VAGINA

JEANS /⌐ ⌐Ġ>⊥Ġ<⊥ ~~/
(Regional: Dundee)

VAGINA /⊓Ġ>∨ ıx Ġ<∨ ˟/

Two Ġ hands: left hand, palm facing right and fingers pointing away from the signer; right hand, palm facing left and fingers pointing away from the signer. Hands, held at lower trunk, move up and down alternately.

Two Ġ hands: left hand, palm facing right and fingers pointing down; right hand, palm facing left and fingers pointing down. Hands, held side by side and contacting at centre of hip area, touch body.

Minimal Pair

PETROL

TEAPOT

PETROL /∅Ġ₁∧ ?/

Right Ġ hand, palm facing the signer and fingers pointing up, is held in neutral space. Hand nods left.

TEAPOT /∅Y₁∧ ?/

Right Y hand, palm facing the signer and fingers pointing up, is held in neutral space. Hand nods left.

G̈ Dez

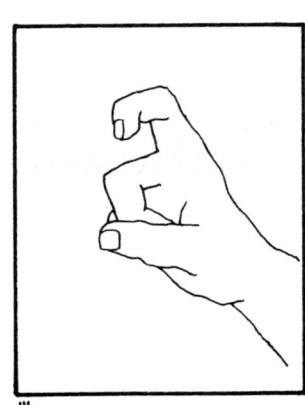
G̈

The main feature of the G̈ dez is that the index finger is extended and bent. It is thus distinguished from the G dez which has the index finger extended but straight. The hand configuration is the same as the letter *x* of the Irish and American manual alphabets and this was the label used for the handshape in <u>Words in Hand 1</u>.

ONION

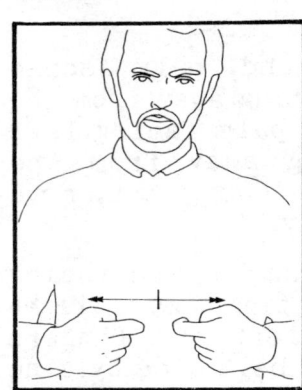
ELASTIC

SISTER

PRETEND

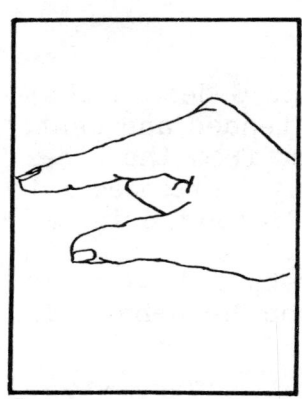
$\bar{\bar{G}}$

PARROT /⌒G̈⊥∧ ᴅ/

ONION /ʊG̈T∧ ᵐx•/

SCREAM /⌒G̈T∧ G̈T∧ ÷/

ELASTIC /øG̈T> ₁G̈T< x÷•/

SISTER /⌒G̈<∧ x•/

PRETEND /⌒G<∧ x•/

Single Dez Signs

Right G̈ hand, palm facing away from the signer and finger pointing up, is held in front of nose. Hand nods forward.

Right G̈ hand, palm facing the signer and finger pointing up, is held below right eye. Finger makes a flexing movement while maintaining contact. The action is repeated.

Double Dez Signs

Two G̈ hands, palms facing the signer and fingers pointing up, are held at mouth. Hands move away from the signer, separating.

Two G̈ hands: left hand, palm facing the signer and finger pointing right; right hand, palm facing the signer and finger pointing left. Hands, held side by side in neutral space, touch then separate. The action is repeated.

Minimal Pair

Right G̈ hand, palm facing left and finger pointing up, taps nose twice.

Right G hand, palm facing left and finger pointing up, taps nose twice.

$\bar{\bar{G}}$ Dez

The $\bar{\bar{G}}$ dez involves the extension of the index finger with the thumb held parallel, and is phonemically distinct from G. The handshape $\bar{\bar{G}}$ was previously known as Ĝ.

Single Dez Signs

VICAR

BONE /√Ḡ̄_{T<} ˇ /

VICAR /π Ḡ̄_{<∧} ˇ /

Right Ḡ̄ hand, palm facing the signer and finger pointing left, is held on the back of the lower forearm. Hand moves down maintaining contact.

Right Ḡ̄ hand, palm facing left and finger pointing up, is held at throat. Hand moves to the right, maintaining contact.

SOCIAL WORKER

POTATO CHIP /ØḠ̄_{>⊥}, Ḡ̄_{<⊥} ǂ[Ĝ Ĝ] /

SOCIAL WORKER/ WELFARE OFFICER /⌐ ⌐ Ḡ̄_{α>} Ḡ̄_{α<} ˇ /

Double Dez Signs

Two Ḡ̄ hands: left hand, palm facing right and finger pointing away from the signer; right hand, palm facing left and finger pointing away from the signer. Hands, held side by side in neutral space, separate and close simultaneously.

Two Ḡ̄ hands: left hand, palm facing up and finger pointing right; right hand, palm facing up and finger pointing left. Hands, held on upper chest, move down, maintaining contact.

THIN

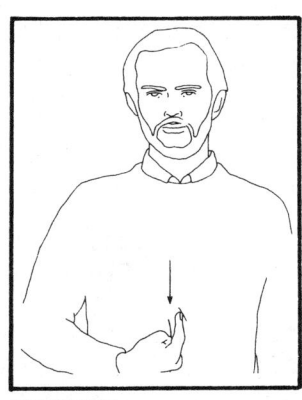
MYSELF

Minimal Pair

THIN /[ ] Ḡ̄_{α<} ˇ /

Right Ḡ̄ hand, palm facing up and finger pointing left, is held on chest. The hand moves down, maintaining contact.

MYSELF /[ ] G̈_{α<} ˇ /

Right G̈ hand, palm facing up and finger pointing left, is held on chest. The hand moves down, maintaining contact.

G̈ Dez

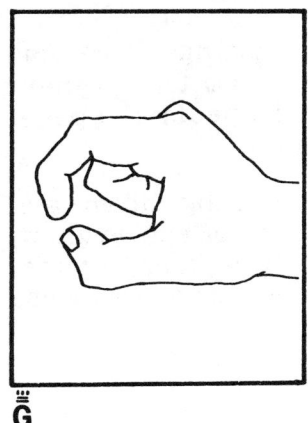
G̈

G̈ has thumb and index finger parallel, then bent, thus creating an almost circular configuration, but without closing. There is some variation in the gap between thumb and finger, but this is not phonemic. In the examples below, the first two signs in each group use a closer variant, the second two have the wider variant, although there is considerable variation from signer to signer. While relatively few signs use this handshape it does appear to be distinctive in BSL.

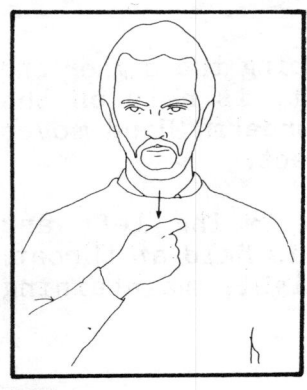
TIE

LAUGH

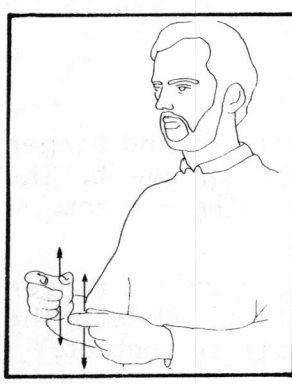
POLITICS

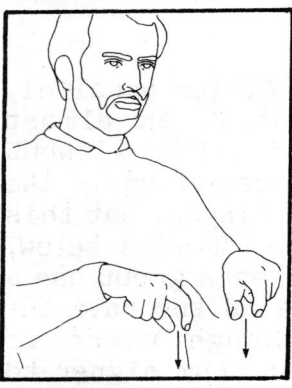
REMAIN

WHISKY /G>∧ G̈⊥∧, >̇/

TIE /πG̈ ˇ×/

APPLE /∪G̈T< ω⊥/

LAUGH /∪G̈T< ωxω/

MISERABLE /∩G̈T> G̈T< ∼̇/

POLITICS /∅G̈>⊥, G̈<⊥ ~~/

CONTINUE /∅G̈b⊥, G̈b⊥ >/

REMAIN /∅G̈b⊥, G̈b⊥ ˇ/

Single Dez Signs

Manual tab G is held with palm facing right and finger pointing up. Right G̈ hand, palm facing away from the signer and finger pointing up, is held behind left hand. Right thumb and index finger move to the right brushing left index finger as they move.

Right G̈ hand, palm facing the signer and finger pointing left, is held on throat. Hand moves down, maintaining contact.

Right G̈ hand, palm facing the signer and finger pointing left, is held in front of mouth. The hand twists in forward movement.

Right G̈ hand, palm facing the signer and finger pointing left, is held touching chin. The hand twists slightly to the right and left, holding contact.

Double Dez Signs

Two G̈ hands: left hand, palm facing the signer and finger pointing right; right hand, palm facing the signer and finger pointing left. Hands are held in front of face with right hand above left hand. Hands separate up and down.

Two G̈ hands: left hand, palm facing right and finger pointing away from the signer; right hand, palm facing left and finger pointing away from the signer. Hands, held side by side in neutral space, move up and down alternately.

Two G̈ hands, palms facing down and fingers pointing away from the signer, are held side by side in neutral space. Hands move to the right.

Two G̈ hands, palms facing down and fingers pointing away from the signer, are held side by side in neutral space. Hands move down in short sharp movement.

Minimal Pair

BULL /⌒G̿ᴛ< ˣ/

Right G̿ hand, palm facing the signer and finger pointing left. Finger and thumb touch nose.

SNOB /⌒Gᴛ< ˣ/

Right G hand, palm facing the signer and finger pointing left. Finger touches nose.

BULL

SNOB

Ĝ G̈ Ĝ̈

Three other related G handshapes occur in BSL. The first two are clearly phonetically conditioned. Ĝ is the closed counterpart of G̿, occurring, for example, as the final handshape in CAN /ʊG̿ᴛʌ #[Ĝ]/ and CHOOSE /∅G̿ᴸᴧ #[Ĝ]/. Unlike B̂ it does not appear to function as a separate phoneme. G̈ has the index finger bent and the thumb prominent. It is relatively rare, occurring in the final configuration of signs such as LOVELY /ʊG̈ᴛ< ˣ᾽[G̈]/ and UNDERSTAND /⌒G̈ᴛ< ˣ᾽[G̈]/ (page 41). Ĝ̈ has the finger bent and thumb and fingertip touching and is often referred to in the American literature as 'baby O'. Although this handshape does occur in signs such as those given below, we have been unable to note any minimal pairs to show that the handshape is distinctive. The contact between thumb and fingertip appears crucial in signs such as WRITE and BONNET and therefore it cannot be regarded as an allophone of Â, despite the physical similarity. Thus its status remains somewhat questionable.

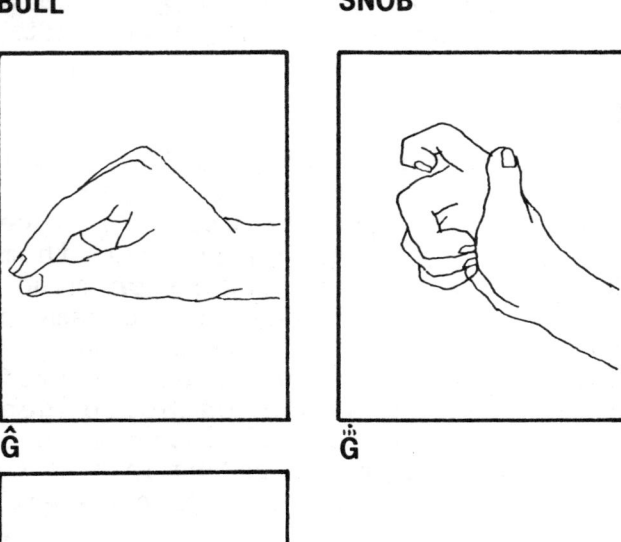
Ĝ   G̈

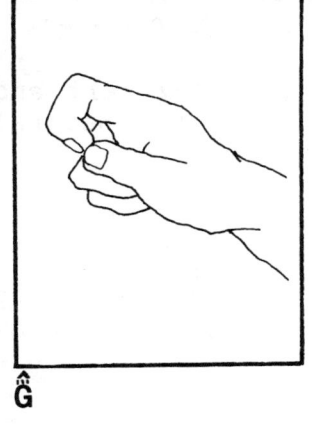
Ĝ̈

Single Dez Signs

Manual tab B is held with palm facing up and fingers pointing right. Right G̈ hand, palm facing down and finger pointing away from the signer, is held above left hand. Right hand moves to and fro and to the right while contacting left palm. The action is repeated.

Right Ĝ̈ hand, palm facing up and finger pointing away from the signer, is held in neutral space. Hand moves up and down in a short sharp action.

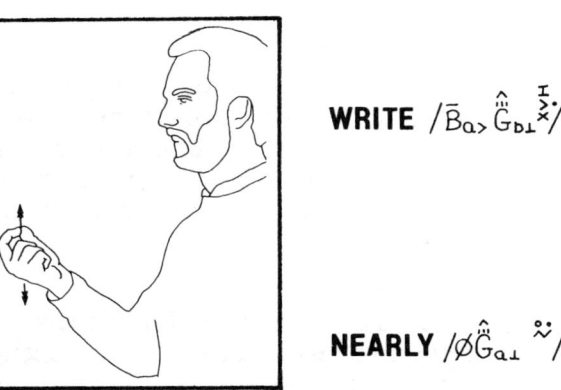
WRITE /B̄ₐ> Ĝ̈ᵦ⊥ ˣ/

NEARLY /∅Ĝ̈ₐ⊥ ˜/

NEARLY

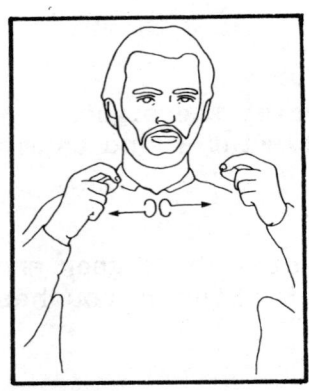
BONNET

SWEAT /⌒Ĝ̂ᴅ> Ĝ̂ᴅ< ⌄[GG]~/

BONNET /⌣Ĝ̂>⊥ Ĝ̂<⊥ ↻̃~÷/

Double Dez Signs

Two Ĝ hands; left hand, palm facing down and finger pointing right; right hand, palm facing down and finger pointing left. Hands, held at either side of forehead, move down alternately, opening to G hands.

Two Ĝ hands: left hand, palm facing right and finger pointing away from the signer; right hand, palm facing left and finger pointing away from the signer. Hands, held side by side under chin, move in alternating circular movement then separate right and left.

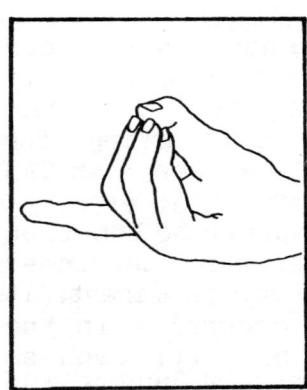
Gd   **Gd**

Gd

A further hand configuration closely related to the different types of G handshape, is that in which the index finger is extended while the thumb touches the three fingers or middle finger. This handshape is the same as the letter *d* of the Irish and American manual alphabets and is only significant within those Catholic deaf communities which use signs such as those given below. These are initial dez signs derived from the Irish alphabet.

DO /∅Gd<∧ ᵇ/

DOCTOR /⌒Gd<∧ ˣ/

Right Gd hand, palm facing left and finger pointing up, is held in neutral space. Hand twists down.

Right Gd hand, palm facing left and finger pointing up, is held with closed fingers touching right forehead. Hand moves towards the signer, maintaining contact.

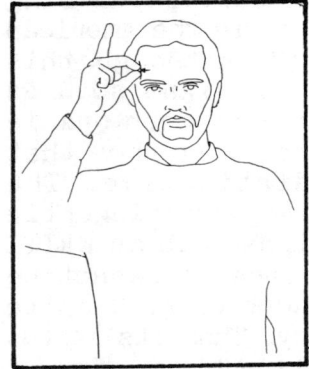
DOCTOR (Irish)

Minimal Pair

DAUGHTER /√Gdᴛ> ≠ Gdᴛ< ~·/

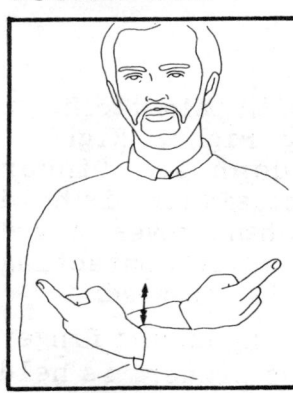 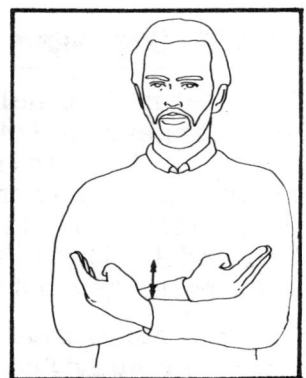
DAUGHTER   **BABY**

Two Gd hands: left hand, palm facing the signer and finger pointing right; right hand, palm facing the signer and finger pointing left. Both forearms are prominent and crossed. Arms move up and down twice.

BABY /√B̈ᴛ> ≠ √B̈ᴛ< ~·/

Two B̈ hands: left hand, palm facing the signer and fingers pointing right; right hand, palm facing the signer and fingers pointing left. Both forearms are prominent and crossed. Arms move up and down twice.

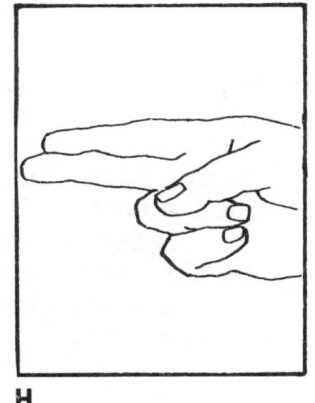
H

H Dez

In this handshape, the index and middle fingers are extended from the closed fist and held together.

Single Dez Signs

BUTTER /B̄ₐ⊥ H_{T<} ^{T.}_x/

Manual tab B is held with palm facing up and fingers pointing away from the signer. Right H hand, palm facing the signer and fingers pointing left. Right hand is held above left hand, then two fingers of right hand stroke left palm in a repeated action.

AFTERNOON

AFTERNOON /∪H_{T∧} ^{xω}/

Right H hand, palm facing the signer and fingers pointing up, is held with fingers touching chin. Hand moves outward in a twisting action so that palm faces away from the signer.

Double Dez Signs

HEREDITARY /∅H̄_{ᴅ>x}H_{ᴅ⊥}[⊻]/

Two H hands: left hand, palm facing down and fingers pointing right; right hand, palm facing down and fingers pointing away from the signer. Hands, held in neutral space with right fingers placed on top of left fingers, move simultaneously down and left.

DEAD

DEAD /∅H_{>⊥} H_{<⊥} ^ȯ_v/

Two H hands: left hand, palm facing right and fingers pointing away from the signer; right hand, palm facing left and fingers pointing away from the signer. Hands, held in neutral space, perform a sharp downward nodding action.

104

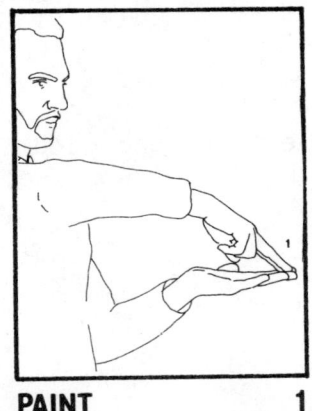
PAINT 1

2

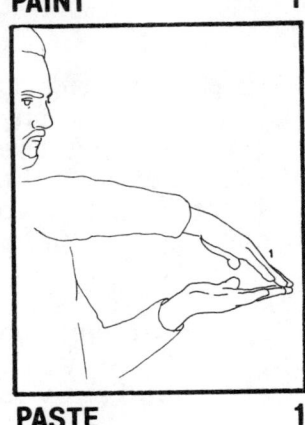
PASTE 1

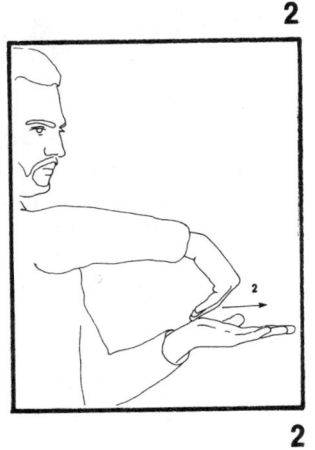
2

Minimal Pair

PAINT /$\bar{B}_{a\perp} H_{b\perp} {}^{T\cap\perp}_{\times\cap\times}$/

Manual tab B is held with palm facing up and fingers pointing away from the signer. Right H hand, palm facing down and fingers pointing away from the signer. Right hand, placed above left hand, moves towards the signer with fingers touching left hand, bends at major knuckles and moves away from the signer with fingers contacting hand.

PASTE /$\bar{B}_{a\perp} B_{b\perp} {}^{T\cap\perp}_{\times\cap\times}$/

Manual tab B is held with palm facing up and fingers pointing away from the signer. Right B hand, palm facing down and fingers pointing away from the signer. Right hand, placed above left hand, moves towards the signer with fingers touching left hand, bends at major knuckles and moves away from the signer with fingers contacting hand.

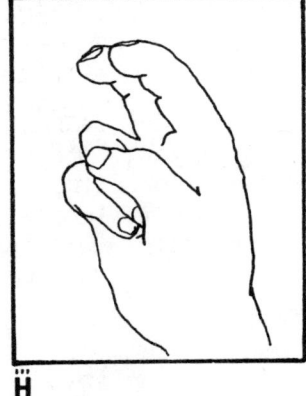
Ḧ

Ḧ Dez

The bent version of H, Ḧ, has the index finger and middle finger extended but bent at both joints. Although less frequently occurring than the straight variety, it is phonemically distinct.

Single Dez Signs

AUNT /$\cup \ddot{H}_{T\wedge}{}^{\times\cdot}$/

Right Ḧ hand, palm facing the signer and fingers pointing up, is held at chin. Fingers contact chin twice.

TRIP

TRIP /$\ddot{H}_{\gg\wedge} {}_{p\times} \ddot{H}_{<\wedge}{}^{\perp}$/

Manual tab Ḧ is held with palm facing right and fingers pointing up. Right Ḧ hand, palm facing left and fingers pointing up, is held in front of, and touching, left hand. Right hand moves forward away from the signer.

RESEARCH

Double Dez Signs

TITLE /∅Ḧ₍>∧₎ Ḧ₍<∧₎ ÷/

Two Ḧ hands: left hand, palm facing right and fingers pointing up; right hand, palm facing left and fingers pointing up. Hands, held side by side in neutral space, move apart.

RESEARCH /∅Ḧ₍▫>₎ Ḧ₍▫<₎ ˣ÷·/

Two Ḧ hands: left hand, palm facing down and fingers pointing right; right hand, palm facing down and fingers pointing left. Hands, held side by side in neutral space, touch then separate downwards in repeated action.

Minimal Pair

CASTLE /∅Ḧ₍>∧₎ Ḧ₍<∧₎ ˇ/

Two Ḧ hands: left hand, palm facing right and fingers pointing up; right hand, palm facing left and fingers pointing up. Hands, held side by side in neutral space, move down in a short action.

SIT /∅H₍>∧₎ H₍<∧₎ ˇ/

Two H hands: left hand, palm facing right and fingers pointing up; right hand, palm facing left and fingers pointing up. Hands, held side by side in neutral space, move down in a short action.

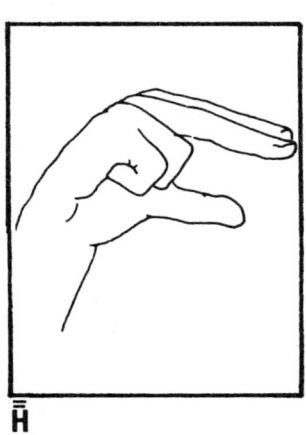
CASTLE

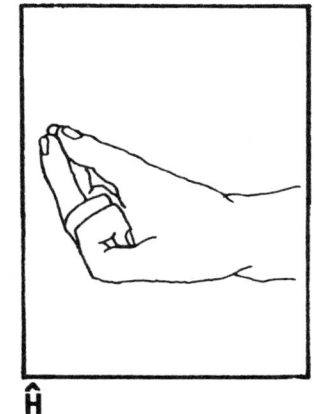
SIT

H̄, Ĥ

Parallel H, H̄, in which the thumb is held parallel to the extended fingers is used primarily in signs demanding an opening or closing action. The related handshape, Ĥ, is used as the closed element in such signs. Because of the existence of such minimal pairs as DUCK /∪H̄₍⊥∧₎ #[Ĥ]·/ and BIRD /∪Ḡ₍⊥∧₎ #[Ĝ]·/ H̄ is presented here as a separate phoneme of BSL.

H̄   Ĥ

STRAWBERRY

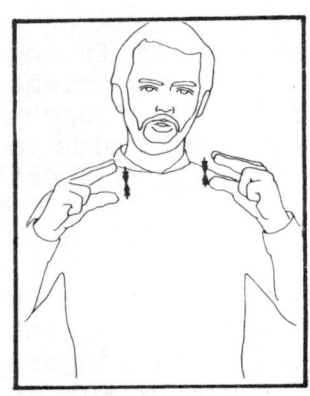
GOSSIP

DUCK

BIRD

Single Dez Signs

PAPER CLIP /H̄>⊥ H̄b⊥ ᵛᴵ/

Manual tab Ḧ is held with palm facing right and fingers pointing away from the signer. Right H̄ hand, palm facing down and fingers pointing away from the signer. Left hand is held below right hand. Right hand moves down to grasp left fingers.

STRAWBERRY /Gₜ>ᴵ H̄<⊥ ⋛#[Ĥ]/

Manual tab G is held with palm facing the signer and finger pointing right. Right H̄ hand, palm facing left and fingers pointing away from the signer. Left index finger is held within right hand. Right hand moves right then closes to an Ĥ hand.

Double Dez Signs

WITH /ØH̿ₜ∧ H̄ₜ∧ ᵡᴵ/

Two H̄ hands, palms facing the signer and fingers pointing up, are held in neutral space. The hands move towards each other and interlink so that the two left fingers are held by the two right fingers and thumb.

GOSSIP /ØH̿>∧ H̄<∧ #[ĤĤ]·/

Two H̄ hands: left hand, palm facing right and fingers pointing up; right hand, palm facing left and fingers pointing up. Hands, held in neutral space, close to Ĥ hands. The action is repeated.

Minimal Pair

DUCK /∪H̄⊥∧ #[Ĥ]·/

Right H̄ hand, palm facing away from the signer and fingers pointing up, is held at the side of the mouth. The thumb and fingers close to an Ĥ hand. The action is repeated.

BIRD /∪Ḡ⊥∧ #[Ĝ]·/

Right Ḡ hand, palm facing away from the signer and finger pointing up, is held at the side of the mouth. The thumb and finger close to a Ĝ hand. The action is repeated.

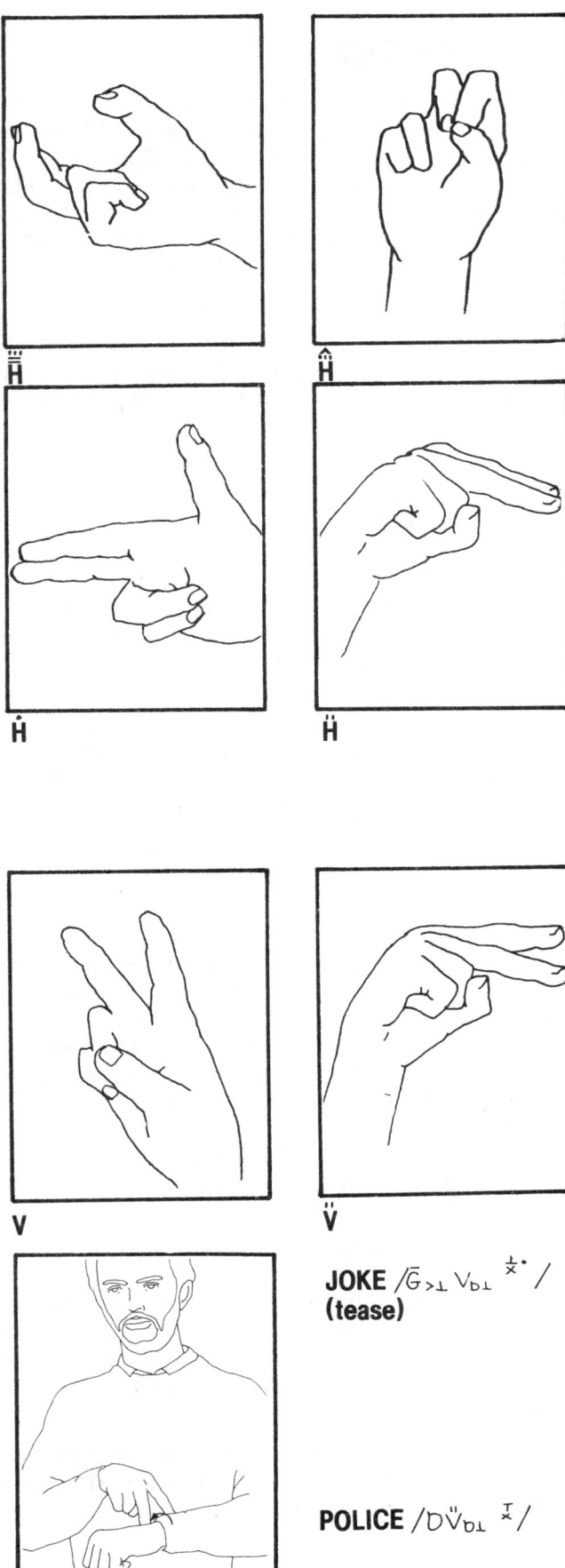

Ḧ Ĥ Ḣ Ḧ

The Ḧ allophone, in which the two fingers and thumb are held parallel and bent, is used only rarely, mainly in signs involving contact, such as PULSE /ɑḦ_b< ͯ / and DOCTOR /ᴅḦ_b< ͯ / (see page 56). A closed version of H, in which the fingers and thumb are bent and contacting, is used as the first element in a number of signs involving an opening action. Examples include BOW-TIE /πĤ_T> ˌ Ĥ_T< ˣ͛[ᵛᵛ]/(see page 48) and STAR /CĤ_ʟ∧ ᵈ[ᵛ] / (see page 65). H, in which the two fingers are extended and the thumb is held at right angles has been noted in very few examples. In all cases it seems to be in free variation with Ġ, for example SHOOT can be transcribed either as /ØḢ_<ʟ ᵐ[Ḧ] / or /ØĠ_<ʟ ᵐ[G̈] /. Ḧ, in which the hand is bent at the knuckles may be the preferred choice in examples such as SUMMER /∪Ḧ_<∧ ˣ˙ / and NEWS /ØḦ_>ʟ ⁹ˣ Ḧ_<ʟ ᵈ˜˙/ where it would be less natural to have the hands completely straight. As in most other examples of the use of this bending at the knuckles, choice depends very much on what is most comfortable for the signer. Thus Ḧ is in free variation with H.

V Dez

This handshape has the index and middle fingers extended and spread. The difference between H and V is thus distinctive in BSL, although in other handshapes the contrast between spread and not spread is non-phonemic. The V̈ variant, with bending at the major knuckles, can be seen in POLICE and TONSILECTOMY.

Single Dez Signs

Manual tab G is held with palm facing right and finger pointing away from the signer. Right V hand, palm facing down and fingers pointing away from the signer. Right hand is placed above left, then moves forward so that the apex of the spread fingers strokes left index finger. The action is repeated.

The wrist, as tab, is held facing down. Right V̈ hand, palm facing down and fingers pointing away from the signer. Fingers contact the dorsal side of wrist and move towards the signer.

JOKE /Ḡ_>ʟ V_bʟ ˣ˙ / (tease)

POLICE /ᴅV̈_bʟ ͯ /

Double Dez Signs

SPECTACLES

WATCH /∅ V̄>⊥× V<⊥ ⋎̈/
(verb)

Two V hands: left hand, palm facing right and fingers pointing away from the signer; right hand, palm facing left and fingers pointing away from the signer. Right hand is held on top of left hand in neutral space. Hands move down in short sharp movement.

SPECTACLES /⊔ V_{T>} V_{T<} ˣ˙/

Two V hands: left hand, palm facing the signer and fingers pointing right; right hand, palm facing the signer and fingers pointing left. Hands, held at the side of each eye, contact face twice.

Minimal Pair

TONSILECTOMY

AWFUL

TONSILECTOMY /π V̈_{T∧} ˣ⊥/

Right V̈ hand, palm facing the signer and fingers pointing up, touches the throat then moves away from the signer.

AWFUL /π 5̈_{T∧} ˣ⊥/

Right 5̈ hand, palm facing the signer and fingers pointing up, touches the throat then moves away from the signer.

V̇ Dez

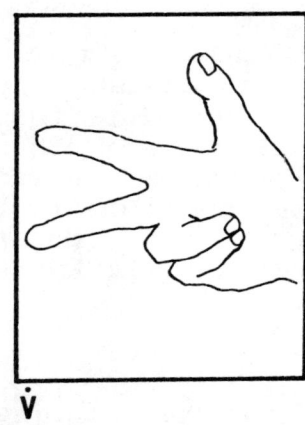
V̇

V̇, in which the first two fingers and the thumb are extended, is used in a number of BSL signs. While examples can be found which show the contrast between V and the other handshapes, no minimal pairs have been noted which distinguish V and V̇, although it is possible to show this handshape contrasting with other handshapes in the language.

Single Dez Signs

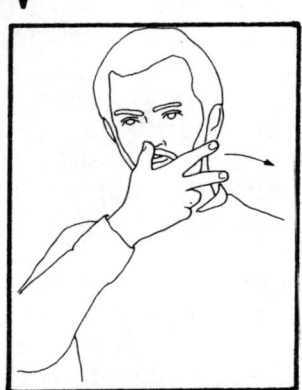
JOKE

DENMARK /[ ] V̇_{T<} ˜ẋ/

Right V̇ hand, palm facing the signer and fingers pointing left, is placed on chest. Hand moves up and down as it moves right, maintaining contact.

JOKE /△ V̇_{T<} ˣ</

Right V̇ hand, palm facing the signer and fingers pointing left. Thumb of right hand touches nose then moves to the left.

109

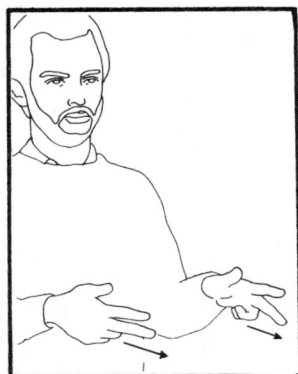
OVERSLEPT

ADDRESS

PROVOKE

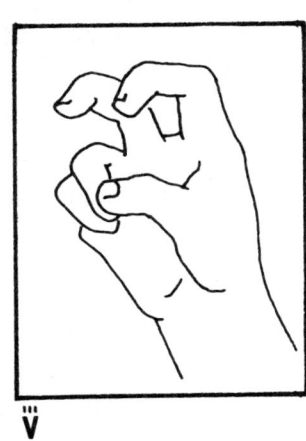
V̈

Double Dez Signs

CARELESS /⌒V̇>⊥ V̇<⊥ ↕̃/

Two V̇ hands: left hand, palm facing right and fingers pointing away from the signer; right hand, palm facing left and fingers pointing away from the signer. Hands, held at either side of the forehead, move in a forward circular action, alternately.

OVERSLEPT /ØV̇⊥<, V̇T< ↙/

Two V̇ hands: left hand, palm facing away from the signer and fingers pointing left; right hand, palm facing the signer and fingers pointing left. Hands, held side by side in neutral space, move to the left in a downward movement.

Minimal Pair

ADDRESS /ØV̇>⊥, V̇<⊥ ⊥·/

Two V̇ hands: left hand, palm facing right and fingers pointing away from the signer; right hand, palm facing left and fingers pointing away from the signer. Hands, held side by side in neutral space, move away in a repeated action.

PROVOKE /ØG>⊥, G<⊥ ⊥·/

Two G hands: left hand, palm facing right and finger pointing away from the signer; right hand, palm facing left and finger pointing away from the signer. Hands, held side by side in neutral space, move away in a repeated action.

V̈ Dez

V̈, in which the index and middle fingers are extended and bent, is phonemically distinct from V as shown in the minimal pair DRUNK and BLIND. The difference between V̈, in which the fingers are bent and spread and Ḧ in which the fingers are bent and close together, can be seen in the minimal pair OLD and NIGHT.

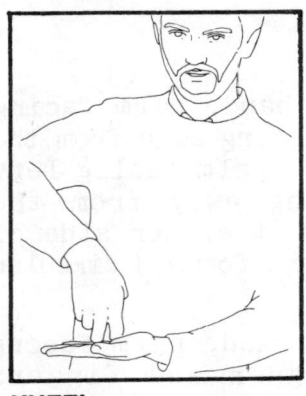
KNEEL

SEEK

DRUNK

BLIND

OLD

NIGHT

IRELAND /$\bar{A}_{D>}\ \ddot{V}_{D\perp}\ ^{x\cdot}$/

KNEEL /$\bar{B}_{a>}\ \ddot{V}_{T v}\ ^{vx}$/

ELICIT /$\emptyset\ \ddot{\bar{V}}_{a\perp}\ \ddot{V}_{b\perp}\ ^{T}_{D}\cdot$/

SEEK /$\emptyset\ \ddot{\bar{V}}_{>\perp x}\ \ddot{V}_{<\perp}\ ^{<<}_{\uparrow\uparrow}$/

Single Dez Signs

Manual tab A is held with palm facing down and fingers pointing right. Right $\ddot{V}$ hand, palm facing down and fingers pointing away from the signer, is held above left hand. Fingers contact back of left hand twice.

Manual tab B is held with palm facing up and fingers pointing right. Right $\ddot{V}$ hand, palm facing the signer and fingers pointing down, is held above left hand. Right hand moves down so that middle phalanx of the bent fingers makes contact with the palm of the left hand.

Double Dez Signs

Two $\ddot{V}$ hands: left hand, palm facing up and fingers pointing away from the signer; right hand, palm facing down and fingers pointing away from the signer. Right hand is held above left hand in neutral space. Hands move towards the signer with fingers flexing. The action is repeated.

Two $\ddot{V}$ hands: left hand, palm facing right and fingers pointing away from the signer; right hand, palm facing left and fingers pointing away from the signer. Right hand is held on top of left in neutral space. Hands move in a right to left arc, maintaining contact.

Minimal Pair

DRUNK /$\Box\ \ddot{V}_{T\wedge}\ ^{z\cdot}$/

Right $\ddot{V}$ hand, palm facing the signer and fingers pointing up, is held in front of eyes. Hand moves from side to side. The action is repeated.

BLIND /$\Box\ V_{T\wedge}\ ^{z\cdot}$/

Right V hand, palm facing the signer and fingers pointing up, is held in front of eyes. Hand moves from side to side. The action is repeated.

Minimal Pair

OLD /$\Box\ \ddot{V}_{T\wedge}\ ^{v}$/

Right $\ddot{V}$ hand, palm facing the signer and fingers pointing up, is held in front of the nose. Hand moves down.

NIGHT /$\Box\ \ddot{H}_{T\wedge}\ ^{v}$/

Right $\ddot{H}$ hand, palm facing the signer and fingers pointing up, is held in front of the nose. Hand moves down.

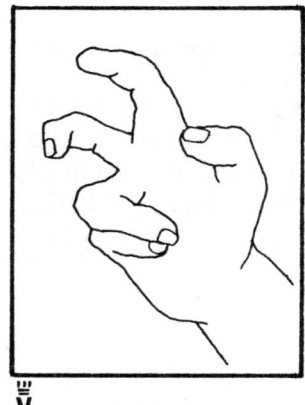
V̈

$\ddot{\overline{V}}$

$\ddot{\overline{V}}$, in which the middle finger, index finger and thumb are all bent, is a separate phoneme in BSL. It is given the label $\ddot{\overline{V}}$ because most typically the thumb is not held at an angle to the other fingers. The handshape can be formed by bringing the thumb into the parallel position, $\overline{V}$, then bending all three digits to produce $\ddot{\overline{V}}$.

Single Dez Signs

WRIST WATCH /D$\ddot{\overline{V}}_{b\perp}$ ³ˣ/

The wrist, as tab, is held with palm facing down. Right $\ddot{\overline{V}}$ hand, palm facing down and fingers pointing away from the signer, is held touching the dorsal side of the wrist. The hand twists, maintaining contact.

TOMATO

TOMATO /G$_{T>}$, $\ddot{\overline{V}}_{<\perp}$ ʬ/

Manual tab G is held with palm facing the signer and finger pointing right. Right $\ddot{\overline{V}}$ hand, palm facing left and fingers pointing away from the signer. Hands are held side by side. Right hand performs a twisting forward movement.

Double Dez Signs

ASTOUNDED /⌐⌐$\ddot{\overline{V}}_{T\wedge}$ $\ddot{\overline{V}}_{T\wedge}$ °ˣ/

Two $\ddot{\overline{V}}$ hands, palms facing the signer and fingers pointing up, are held in front of eyes. Hands move away from the signer in a short sharp movement.

ARGUE

ARGUE /⌀$\ddot{\overline{V}}_{>\wedge}$, $\ddot{\overline{V}}_{<\wedge}$ ~~/

Two $\ddot{\overline{V}}$ hands: left hand, palm facing right and fingers pointing up; right hand, palm facing left and fingers pointing up. Hands, held side by side in neutral space, move up and down alternately. The action is repeated.

Minimal Pair

CAPTAIN /⌐⌐$\ddot{\overline{V}}_{bT}$ ˣ·/

Right $\ddot{\overline{V}}$ hand, palm facing down and fingers pointing towards the signer. The fingers touch the top of the left shoulder twice.

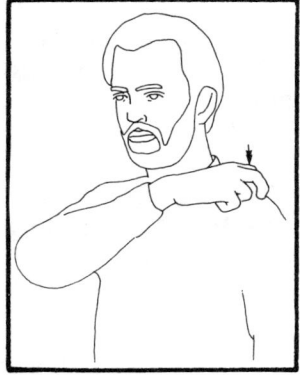
CAPTAIN

OFFICER

OFFICER /⌐⌐V$_{bT}$ ˣ·/

Right V hand, palm facing down and fingers pointing towards the signer. The fingers touch the top of the left shoulder twice.

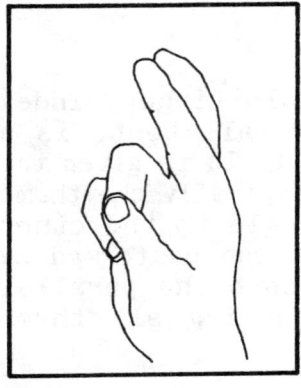
R

WISH

HOPE

RELIGION

WHY

R Dez

This handshape has both the index and middle fingers extended and crossed. It is the same configuration as the letter *r* of the Irish and American manual alphabets. The R dez is used very rarely in BSL, although within the Catholic deaf community it is found in initial dez signs.

Single Dez Signs

READY /√R_T< ˣ/
(RC sign)

Right R hand, palm facing the signer and fingers pointing left, is placed on left lower arm. Right hand moves down, maintaining contact.

WISH /∅R_⊥∧ ∅/

Right R hand, palm facing away from the signer and fingers pointing up, is held in neutral space without moving.

Double Dez Signs

REST /∨√R_T>≠√R_T<ˣ/
(RC sign)

Two R hands: left hand, palm facing the signer and fingers pointing right; right hand, palm facing the signer and fingers pointing left. Arms are crossed so that right hand touches left upper arm and left hand touches right upper arm.

HOPE /∅R_b⊥ R_b⊥ ∅/

Two R hands, palms facing down and fingers pointing away from the signer, are held in neutral space without moving.

Minimal Pair

RELIGION (RC sign) /⌐⌐R_b< ˣ/

Right R hand, palm facing down and fingers pointing left, is held touching left side of upper trunk.

WHY /⌐⌐G_b< ˣ/

Right G hand, palm facing down and finger pointing left, is held touching left side of upper trunk.

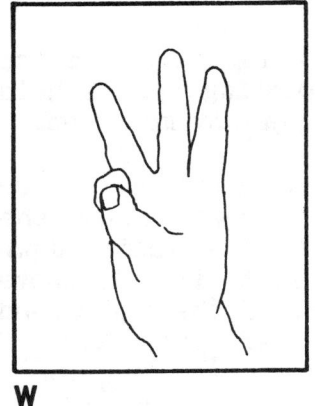
W

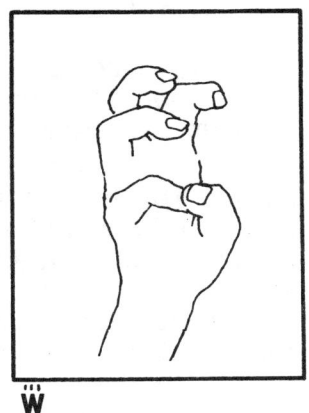
Ẅ

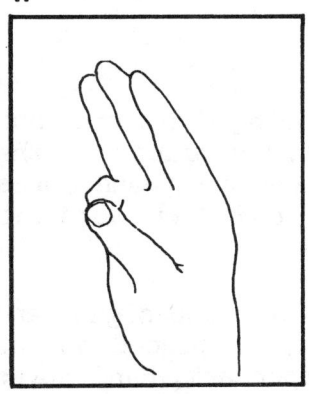
Wm

W Dez

The W dez, which has three fingers extended and spread, is the same as the letter *w* of the Irish and American manual alphabets. This is a relatively infrequent handshape. The main allophonic variants are Ẅ, in which the three fingers are extended, spread and bent, and Wm, in which the three fingers are extended but held together. Wm is the same as the right handshape of the letter *m* in the British manual alphabet and this variant is used in initial dez signs. The Catholic community also makes use of initial dez signs based on the letter W.

Single Dez Signs

FOREMAN /⌀W$_{a⊥}$ $^{ɒ×}$/

The wrist, as tab, is held with palm facing down. Right W hand, palm facing up and fingers pointing away from the signer, is held above left wrist. The right hand twists over to make contact with dorsal side of left wrist.

WALES /⌀Ẅ$_{⊥∧}$ $^{˅}$/

Right Ẅ hand, palm facing away from the signer and fingers pointing up, is held in neutral space. The hand moves down in a short movement.

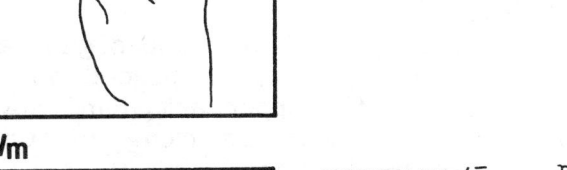
WALES

Double Dez Signs

WAY /⌀W$_{>⊥}$,W$_{<⊥}$ $^{⊥}$/
(RC sign)

Two W hands: left hand, palm facing right and fingers pointing away from the signer; right hand, palm facing left and fingers pointing away from the signer. Hands, held side by side in neutral space, move away from the signer.

SHIPYARD /⌀W$_{>∧}$,W$_{<∧}$ $^{⊥∼}$/

Two W hands: left hand, palm facing right and fingers pointing up; right hand, palm facing left and fingers pointing up. Hands, held side by side in neutral space, move to and fro alternately.

SHIPYARD

MOTHER

BOY SCOUT /∅W$_{m⊥∧}$ ∅/

MOTHER /B̄$_{a⊥}$ W$_{m▷<}$ ˣ˙/

SERGEANT   CORPORAL

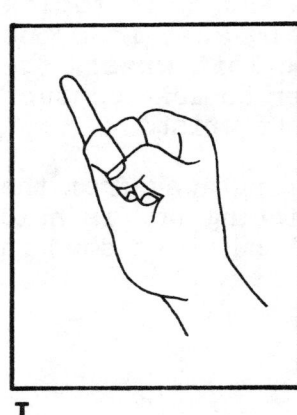
I

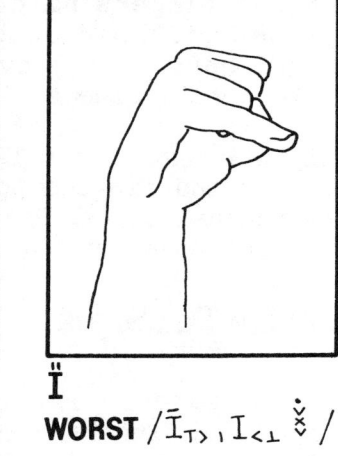
Ï

WORST /Ī$_{T>}$, I$_{<⊥}$ ˣ˙/

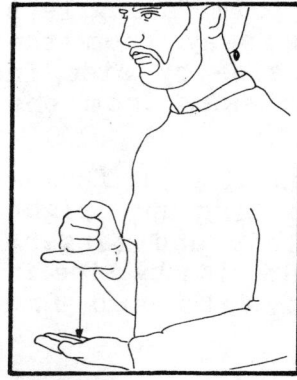
WRONG

WRONG /B̄$_{a>}$ I$_{<⊥}$ ᵛˣ/

W$_m$ Variant

Right W$_m$ hand, palm facing away from the signer and fingers pointing up, is held in neutral space without any movement.

Manual tab B is held with palm facing up and fingers pointing away from the signer. Right W$_m$ hand, palm facing down and fingers pointing left, is held above left hand. The fingers of the right hand make contact with the left palm twice.

Minimal Pair

SERGEANT /⋏W$_{T<}$ ᵛˣ/

Right W hand, palm facing the signer and fingers pointing left, is placed on the dorsal side of the upper arm. Hand moves down and up, maintaining contact (illustrating stripes).

CORPORAL /⋏V$_{T<}$ ᵛˣ/

Right V hand, palm facing the signer and fingers pointing left, is placed on the dorsal side of the upper arm. Hand moves down and up, maintaining contact (illustrating stripes).

I Dez

The essential feature of this hand configuration is that the little finger is extended from the closed fist. As indicated in Chapter 1 (page 23), the handshape is frequently associated with meanings related to the notion of 'badness'. The Ï variant, with bending at the knuckles, is also common.

Single Dez Signs

Manual tab I is held with palm facing the signer and finger pointing right. Right I hand, palm facing left and finger pointing away from the signer. Hands are held side by side with right hand slightly above left. Right hand moves down so that little finger contacts the left little finger sharply, then continues downward.

Manual tab B is held with palm facing up and fingers pointing right. Right I hand, palm facing left and finger pointing away from the signer, is placed above left hand. Right hand moves down and touches left palm.

Double Dez Signs

WORSE

TEMPTATION /[]Ï_{a>1}Ï_{a<}^{x•}/ Two Ï hands: left hand, palm facing up and finger pointing right; right hand, palm facing up and finger pointing left. Hands are held side by side at left side of chest. Hands make contact with chest. The action is repeated.

WORSE /ØI_{T>1x}I_{T<}^{¥•}/ Two I hands: left hand, palm facing the signer and finger pointing right; right hand, palm facing the signer and finger pointing left. Hands, held side by side in neutral space with tips of little fingers touching, separate moving downwards.

Minimal Pair

POISON

EMPTY

POISON /Ō_{>⊥}∘Ï_{b⊥}^{e/x}/
Manual tab O is held with palm facing right and fingers pointing away from the signer. Right Ï hand, palm facing down and finger pointing away from the signer. Little finger of right hand is placed within circle of left O hand. Little finger makes circular motion, maintaining contact.

EMPTY /Ō_{>⊥}∘G̈_{b⊥}^{e/x}/
Manual tab O is held with palm facing right and fingers pointing away from the signer. Right G̈ hand, palm facing down and finger pointing away from the signer. Index finger of right hand is placed within circle of left O hand. Index finger makes circular motion, maintaining contact.

Y Dez

Y

This handshape, which has the thumb and little finger extended from the closed fist is the same as the letter *y* of the Irish and American manual alphabets.

Single Dez Signs

MAYBE /ØY_{b⊥}^{ω•}/ Right Y hand, palm facing down and fingers pointing away from the signer, is held in neutral space. Hand twists in a repeated action.

WHICH /ØY_{b⊥}^{z•}/ Right Y hand, palm facing down and fingers pointing away from the signer, is held in neutral space. Hand moves from side to side in a repeated action.

WHICH

CARDBOARD

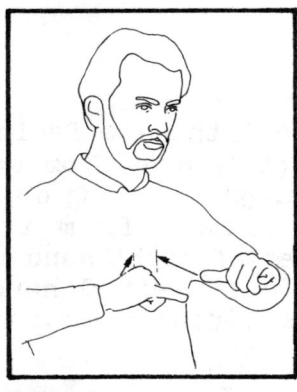
BOSS

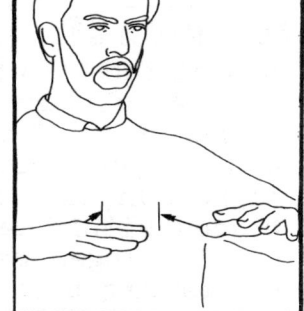
READY

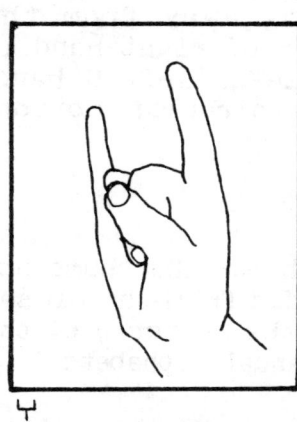
ꟼ

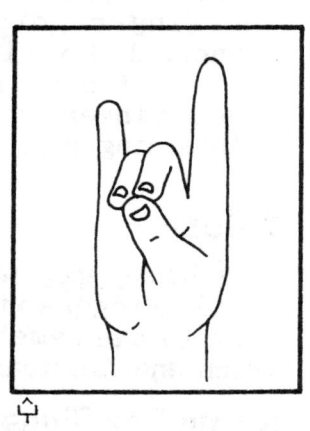
ꟼ̂

ꟼ̇

Double Dez Signs

PARTY /∅ Y₌ₐ Y₌ₐ ⁺·/

Two Y hands: left hand, palm facing right and fingers pointing up; right hand, palm facing left and fingers pointing up. Hands, held in neutral space, perform a repeated twisting action.

CARDBOARD /∅ Y₌₁ Y₌ ÷/

Two Y hands: left hand, palm facing down and fingers pointing right; right hand, palm facing down and fingers pointing left. Hands are held side by side in neutral space then separate.

Minimal Pair

BOSS /⌐ ⌐ Y₌ Y₌ ˣ·/

Two Y hands: left hand, palm facing down and fingers pointing right; right hand, palm facing down and fingers pointing left. Hands are held at upper trunk. Thumbs touch upper trunk twice.

READY /⌐ ⌐ 5₌ 5₌ ˣ·/

Two 5 hands: left hand, palm facing down and fingers pointing right; right hand, palm facing down and fingers pointing left. Hands are held at upper trunk. Thumbs touch upper trunk twice.

ꟼ Dez

The ꟼ configuration has both the index and little fingers extended from the closed fist. This dez, sometimes known as the 'horns' handshape, is distinctive in BSL, although in ASL it is classified by Stokoe (1978) as a phonetic variant of Y. The ꟼ dez is the same as the letter h of the Irish manual alphabet and is used within the Catholic community for initial dez signs. A variant, ꟼ̂, in which the two middle fingers are extended and held contacting the thumb, can be found in a number of signs including KISS /∪ ꟼ̂ₜₐ ᵀˣ/ and SHY /3ꟼ̂₌ₐ ᵉ̇ₓ/. The handshape in which the thumb, index finger and little finger are all extended, can be regarded as a variant of either Y or ꟼ: here it is arbitrarily placed under ꟼ. This handshape, given the symbol ꟼ̇, occurs rarely.

DEVIL

FOOTBALL PITCH

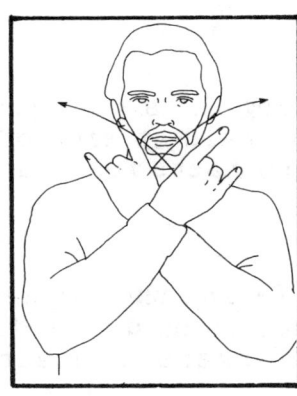 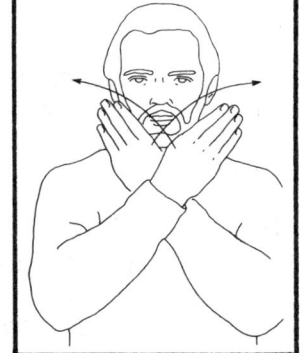
HEAVEN   **LIGHT/DAY**

GOAL /∅ Ψ<∧ ∅/
(object)

DEVIL /∩ Ψ⊔⊥ Ψˣ/

HURRY UP /∅ Ψ>⊥ Ψ<⊥ ~~/
(RC sign)

FOOTBALL PITCH
/∅ Ψ>∧ Ψ<∧ ÷/

Single Dez Signs

Right Ψ hand, palm facing left and fingers pointing up, is held in neutral space without any movement.

Right Ψ hand, palm facing down and fingers pointing away from the signer, is held in front of forehead. Hand nods so that back of hand touches forehead.

Double Dez Signs

Two Ψ hands: left hand, palm facing right and fingers pointing away from the signer; right hand, palm facing left and fingers pointing away from the signer. Hands, held in neutral space, move up and down alternately.

Two hands: left hand, palm facing right and fingers pointing up; right hand, palm facing left and fingers pointing up. Hands are held side by side in neutral space then separate.

Minimal Pair

HEAVEN /⊃ Ψ⊤> ⊋ Ψ⊤< ≑/

Two Ψ hands: left hand, palm facing the signer and fingers pointing right; right hand, palm facing the signer and fingers pointing left. Hands are held in front of face. Left hand is held behind, and touching, right hand. Hands move up separating.

LIGHT/DAY /⊃ B⊤> ⊋ B⊤< ≑/

Two B hands: left hand, palm facing the signer and fingers pointing right; right hand, palm facing the signer and fingers pointing left. Hands are held in front of face. Left hand is held behind, and touching, right hand. Hands move up separating.

λ Dez

The symbol λ has been added here to Stokoe's original list of handshapes to represent the hand configuration in which the middle finger is extended from the closed fist (see Chapter 1, page 4). This handshape is used in relatively few BSL signs, but it is phonemically distinct. Again, some signers may prefer to use a λ variant with bending at the knuckles.

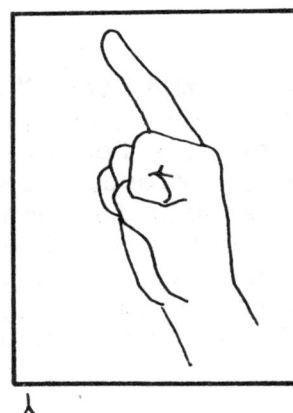 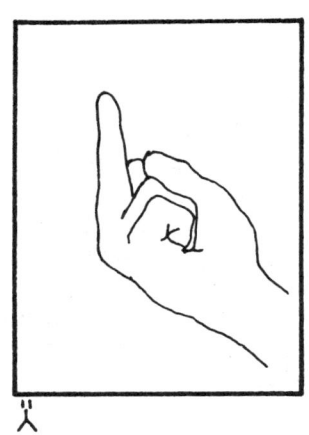
λ   λ̈

118

UNEMPLOYED

LAZY

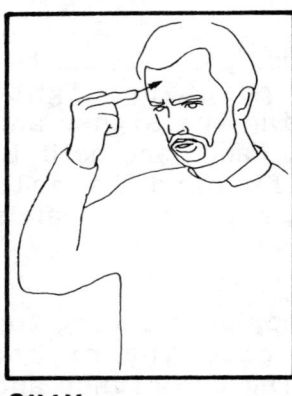
SILLY

MAD

IDLE /∅λ̈ₐ⌐ ~· /

UNEMPLOYED /∅λ̈ₐ⌐ ẽ· /

HOLIDAY /∅λ̈ₐ⌐ λ̈ₐ⌐ ẽ· /

LAZY /∅λ̈ₐ⌐·λ̈ₐ⌐ ~· /

Single Dez Signs

Right λ̈ hand, palm facing up and finger pointing away from the signer, is held in neutral space. Hand moves up and down twice.

Right λ̈ hand, palm facing up and finger pointing away from the signer, is held in neutral space. Hand makes a circular movement twice.

Double Dez Signs

Two λ̈ hands, palms facing up and fingers pointing away from the signer, are held in neutral space. Hands make circular motion while separating. The action is repeated.

Two λ̈ hands, palms facing up and fingers pointing away from the signer, are held in neutral space. Hands move up and down twice.

Minimal Pair

SILLY /⌒λ̈_{T⌃} ×· /

Right λ̈ hand, palm facing the signer and finger pointing up, is held at side of forehead. The finger contacts forehead twice.

MAD /⌒Ẅ_{m T⌃} ×· /

Right Ẅ_m hand, palm facing the signer and fingers pointing up, is held at side of forehead. The fingers contact forehead twice.

Prominent Forearm

In some signs the positioning of the arms as well as the actual dez realisations may be important. In most cases, this feature is demanded by the other parameters, particularly orientation. It would be extremely awkward to produce the sign for CHAIRMAN, which has palms down and fingers pointing right and left, with the elbows at the side of the body. No minimal pairs have been noted which are distinguished only by the feature 'prominent forearm'. Nevertheless, this feature is important enough in some signs to warrant the inclusion of a separate symbol. In such signs, the symbol √, as used for the forearm tab, is placed in front of the appropriate dez.

CHAIRMAN

DRAMA /[ ]√A₋ₐ √A₍ₐ ᴵ~/ Two A hands: left hand, palm facing right and fingers pointing up; right hand, palm facing left and fingers pointing up. Forearms are prominent, ie raised so that they are horizontal and parallel to the body. Hands, held in front of chest, move to and fro alternately.

CHAIRMAN /∅√Aᵦ₎ √Aᵦ₍ ᵛ/ Two A hands: left hand, palm facing down and fingers pointing right; right hand, palm facing down and fingers pointing left. Forearms are prominent, ie raised so that they are horizontal and parallel to the body. Hands, held in neutral space, move down in a short sharp movement.

Initial Dez Signs

Throughout this chapter we have made reference to the use of particular handshapes for signs apparently derived from a particular letter of the manual alphabet. The main examples are those linked with the Irish manual alphabet, although initial dez signs do exist which derive from the British manual alphabet. As indicated in Chapter 1, such signs may be deliberately 'created' for educational reasons, or may have developed naturally, because of the co-existence of signs and alphabet. There does seem to be some evidence that just as signs can move away from their iconic origins, they may similarly move away from their alphabetic origins. The sign used within the world of the Scottish Catholic community for READY is /√R_T< ˣ /, clearly an initial dez sign. However, we have also noted its use with an H hand. Every other aspect of the sign remains the same.

Phonemic Inventory

The examples in the preceding sections show that BSL has 33 distinctive dez phonemes, together with 24 main allophonic variants. The list of allophonic variants is not exhaustive although the evidence available suggests that those given here are the most typical alternative realisations of the dez phonemes. Some signs make use of more than one handshape. Complex signs often involve opening or closing to a different handshape.

Complex Signs

DISAGREE

FAMOUS /◡G₋ₐG₍ₐ ᵈ⁽⁵⁵⁾/ Two G hands: left hand, palm facing right and finger pointing up; right hand, palm facing left and finger pointing up. Fingers, held at either side of mouth, move away from the signer changing to 5 hands.

DISAGREE /∅Ȧ₋ᴸᵢ Ȧ₍ᴸ ˣᵉ⁽⁵⁵⁾/ Two Ȧ hands: left hand, palm facing right and fingers pointing away from the signer; right hand, palm facing left and fingers pointing away from the signer. Hands, held side by side in neutral space, touch then separate opening to two 5 hands.

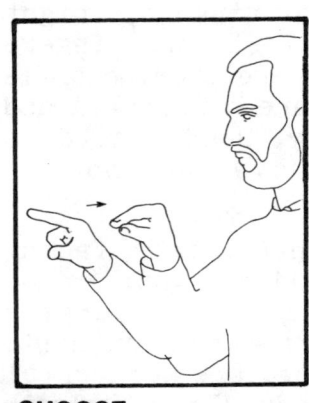
CHOOSE

MISS /⊃H̿>∧ H̿<∧ ≠[ĤĤ]/ Two H̿ hands: left hand, palm facing right and fingers pointing up; right hand, palm facing left and fingers pointing up. Hands, held at either side of head, cross closing to Ĥ hands.

CHOOSE /∅Ḡ̄⊥∧ ≠[Ĝ]/ Right Ḡ̄ hand, palm facing away from the signer and finger pointing up, is held in neutral space. Hand moves towards the signer closing to a Ĝ hand.

Compound Signs

The use of the term 'compound' here begs a number of questions about the nature of 'true' compounds in BSL. Compounding is a productive process which allows two words to come together to form new lexical items in the language. In English, from examples such as "hotdog", "frogman" and "highbrow", it can be seen that the new created items have a different meaning from the combined meaning of the original words. Research by Klima and Bellugi (1979), Liddell (1983) and Bergman (1977) has shown the existence of compounds in sign languages too. Our own limited work in this area shows their existence in BSL also, although we are only just beginning to examine the special temporal properties of such signs. One of the problems in relation to the transcription system is to decide whether a particular item is a 'true' compound or not. Some complex signs, involving changes in the major parameters, may or may not be compound in the sense mentioned above. For the purposes of transcription it does seem useful to make use of the dotted oblique lines when it is clear that a sign can be separated into distinct sequential elements, even if the sign is not necessarily a compound in the true sense. The following examples will show how this convention is used and also illustrate some of the compounds in BSL (see also discussion in Chapter 8).

REMEMBER

REMEMBER /⌒G<∧ ×⫽Ā₀>A▷ᴸ ᵛˣ/ Right G hand, palm facing left and finger pointing up, is held at forehead. Index finger touches right side of forehead. Manual tab A is held with palm facing up and fingers pointing right. Right hand moves down changing to an A hand with palm facing down and fingers pointing away from the signer. Right hand is placed on top of left.

FORGIVE

FORGIVE
/⌣G_T∧ ˣ⫽ B_a> B_b⊥ ˣ⁺ᵉ/

Right G hand, palm facing the signer and finger pointing up, is held at the side of the mouth. Index finger touches mouth. Manual tab B is held with palm facing up and fingers pointing right. Right hand moves down changing to a B hand with palm facing down and fingers pointing away from the signer. Right hand, placed on top of left, makes circular motion towards the signer, maintaining contact.

BELIEVE
/⌒G_<∧ ˣ⫽ B_a> B_<⊥ ᵛˣ/

Right G hand, palm facing left and finger pointing up, is held at forehead. Index finger touches right side of forehead. Manual tab B is held with palm facing up and fingers pointing right. Right hand moves down from forehead changing to a B hand with palm facing left and fingers pointing away from the signer. Right hand edge makes contact with left palm.

CHECK

CHECK /ʊ ᵉȲ_<∧ ˣ⫽ ∅ Y_<∧ ᵉ⸱/

Right Ȳ hand, palm facing left and fingers pointing up, is held contacting face under right eye. Hand changes to a Y hand, with palm facing left and fingers pointing up. Hand moves away and to the right while making short repeated twisting movements.

Notes

CHAPTER FIVE

Orientation

Orientation is the relationship of the hand(s) to the signer's body. As this is one of the most controversial areas in current sign language research, it is necessary here to delve a little further into the theoretical issues. (See also Chapter 1, pages 5-6; Chapter 2, page 28). This chapter has three main sections: firstly, the background to the establishment of the orientation parameter is presented; secondly, examples from BSL are given to illustrate the specific orientation choices within the system; finally, some practical guidelines to the interpretation of the orientation symbols in relation to specific handshapes are outlined.

Theoretical Background

As indicated in previous chapters, Stokoe's original analysis (1960, 1965, 1972), distinguished three significant aspects of sign activity: what acts, the action and the location, ie dez, sig and tab. In the revised version of Sign Language Structure (1978, p40), Stokoe comments:

> *"To suppose that the three aspects are independent parameters is to mistake the nature of sign activity or to confuse it with the sequential way that segments of sound in speaking follow one another to build a morpheme or a word."*

Similarly, in his review of Wilbur (Stokoe, 1979, pp184-5), he suggests that:

> *"Like the last addition to a house of cards, the adding of 'orientation' collapses the whole parametrical edifice. Since what acts, where it acts and what it does are inseparable except by the imaginative act of considering one of these aspects at a time, the attempt to introduce orientation misses both the nature of the original aspectual analysis and any pretence of empirical investigation."*

These are strong words and obviously anyone engaged in an examination of the internal structure of signs must take note of this forceful opposition to the addition of orientation from the originator of the theoretical framework. However, a close reading of the literature suggests that part of the problem may lie in conflicting interpretations of the notion of a 'separate parameter'. It may, therefore, be useful to note the way in which this term has been used within phonetics and phonology.

Abercrombie defines a parameter as *"a variable, an ingredient which is constantly present but changing in value."* (Abercrombie, 1965, p123). The parametric approach thus *"recognises the physiological system for speech as a single complex system in which the continuous interacting activities of the various linked components are intricately co-ordinated in time."*

(Laver, 1970, p60). It is fascinating to observe that the parametric approach developed out of a dissatisfaction with the purely segmental and sequential analysis of speech. Rather than speech being regarded as consisting of sequences of fairly static articulatory postures, it is viewed as a dynamic process involving a number of intricately co-ordinated activities. Stokoe has stressed again and again the inadequacy and indeed the inapplicability of segmental analysis to sign phonology. The parametric approach forces us to recognise the interdependence of those ingredients which are ever-present in the production of a sign: the claim here is that these ingredients include the orientation parameter. Extricating orientation for specific analysis is an artificial process just as it is artificial to separate what acts from the action. Nevertheless, this can be useful so long as an attempt is then made to characterise the way in which the choices from each parameter are interrelated, eg certain combinations are physically impossible, others are language specific. Stokoe is surely right (Stokoe, 1979, p182) to doubt whether we have reached a stage of precision in measurement and analysis that would allow us to be completely confident in isolating not only the significant parameters but the particular sets of values which realise these parameters. Certainly it is rather more difficult to provide evidence for the specific values given for orientation than it is for the other parameters. However, orientation is a consistent ingredient of sign production: it is not possible to produce a sign without placing the hand(s) in a particular orientation in relation to the signer's body. As with the sig parameter, it sometimes appears that the separation into specific values is relatively arbitrary, but similar problems of categorisation are also found in spoken language phonology.

Another of Stokoe's criticisms (Stokoe, 1978, p85) is that four parameter analysis goes against the signer's intuitions in that generally the signer is unconcerned with where the palm of the hand is facing: other factors such as muscular activity and the feel of the contacting surfaces are more important. A comment by Abercrombie in relation to the physiological parameters of speech may provide a partial answer:

"I am not suggesting that we normally listen to these parameters. We hear the medium as a single unanalysed continuing noise fluctuating in quality . . . but we can learn to listen in terms of the physiological parameters . . . so that failure to master the medium can be described in these terms and so can the development of speech in the child."

(Abercrombie, 1965, p124)

Whether we take an aspectual or a parametric approach, we are isolating descriptive categories whose realisations in actual production and reception are inseparable from other aspects. Of course, there is a link between the descripive categories posited and our observation of language behaviour. We can learn to observe and record in terms of the categories we propose, so long as these bear some relation to the actual activity. Similarly, if we make the wrong choices as to the essential and distinctive categories, our observations will be distorted and we may miss important information.

As indicated in Chapter 2, two main factors have influenced our decision to regard orientation as a separate parameter: the fact that orientation alone distinguishes pairs of otherwise identical signs and the fact that transcriptions excluding orientation have proved descriptively inadequate. In practical sessions with non-signers, in which full information on tab, dez and sig was given, we found that incorrect reproductions consistently manifested orientation errors. A lack of detailed phonetic information can also lead to incorrect or 'odd' reproduction of English words, yet this does not necessarily lead us to the conclusion that our phonemic analysis as such is inadequate. However, in sign language, orientation information does seem to be a consistent requirement both for the learner and the researcher. Our own experience of trying to reproduce transcribed signs from other sign languages has also shown how easy it is to make errors if orientation information is not available.

Within this account of BSL two types of orientation are seen as essential: palm ori, the attitude of the palm in relation to the signer's body, and finger ori, the direction of the fingers in relation to the signer's body. It has been possible to find minimal pairs of signs which are distinguished only by orientation, whether by palm ori alone (SOME:FLOUR), finger ori alone (CHEAT:SLY), or a combination of both palm and finger ori (BALL:CLASS).

Minimal Pairs
Palm Ori

SOME /∅$\hat{B}_{α⊥}$ ⁻/

Right $\hat{B}$ hand, palm facing up and fingers pointing away from the signer, is held in neutral space. Fingers perform a crumbling action.

FLOUR /∅$\hat{B}_{D⊥}$ ⁻/

Right $\hat{B}$ hand, palm facing down and fingers pointing away from the signer, is held in neutral space. Fingers perform a crumbling action.

SOME

FLOUR

Finger Ori

CHEAT /3$\dot{A}_{<∧}$ ˣ/

Right $\dot{A}$ hand, palm facing left and fingers pointing up, is held with thumb touching cheek. Hand moves down, maintaining contact.

SLY /3$\dot{A}_{<⊥}$ ˣ/

Right $\dot{A}$ hand, palm facing left and fingers pointing away from the signer, is held with thumb touching cheek. Hand moves down, maintaining contact.

CHEAT

SLY

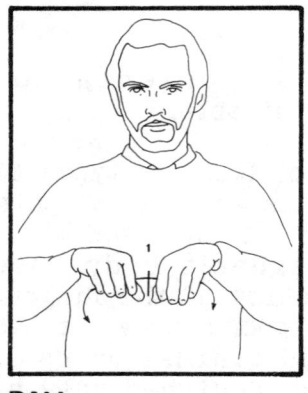

BALL

CLASS

Palm Ori/Finger Ori

BALL /⌀C₆⊥ ıx C₆⊥ ᵃˣ/

Two C hands, palms facing down and fingers pointing away from the signer, are held side by side and touching in neutral space. The hands twist and then touch.

CLASS /⌀C⊥∧ ıx C⊥∧ ᵂˣ/

Two C hands, palms facing away from the signer and fingers pointing up, are held side by side and touching in neutral space. The hands twist and then touch.

Orientation Choices within BSL

The following options are available within the palm ori and finger ori components which together realise the orientation parameter in BSL signs:

Palm Ori	Finger Ori
ɑ up	∧ up
ҍ down	∨ down
⊤ towards the signer	⊤ towards the signer
⊥ away from the signer	⊥ away from the signer
> right	> right
< left	< left

It would be an exaggeration to suggest that the primes of the orientation parameter can be established in quite the same way as for tab and dez. The two components, palm ori and finger ori, together provide the distinctive choices. As yet we have been unable to do enough work on the combination realisations which occur in BSL to be sure that the categories we posit are the essential ones. In the coming months and years this task should be aided by computer processing (see Carter and Maddix, 1980). As illustrated above, one of the orientation components alone may provide the distinguishing feature between pairs of signs. It is, therefore, possible to cite minimal pairs which illustrate the specific choices available for palm ori. Our evidence so far suggests that finger ori alone accounts for very few minimal pairs.

A further problem is that in some signs it is clear that one of the orientation components is relatively arbitrary. In signs such as SEE /⊐G⊤∧ ˣ⊥/ and SAY /ꭒG⊤∧ ˣ⊥/ the finger ori component can be regarded as the primary orientation feature: it is probably unimportant whether the palm faces the signer, as in the transcription, or to the left. Yet it would be noticeably 'odd' to have palm ori away from the the signer. The somewhat arbitrary nature of the secondary ori component in some signs has caused considerable difficulty in deciding upon the citation form of signs such as SEE and SAY. Every effort has been made to use information available from deaf informants in making these decisions. It is also important to remember that a citation form is in any case, whether spoken or signed, an idealised representation of a linguistic unit.

In many cases, orientation and movement combine to distinguish pairs of otherwise similar signs. SEND /∅B̂⊥∧ ᵇ[5]/ has palm facing away from the signer's body and fingers pointing up, while PUT /∅B̂ᵦ⊥ ˇ[5]/ has palm facing down and fingers pointing away. The sig in each case mirrors the palm ori so that the movement in SEND is away from the signer, while the movement in PUT is down. The two signs SPIT /ᴗG⊥∧ ᴅ[G̃]/ and CLIPE /ᴗG̃<∧ ²[G̃]/ are also distinguished by a combination of orientation and movement. Here again, palm ori is particularly important and the movement corresponds with the direction of the palm. Thus even where orientation is not the only distinguishing feature, it nevertheless plays an important role.

If the transcription for WHICH was simply given as /∅Yᶻ·/ we would know that the Y handshape was held in neutral space and moved from side to side repeatedly, but learners could produce it with palm up or to the left or away from the signer. At the very least such productions would appear very strange to the native signer. The transcription given here, /∅Yᵦ⊥ᶻ·/, gives us precise information on orientation and allows us to produce signs that look like those produced by deaf people. Similarly, if the transcription for DELAY was simply /∅F,F ⊥/ a whole range of orientation positions would be possible. To produce the sign with palms up and fingers pointing away would look very odd: to produce the sign with palm facing towards the signer and fingers pointing up would render the sign quite meaningless. Thus, as indicated earlier, descriptive adequacy demands the use of orientation information.

WHICH **DELAY**

Possible Error 1 **Possible Error** 1

Possible Error 2

Possible Error 2

Orientation alone is able to distinguish MEET from at least two other BSL signs, SAME and THING. This set of three signs illustrates particularly well the way in which realisations of palm and finger ori combine to create significant orientation choices.

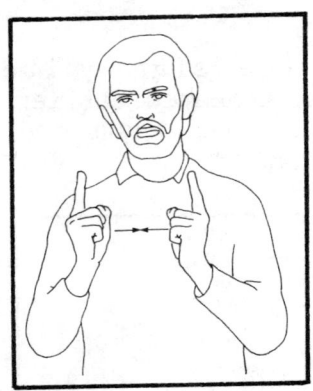
MEET

MEET /⌀G₊∧, G₍∧ ᵡ/ Two G hands: left hand, palm facing right and finger pointing up; right hand, palm facing left and finger pointing up. Hands, held side by side in neutral space, move towards each other and touch.

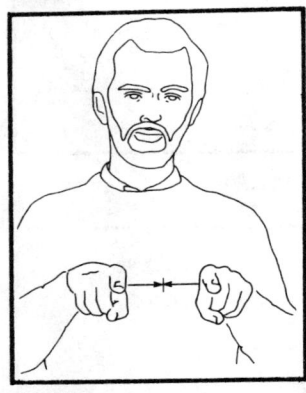
SAME

SAME /⌀G▽⊥, G▽⊥ ᵡ/ Two G hands, palms facing down and fingers pointing away from the signer, are held side by side in neutral space. Hands move towards each other and touch.

THING

THING /⌀G⊤∧, G⊤∧ ᵡ/ Two G hands, palms facing the signer and fingers pointing up, are held side by side in neutral space. Hands move towards each other and touch.

The following minimal pairs will provide some indication of the range of orientation realisations which can be distinctive in BSL signs.

Minimal Pairs
Palm Ori

RABBIT /⌒H⊥∧ H⊥∧ ṁ·/

Two H hands, palms facing away from the signer and fingers pointing up, are held on either side of forehead. Fingers perform a waving action while hands retain contact.

HARE /⌒H⊤∧ H⊤∧ ṁ·/

Two H hands, palms facing the signer and fingers pointing up, are held on either side of forehead. Fingers perform a waving action while hands retain contact.

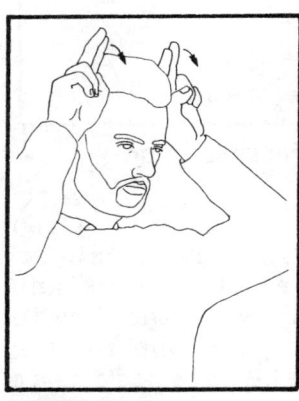
RABBIT

HARE

ROLLER SKATING

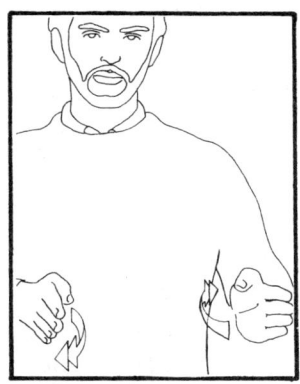
ICE SKATING

Palm Ori

ROLLER SKATING /∅B$_{\text{⊳⊥}}$, B$_{\text{⊳⊥}}$ $\overset{\div}{}$ ~·/

Two B hands, palms facing down and fingers pointing away from the signer, are held side by side in neutral space. Hands move away and separate in a repeated alternating action.

ICE SKATING /∅B$_{\text{>⊥}}$, B$_{\text{<⊥}}$ $\overset{\div}{}$ ~·/

Two B hands: left hand, palm facing right and fingers pointing away from the signer; right hand, palm facing left and fingers pointing away from the signer. Hands, held side by side in neutral space, move away and separate in a repeated alternating action.

BANK

PRINT

Palm Ori

BANK /B̄$_{\text{α>}}$ A$_{\text{<⊥}}$ $^{\vee \times α}_{\wedge}$/

Manual tab B is held with palm facing up and fingers pointing right. Right A hand, palm facing left and fingers pointing away from the signer, is held above left hand. Right hand moves down to make contact with left palm, then twists upwards.

PRINT /B̄$_{\text{α>}}$ A$_{\text{⊳⊥}}$ $^{\vee \times α}_{\wedge}$/

Manual tab B is held with palm facing up and fingers pointing right. Right A hand, palm facing down and fingers pointing away from the signer, is held above left hand. Right hand moves down to make contact with left palm, then twists upwards.

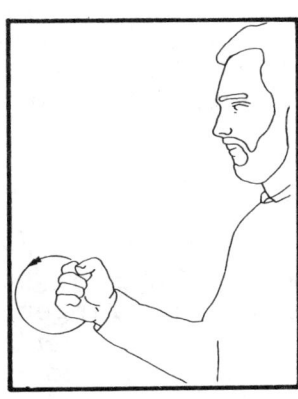
TRAIN

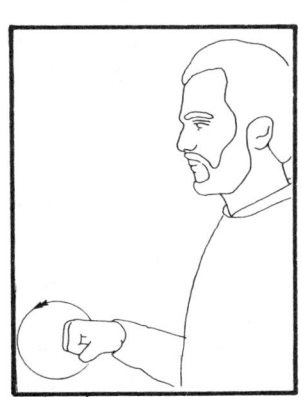
MANGLE

Palm Ori

TRAIN /∅A$_{\text{<⊥}}$ $\overset{e}{\underset{\vee}{}}$·/

Right A hand, palm facing left and fingers pointing away from the signer, is held in neutral space. Hand makes repeated forward circular action.

MANGLE /∅A$_{\text{⊳⊥}}$ $\overset{e}{\underset{\vee}{}}$·/

Right A hand, palm facing down and fingers pointing away from the signer, is held in neutral space. Hand makes repeated forward circular action.

130

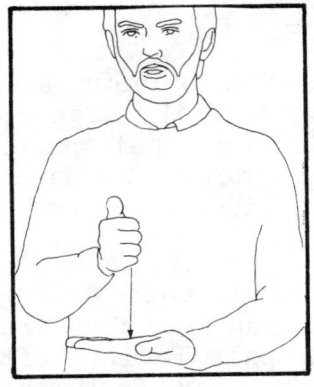
REAL

PROPERLY

Palm Ori

REAL /B̄ₐ₎ Ȧ₍⊥ ˇˣ/

Manual tab B is held with palm facing up and fingers pointing right. Right À hand, palm facing left and fingers pointing away from the signer, is held above left hand. Right hand touches left sharply.

PROPERLY /B̄ₐ₎ Ȧ_b⊥ ˇˣ/

Manual tab B is held with palm facing up and fingers pointing right. Right À hand, palm facing down and fingers pointing away from the signer, is held above left hand. Right hand touches left hand sharply.

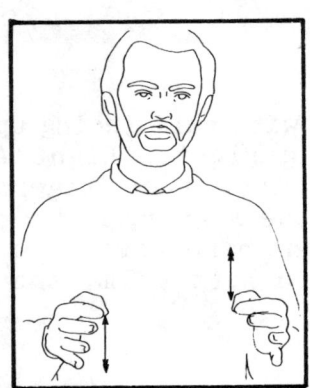
BANQUET

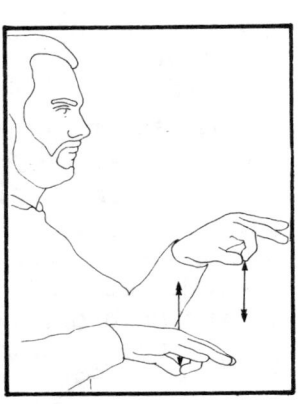
STRING PUPPET

Palm Ori

BANQUET /ØF_>⊥, F_<⊥ ~~·/

Two F hands: left hand, palm facing right and fingers pointing away from the signer; right hand, palm facing left and fingers pointing away from the signer. Hands, held side by side in neutral space, move up and down in repeated alternating action.

STRING PUPPET /ØF_b⊥, F_b⊥ ~~·/

Two F hands, palms facing down and fingers pointing away from the signer, are held side by side in neutral space. Hands move up and down in repeated alternating action.

CHAIR

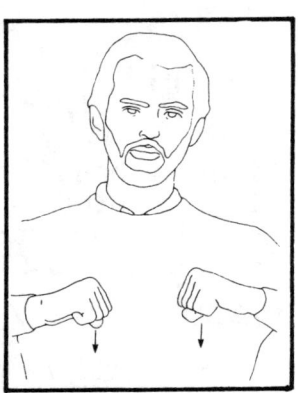
CHAIRMAN

Finger Ori

CHAIR /ØA_b⊥ A_b⊥ ˇ̈/

Two A hands, palms facing down and fingers pointing away from the signer, are held in neutral space. Hands move down.

CHAIRMAN /Ø√A_b> √A_ᴅ< ˇ̈/

Two A hands: left hand, palm facing down and fingers pointing right; right hand, palm facing down and fingers pointing left. Forearms are prominent. Hands, held in neutral space, move down. (The feature prominent forearm is non-phonemic - see page 118).

KNITTING MACHINE

IRON

Palm and Finger Ori

KNITTING MACHINE /∅A$_{D\perp}$ $^{z\cdot}$/

Right A hand, palm facing down and fingers pointing away from the signer, is held in neutral space. Hand moves right and left in repeated action.

IRON /∅A$_{T\vee}$ $^{z\cdot}$/

Right A hand, palm facing the signer and fingers pointing down, is held in neutral space. Hand moves right and left in repeated action.

PEACE

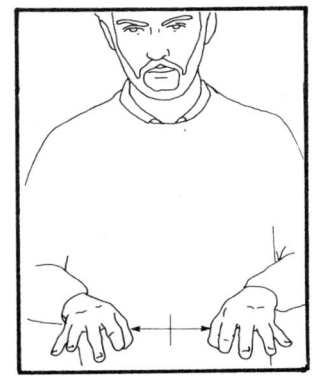
QUIET

Palm and Finger Ori

PEACE /∅F$_{\perp\wedge}$ $_{1x}$ F$_{\perp\wedge}$ $^{\div}$/

Two F hands, palms facing away from the signer and fingers pointing up, are held side by side and touching in neutral space. Hands separate.

QUIET /∅F$_{D\perp}$ $_{1x}$ F$_{D\perp}$ $^{\div}$/

Two F hands, palms facing down and fingers pointing away from the signer, are held side by side and touching in neutral space. Hands separate.

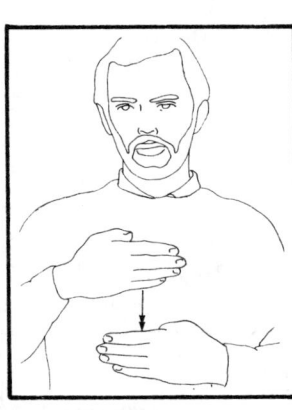
PANTOMIME

WORK

Palm and Finger Ori

PANTOMIME /B̄$_{T>}$ B$_{T<}$ $^{x\cdot}$/

Manual tab B is held with palm facing the signer and fingers pointing right. Right B hand, palm facing the signer and fingers pointing left, is held above left hand. Right hand contacts left hand twice.

WORK /B̄$_{T>}$ B$_{<\perp}$ $^{x\cdot}$/

Manual tab B is held with palm facing the signer and fingers pointing right. Right B hand, palm facing left and fingers pointing away from the signer, is held above left hand. Right hand contacts left hand twice.

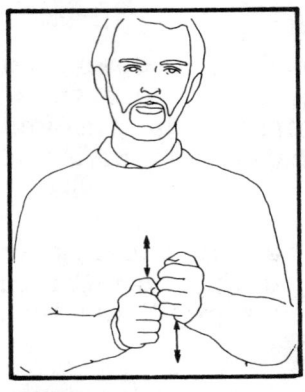
BROTHER

PISTON ENGINE

Palm and Finger Ori

BROTHER /ØA$_{>⊥}$ ıx A$_{<⊥}$ $\tilde{x}$~·/

Two A hands: left hand, palm facing right and fingers pointing away from the signer; right hand, palm facing left and fingers pointing away from the signer. Hands, held side by side and touching in neutral space, move up and down alternately in a repeated action, maintaining contact.

PISTON ENGINE /ØA$_{T∧}$ ıx A$_{T∧}$ $\tilde{x}$~·/

Two A hands, palms facing the signer and fingers pointing up, are held side by side and touching in neutral space. Hands move up and down alternately in a repeated action, maintaining contact.

Guidelines to Interpreting Orientation

In Chapter 2 (page 28), several guidelines were presented which should aid in the interpretation and use of the orientation symbols mentioned above. Here it may be useful to provide further explication of the need for these guidelines and a more detailed account of their applications.

The major difficulty in interpreting orientation is that, as illustrated in the previous chapter, BSL makes use of a wide range of different handshapes. Some of these handshapes are fully closed, others fully open; some involve extension of the thumb and one or more fingers, others involve extension of fingers but not thumb. If, as in the F dez, some digits point in one direction and some in the other, how can we possibly decide what the finger ori is? One answer to this problem would be to define palm and finger ori for each individual handshape (cf Friedman, 1977). However, given that we are dealing with approximately 50 regularly occurring handshapes in the language, this would involve placing an unacceptable burden on the individual learning the system. A more economical answer, in terms of lessening this burden, seemed to be the development of several interpretive rules which could be applied in all cases - the fewer rules the better. After considerable experimentation with different sets of rules, it was decided that the rules presented below were the most effective. We recognise that as we become more and more informed about the orientation choices within BSL it may be possible to refine these rules still further. However, these rules have proved adequate for the vast majority of BSL signs.

Palm Ori

> If there is any problem in deciding on the orientation of the palm, the direction of the wrist should be taken as decisive.

As illustrated in Chapter 2 (page 28), the few problems which do arise in relation to palm ori usually occur when the hand is partially bent at the wrist and the hand is at an angle. Typical examples are WHY /⌐⌐G$_{b<}$ ^{x}/ where the

WHY

I

palm is partly down and partly left, and I /[ ]G̈_T< ˣ/ where the palm is partly facing the signer and partly pointing right. This, of course, illustrates a fundamental problem in orientation, namely that the hand can actually turn 180° in the vertical plane and 180° in the horizontal plane, and in actual production the hand may be at virtually any angle, ie neither completely right nor left, completely supinated nor pronated and so on. The wrist is the most stable indication of the orientation of the whole hand and the decision to use the wrist has eliminated palm ori problems in all the examples so far transcribed.

Finger Ori

The primary interpretive rules are those presented in Chapter 2:

1. The direction of the four fingers takes precedence over the thumb.

2. In closed or bent handshapes, finger ori is the direction of the fingers when straightened.

The main reason for the first rule is that it is always possible to predict the direction of the thumb given the specific handshape and information on finger direction. Thus the G dez, which may seem a particularly awkward example, presents no problem at all once this rule is applied. This is also true in a handshape such as F. If we take the straightened fingers as decisive, we know that the thumb and index finger will always be at a 90° angle to the fingers, therefore it is easy to predict the position of the thumb and index finger. If the three fingers are pointing forward and the palm is facing down, then the finger-thumb circle must be pointing down; if the three fingers are pointing away from the signer and the palm is facing left, then the finger-thumb circle must be pointing left.

The second finger ori rule demands that where the fingers are bent, either partially as in G̈, or completely folded into the hand, as in the 'closed' handshape A, the fingers should be unbent in order to decide on finger ori. Thus in a sign like PRACTISE /ØO>⊥ ᵢˣ O<⊥ ᴵ˙/ the fingers when straightened point away from the signer; similarly, with ROB /Ø5̈ᵦ⊥ 5̈ᵦ⊥ ᵀ/ , although the tips of the fingers

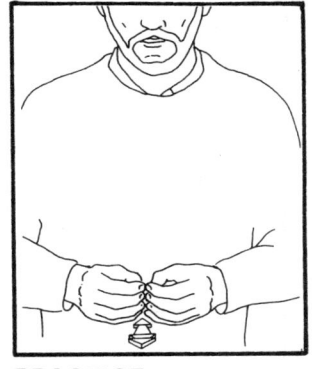
PRACTISE

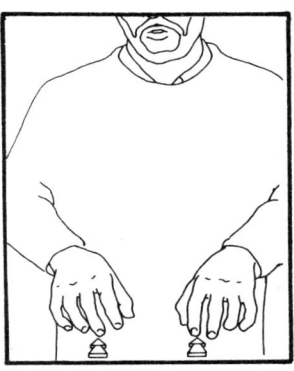
ROB

actually point down, the rest of the fingers point away from the signer. Once we apply the rule that the fingers must be straightened there is no problem: finger ori is away from the signer.

In <u>Words in Hand 1</u> (pages 174-5), we referred to the particular difficulties for interpreting ori in those handshapes which have optional bending at the major knuckles. We noted that in handshapes such as G, I, ⋏, and V, the hand may be held straight or with the extended fingers held at an angle to the palm.

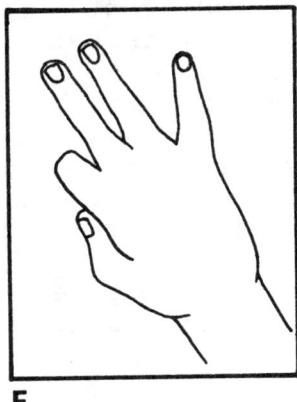
F

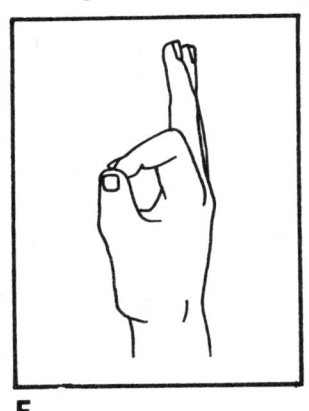
F

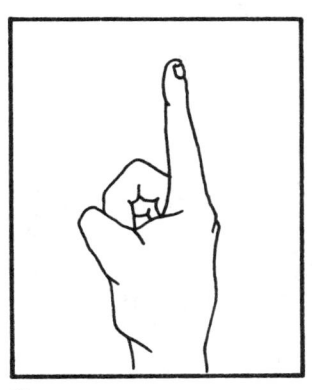
G

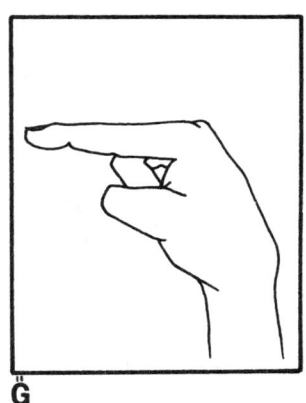
G̈

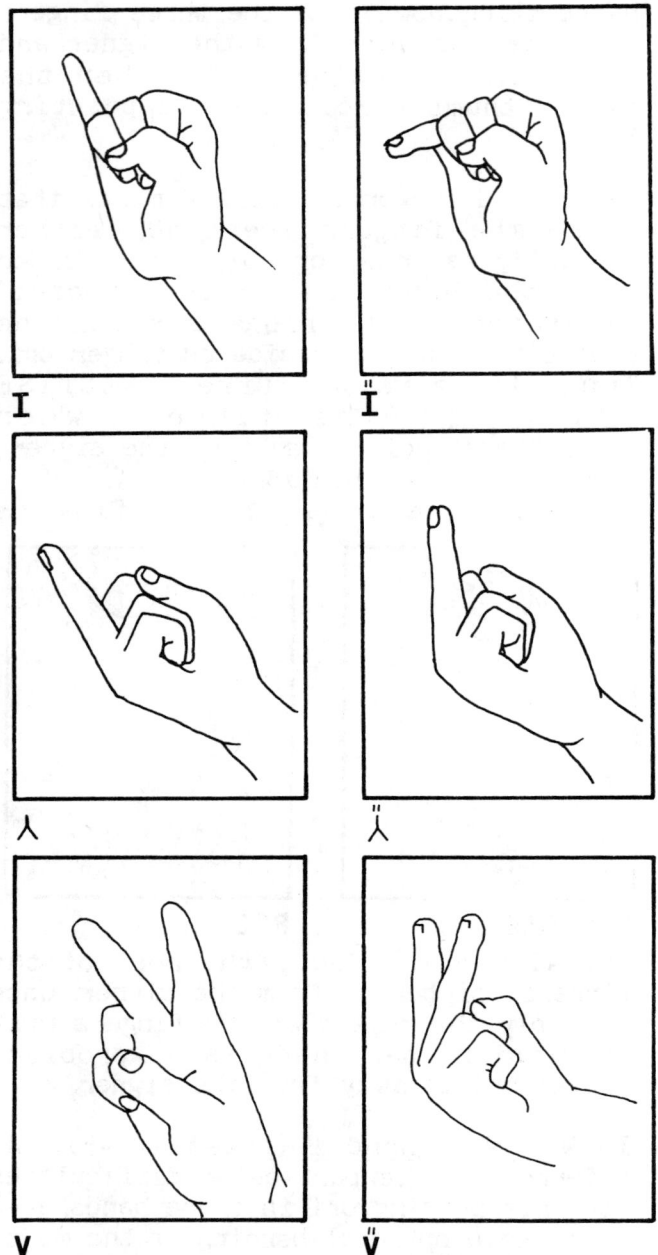

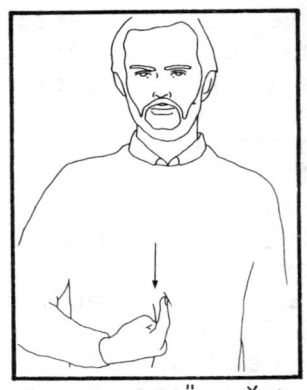 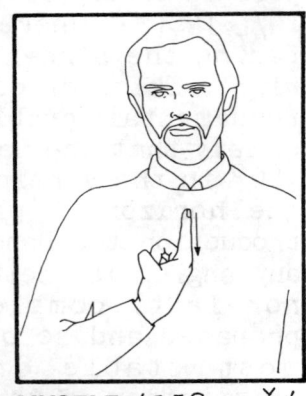

MYSELF /[ ]G̈ₐ< ˘/   **MYSELF** /[ ]G<∧ ˘/

This clearly caused problems in the interpretation of finger ori as in a sign such as MYSELF /[ ]G̈ₐ< ˘/ the orientation would be different depending on which variant was used. Thus on the rules established so far it would be 'up' when the straight variant was used, ie /[ ]G<∧ ˘/ and 'to the left', ie /[ ]G̈ₐ< ˘/ when the angled variant was used. Our answer to the problem in <u>Words in Hand 1</u> was to establish a further rule which required that if a handshape involved both optional bending at the major knuckles and finger extension, the direction of the extended finger would be counted for ori. This at least meant that the finger ori was the same for both variants, although it went against the rule already established for bent handshapes.

An early response from fellow researchers in several countries was to ask why we had not simply accepted that the variants with optional bending were just that, variants, in free variation and not phonemically distinctive. Once we accepted this then we could use some label to show which particular choice had been made by the signer and follow the same orientation rules as before. Indeed, why should we treat these handshapes as a special group? There was no theoretical justification for this. It now seems to us that our fellow researchers were correct in this. What is more, we have found that those learning the system do have difficulty in using the extra rule for finger orientation. Thus, as will have been seen in Chapter 4, we have now incorporated the new labels for these angled handshapes into our description. We treat then exactly the same as all handshapes involving bending, so that finger ori is the direction of the finger when the hand is straightened. Researchers will thus note that SILLY which was earlier transcribed as /⌒⋏ₜₜ ˣ·/ is now written as /⌒⋏̈ₜ∧ ˣ·/ and ILL which in <u>Words in Hand 1</u> was written as /[ ]Iₐ∧ Iₐ∧ ˘/, is now written as /[ ]Ïₐ> Ïₐ< ˘/. The change means that users of the system will have to learn the new labels for the handshapes, but both in the labelling and in the interpretation of orientation, we are now able to recognise more consistency across the system.

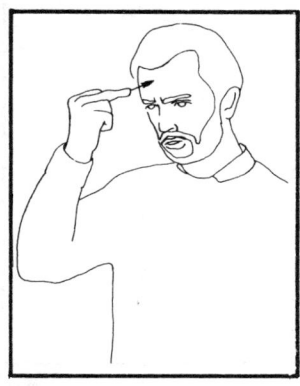 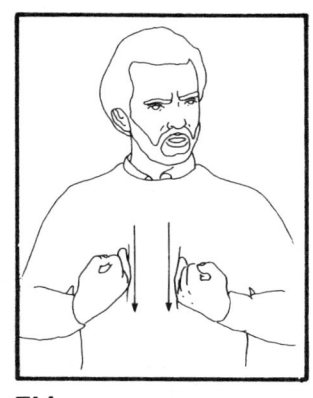  

SILLY   **ILL**   **DEVIL**   **HEAVY**

Several other points may be noted in relation to the transcription of orientation in BSL. Firstly, in this account, the realisation of the two components, palm and finger ori, are always given separately, even when both realisations are the same. Using the original rules, it was possible for orientation realisations to be identical and we could therefore have used one symbol. However, in practice, it proved just as easy to fill both 'slots' and the advantage of complete consistency seemed more important than 'saving' on symbols. The regularity of the patterning aids learners in using the system and should facilitate the computer processing of sign transcriptions.

In so far as it can be determined, the initial orientation is always given, although the realisation of the sig parameter frequently brings about a change in orientation. In the sign DEVIL /⌒Ҷ_{DL} ?×/, the Ҷ hand is held with palm down and fingers, when straightened, pointing away from the signer. The sig realisation requires the hand to move upwards and touch the brow. The initial position means that final contact is between the back of the hand and the brow. Therefore, at the end of the sign, the palm is facing away from the signer and the fingers are pointing up. Once we know the initial ori, the sig allows us to predict what the final ori will be.

It may also be noted that the symbols used to represent palm up and palm down, ie ɑ and ᴅ, are different from those used to indicate finger up and finger down. This decision was made in order to make manifest within the system the physical links between supination and pronation as realisations of the orientation parameter and supination and pronation as realisations of the sig parameter (cf Stokoe, 1978, 1979). In making these inter-parametric links explicit we are losing a certain consistency between the two components of orientation: it seems odd to use exactly the same symbols for both palm and finger ori in the other four cases, while using quite separate symbols for the up/down choices. The decision by Carter and Maddix (1980) to use ∧ and ∨ for both palm and finger ori may be more sensible, but as learners appear to find no particular problem with the use of ɑ and ᴅ and can in some cases be helped by the links between sig and ori symbols, we have decided not to change the system. If particular users wish to change to ∧ and ∨ this should not cause any major difficulties.

In this account, orientation information is given for both hands in double dez signs. Again, given the symmetry already noted in double dez signs, it may have been possible to provide orientation information for both hands at once, possibly after the second dez symbol. A sign like HEAVY (see pages 5 and 30) would thus be transcribed as /∅B̈ B̈_{ɑ⊥} ˅/ rather than /∅B̈_{ɑ⊥} B̈_{ɑ⊥} ˅/ . This may have been feasible for the up/down, towards/away options but would have been more problematic for left/right. A symbol indicating sideways, eg ≥ could have been used, implying that the left hand faced right and the right hand faced left. This may have worked in a sign such as AGREE which could be written /ØȦ Ȧ$_{z\perp}$ ˣ/. However, the inadequacy of this approach can be seen in a sign such as SEAL /ØB$_{<v}$ ı B$_{>v}$ˣ·/ where the left palm faces left and the right palm faces right, rather than the more usual situation of right palm facing left and left palm facing right. Moreover, the placing of each set of orientation symbols directly after each dez, seems to act as a visual aid to the learner.

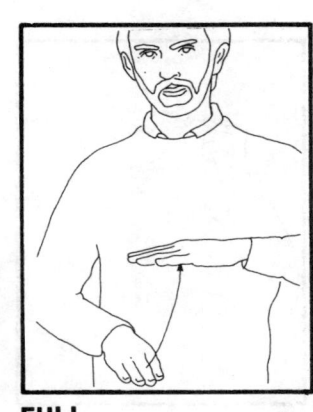
DIFFICULT **FULL**

AGREE **SEAL**

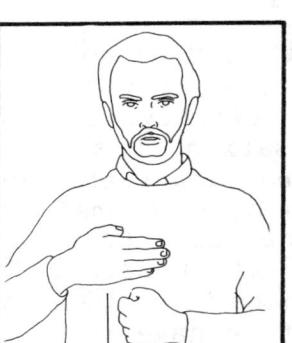
NEVER

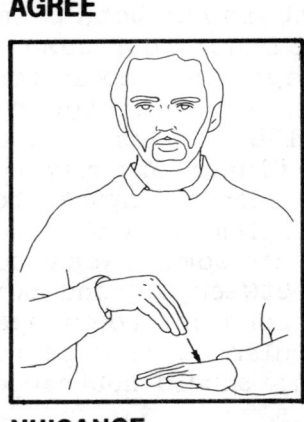
NUISANCE **CAKE**

So far, we have presented guidelines for indicating orientation realisations of the active dez. It has also been found necessary to include the same kind of information for the non-dominant hand acting as tab. Readers will already have noted that in some signs, eg NUISANCE /B̄$_{b>}$ B̈$_{b\perp}$ ᵛˣ·/ and CAKE /B̄$_{b>}$ 5̈$_{b\perp}$ ˣ·/, the hand acting as tab is pronated, while in other examples, in fact the majority, the tab is supinated: examples include WRONG /B̄$_{a>}$ I$_{<\perp}$ ᵛˣ/ and TRUE /B̄$_{a>}$ B$_{<\perp}$ ᵛˣ/. In fact the manual tab can express a number of different realisations of palm and finger ori: DIFFICULT /B$_{>\perp}$ ıˣ Ȧ$_{b\perp}$ ⸚/ has palm facing right and fingers pointing away from the signer; FULL /B̲$_{b>}$ B$_{b\perp}$ ^ˣ/ has palm facing down and fingers pointing right; NEVER /Ā$_{T>}$ ꝯ B$_{T<}$ ⸚/ has palm facing the signer and fingers pointing right. In a large number of cases the exact realisation of finger ori seems relatively arbitrary: in signs such as TRUE and WRONG it simply does not matter whether finger ori is right, away from the signer or at some point in between, although it would be definitely incorrect for finger ori to be towards

TRUE **WRONG**

the signer. The crucial point in these two signs is that the active dez is placed at right angles to the manual tab. Thus if manual tab ori is palm facing up, fingers pointing right, then dez ori for TRUE will be palm facing left, fingers pointing away from the signer: if manual tab ori is palm facing up, fingers pointing away from the signer, then dez ori must be palm facing the signer, fingers pointing left. As indicated earlier, our decision as to which should be regarded as the citation form has been guided by our observations of deaf informants, although so many variables are involved that, at least in some cases, the decision has been relatively arbitrary. The primacy of palm ori in relation to the manual tab can be shown in that although minimal pairs of signs have been noted which are distinguished only by the palm ori of the manual tab (eg TRANSLATE:BASTARD). No comparable pairs have been noted which are distinguished only by finger ori of the manual tab.

TRANSLATE $/\bar{B}_{a>} \, B_{b\perp}{}^{x a x}/$

Manual tab B is held with palm facing up and fingers pointing right. Right B hand, palm facing down and fingers pointing away from the signer. Right hand is placed on top of left hand then twists to palm up position and touches palm again.

TRANSLATE   1   2

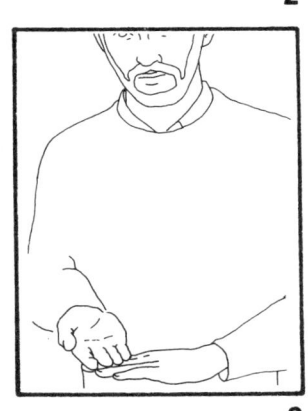

BASTARD $/\bar{B}_{b>} \, B_{b\perp}{}^{x a x}/$

Manual tab is held with palm facing down and fingers pointing right. Right B hand, palm facing down and fingers pointing away from the signer, is held on left hand. Right hand twists so that palm faces up and touches hand again.

BASTARD   1   2

Finally, it should be noted that all of the above comments relate to the manual signs of BSL. As indicated in Chapter 1 (page 2), while we recognise the importance of non-manual activity and the possibility of non-manual signs in BSL, this initial account of BSL sign structure concentrates on those signs which are clearly manual. It may be, as Stokoe suggests (Stokoe, 1978b, p139), that a tri-aspectual analysis of signs, ie one which excludes orientation, would allow for generalisations to be made about sign structure which would include both manual and non-manual signs. This claim will be discussed further in the final chapter. In this chapter we have tried to show that explicit information on orientation in BSL signs is in many cases a descriptive necessity and we have been prepared to err on the side of explicitness in description, rather than economy of description. At some future date, it may be possible to provide an analysis which is optimally efficient and economical and which allows an integrated approach to manual and non-manual systems. Such an approach awaits more detailed descriptions of all aspects of BSL signs, especially systematic non-manual activity.

Notes

CHAPTER SIX

Signation

The analysis of the sig parameter, which expresses the significant movements used in BSL signs, is one of the most difficult tasks in relation to BSL sign structure. Stokoe comments that the action aspect of sign phonology

> *"would present a bewildering maze of movement, were it not possible to apply to this part of the system the clearly formulated methods of structural linguistics. Operating for each user of the language, in the midst of a literally infinite variety of action, is the principle of significant contrast."*
>
> (*Stokoe, 1978, p51*)

Although Stokoe himself has expressed dissatisfaction with the analysis of sig (personal communication), it is nevertheless remarkable that virtually all the contrastive movement/action types, isolated for ASL in Stokoe's original account, are also exploited in a significant way in BSL. The analysis presented here thus stays close to the original approach although it is fully recognised that alternative analyses of the sig parameter are required. The material presented in this chapter should provide an adequate basis for the construction of alternative descriptive frameworks.

Before presenting the sig choices available in BSL, it may be worth examining in closer detail the problems involved in tackling a linguistic description of movement. We may find a clue to the nature of the problem by looking at the analysis of movement within the non-linguistic, but meaningful, medium of dance. "Labanotation", the dance notation system originating in the work of Rudolf Laban (Laban, 1950; Hutchinson, 1977), describes movement in terms of:

the body	the specific parts that move
space	the particular direction, level distance and degree of movement
time	the amount of time taken to produce specific movements
dynamics	the quality and texture of the movement, partly conditioned by the type and degree of muscular energy.

There is little doubt that these four elements are also crucially important within sign language structure. The first two have received most attention yet even here certain aspects such as degree and distance of movement remain largely unexplored. Temporal and dynamic features have received least attention. Certainly temporal factors are probably more important in relation to grammatical and lexical modulations of signs and to the patterning of sign sequences. However, they may also be relevant to the internal structure of signs: it would clearly be incorrect to use a slow measured movement in the sign QUICK /Ḡ_T> G_<⊥ ⸗×ᴧ / yet there is no explicit indication of this within the notation system. Similarly the sign SHOULD /ØȦ_ᴅ⊥ ⸗/ must be produced with a high degree of muscular tension although there is nothing in the transcription to inform us of this. Obviously there is considerable scope for the development of an appropriate descriptive framework to indicate temporal and dynamic aspects. Nevertheless, despite their importance it should be noted that few, if any, minimal pairs of signs are distinguished by such factors alone. Present evidence supports the view that these aspects are crucially important to an account of modulations and syntactic structure, but comparatively less important to the internal structure of individual citation forms.

Much more attention has been given to the other two factors, ie what moves and the direction and type of movement. Again it is clear that the type of movement may in part be conditioned by what is performing the action. This is especially true if we move out beyond our present analysis to a description of non-manual movement. Several researchers have attempted to separate the direction of the movement in manual signs from the actual type of movement involved. Friedman (1977) develops a feature analysis of movement in terms of four fundamental aspects:

interaction   whether one or both hands move, and, if both hands move, whether they perform exactly the same movement or interact with each other

contact   whether or not there is contact with the body, and if so, the type of contact, eg continuous, final, etc

direction   the direction of the movement in space described in terms of three axes, vertical, horizontal-width and horizontal-depth

manner   the type of movement, in terms of the movement of the entire arm (macro) or the joints of the hand and wrist (micro).

She distinguishes five interactive types of movement, six values expressing direction and nine features indicating manner (Friedman, 1977, p35).

It should be stressed that virtually all the features found in Friedman's system can be indicated within the Stokoe Notation System (SNS). The main innovative component of Friedman's account is the set of contrasts given under the heading 'contact'. Friedman notes that contact may be made at the onset of a sign's production, as in BSL NAME /⌒H_T∧ ×Ψ/ or as the final element in a sign like BSL HARD /◡G̈_<∧ Ψ×/. The contact may be continuous so that the hands touch the body throughout the sign, even though they move from one point to another, eg BSL INTERESTING /[]ᵒ_T> ᵒ_T< ×~/. A holding contact involves one part of the dez maintaining contact while the rest of the dez moves, eg in BSL LATE /B_>⊥ ɪ× Ġ ᵇ/ the thumb maintains contact with the palm while the wrist performs a nodding action. Double contact signs involve the hand(s) making two separate contacts with the body, as in BSL SOLDIER /⌐⌐B_<∧ ×>×/ and non-contact signs are those in which there is no contact whatsoever, as in BSL EMBARRASS /◯5_T∧ ̊/.

While Friedman's account focuses attention on the importance of different types of contact, most of these contrasts are describable within the SNS by appropriate placing of the symbols. As illustrated in Chapter 2, by placing the sig symbols one below the other, it is possible to show simultaneous action including simultaneous movement and contact. Normally the contact symbol is placed below the other symbols, but for holding contact, the symbol is placed in the top position. The fact that the contacting digit does not change position is usually obvious from the type of sig action involved, typically nodding, as in EARLY /B_>⊥ ɪ× Ġ_ᴅ⊥ ̊/ or twisting, as in SWEET /∪G<∧ ⚯/. In these examples the contacting digit also twists slightly but on the same position. In EARLY, the initial position has the back of the thumb facing the signer's body, the final position has the back of the thumb facing downward. But in both cases the place of contact is the centre of the left palm. Initial, final and double contact can be shown by filling the appropriate slot in the sequential ordering of sig symbols.

A further type of contact, labelled here 'brushing contact', occurs when the movement involves temporary contact with the tab and the contact is preceded and followed by non-contact. In signs such as NEVER /Ā_{T>} ⋅ B_{T<} ⚯/ and EGG /Ō_{>⊥} ⋅ H_{α⊥} ⚯/, the active hand is not initially in contact with the tab, nor is it at the end of the sign. It would be possible to show this by sequential placing of the symbols, eg ∨ and ×, but this gives a somewhat false impression, suggesting a less fluid movement than actually occurs. Frequently the contact itself is very slight, hence the use of the label 'brushing contact'. It has been thought useful to distinguish this as a separate type of contact by placing the sig symbols vertically, with the contact symbol placed centrally between the two directional symbols. This allows us to stress the 'coherence' of the action. The following examples should illustrate the different types of contact distinguished here and the associated transcription conventions.

NAME

NAME /⌒H_{T∧} ×⚲/

Initial Contact

Right H hand, palm facing the signer and fingers pointing up, touches right side of forehead then moves outwards in a twisting movement so that the palm faces away from the signer.

HARD

HARD /∪G̈_{<∧} ω×/T/

Final Contact

Right G̈ hand, palm facing left and finger pointing up, twists towards chin and touches chin sharply.

142

LIFE

LIFE /[]ȣ_T< ˣ₹/

Maintaining Contact

Right ȣ hand, palm facing the signer and finger pointing left. Middle finger touches chest and moves up and down in a short movement while maintaining contact with chest.

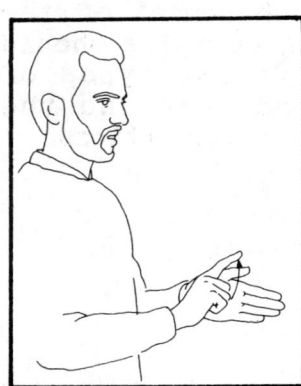
EARLY

EARLY /B_>⊥ ıx Ġ_D⊥ ˣ₹/

Holding Contact

Manual tab B is held with palm facing right and fingers pointing away from the signer. Right Ġ hand, palm facing down and finger pointing away from the signer, is held close to left hand so that thumb of right hand contacts the centre of the left palm. The hand then nods upward, with the thumb holding the contact in exactly the same position.

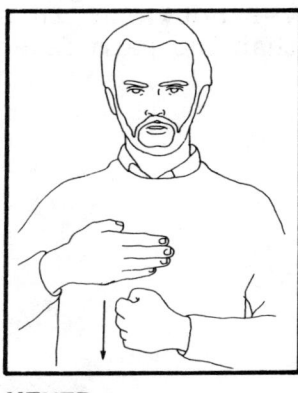
NEVER

NEVER /Ā_T> ꜉ B_T< ˣ̌/

Brushing Contact

Manual tab A is held with palm facing the signer and fingers pointing right. Right B hand, palm facing the signer and fingers pointing left, is held slightly above and in front of the left hand. Right hand moves downward in sharp action so that palm of right hand brushes against the back of the left hand.

SOLDIER

SOLDIER /⌐⌐ B_<∧ ˣ˃ˣ/

Double Contact

Right B hand, palm facing left and fingers pointing up, makes contact with left shoulder and hand moves right to touch right shoulder.

EMBARRASS

EMBARRASS /C5T∧ ⚬/̊

Non-Contact

Right 5 hand, palm facing the signer and fingers pointing up, is held in front of face. Hand moves up and towards the face in a short movement.

It is worth stressing that the distinctions in types of contact are not in themselves phonemically contrasting. Even pairs of signs which at first sight seem to contrast primarily in terms of their contact type, turn out to be distinguished by the movement action as a whole. Thus THEATRE /B̄b>x ʊbㅗ ẍ·/ and BLUE /B̄b>x ʊbㅗ ẍ·/ each involve contact of the middle finger of the ʊ hand on the back of the left hand. In BLUE the finger moves from side to side, maintaining contact; in THEATRE a holding contact is used, and although the hand moves from side to side, it does so with a twisting action, allowing the middle finger to stay in the same position. The type of movement and the type of contact are frequently closely linked, so although contact is important it needs to be interpreted within the context of other elements within the movement parameter.

Klima and Bellugi extend the notion of 'contact' to include abstract points on what they term the horizontal, vertical and bilateral planes, hence treating these planes "as if they were tangible surfaces" (Klima and Bellugi, 1979, p60). This development is probably most relevant to a description of grammatical and lexical modulations. However, it also focuses on the fact that categorisations such as 'circular' can be inadequate. It is necessary to know on which plane the circular movement is operating. Again it is possible to show these distinctions by appropriate manipulation of the sig symbols as illustrated below. In the following sections, sets of minimally differentiated BSL signs will be used to illustrate the appropriateness of the sig distinctions employed here.

Directional Movement

The contrasts used by Stokoe show three dimensions of movement.

Vertical	up	∧
	down	∨
	up and down	∧∨
Bilateral (horizontal-width)	right	>
	left	<
	side to side	z
Horizontal (horizontal-depth)	towards the signer	T
	away from the signer	⊥
	to and fro	I

Stokoe also includes circular movement under directional movement, while Friedman regards circular as a type of macro action. Circular motion is here discussed under 'Manner', as this then allows manner choices and direction choices to be combined to produce, eg circular action in a vertical plane as opposed to circular action in the horizontal plane. The following examples illustrate significant choices realising directional movement.

Minimal Pairs
Right: Left
CLEVER /⌒Ȧ<∧ ⇄/

Right Ȧ hand, palm facing left and fingers pointing up, is held with thumb touching forehead. Hand moves to the right with thumb maintaining contact.

WISE /⌒Ȧ<∧ ⇆/

Right Ȧ hand, palm facing left and fingers pointing up, is held with thumb touching forehead. Hand moves to the left with thumb maintaining contact.

CLEVER **WISE**

Right: Side to Side
BUT /ØG⊥∧ ⇉/

Right G hand, palm facing away from the signer and finger pointing up, is held in neutral space. Hand nods sharply to the right.

WHAT /ØG⊥∧ ⇌/

Right G hand, palm facing away from the signer and finger pointing up, is held in neutral space. Hand nods sharply from side to side.

BUT **WHAT**

Away: Towards
TOMORROW /⌣G⊤∧ ×⊥/

Right G hand, palm facing the signer and finger pointing up, is held with finger touching chin. Hand moves away from the signer.

YESTERDAY /⌣G⊤∧ ×⊤/

Right G hand, palm facing the signer and finger pointing up, is held with finger touching chin. Hand moves towards the signer.

TOMORROW **YESTERDAY**

Away: To and Fro

TRIP /Ḧ>∧ ᵩx Ḧ<∧ ⊥/

Manual tab Ḧ is held with palm facing right and fingers pointing up. Right Ḧ hand, palm facing left and fingers pointing up, is held in front of and touching left hand. Right hand moves away from the signer.

RETURN TRIP /Ḧ>∧ ᵩx Ḧ<∧ ᴵ/

Manual tab Ḧ is held with palm facing right and fingers pointing up. Right Ḧ hand, palm facing left and fingers pointing up, is held in front of and touching left hand. Right hand moves to and fro, returning to initial contact position.

TRIP

RETURN TRIP

Up: Down

LAST /I_T>, I<⊥ ˣ̌/

Manual tab I is held with palm facing the signer and finger pointing right. Right I hand, palm facing left and finger pointing away from the signer. Hands are held side by side with right hand slightly below left. Right hand moves up so that the little finger contacts the left little finger sharply then continues up.

WORST /Ī_T>, I<⊥ ˣ̌/

Manual tab I is held with palm facing the signer and finger pointing right. Right I hand, palm facing left and finger pointing away from the signer. Hands are held side by side with right hand slightly above left. Right hand moves down so that the little finger contacts the left little finger sharply then continues downward.

LAST

WORST

Down: Up and Down

CHILD /∅B_b⊥ ˇ/

Right B hand, palm facing down and fingers pointing away from the signer, is held in neutral space. Hand moves down.

BOUNCE /∅B_b⊥ ∼/

Right B hand, palm facing down and fingers pointing away from the signer, is held in neutral space. Hand moves up and down.

CHILD

BOUNCE

Interaction

When two hands are involved in the production of a sign, they may perform exactly the same action simultaneously or they may interact in various ways. The hands may approach each other or separate, change places or move alternately, cross each other, touch or interlink. In most cases, other sig choices must also be realised, eg the hands may move to and fro alternately, side to side alternately, up and down alternately, and so on. One type of interaction distinguished by Stokoe, entering, normally occurs only in single dez signs where the active dez hand enters the tab as in BSL IN /C̄$_{>⊥}$ B̈$_{D⊥}$ °/ and PARTICIPATE /C$_{>⊥}$, B̈$_{D⊥}$ °/. So far we have noted no minimal pairs which are distinguished by this feature alone and as this type of interaction cannot occur in double dez signs it may be regarded as a somewhat peripheral feature. The other interaction symbols used in the SNS are:

approach	⊃⊂
separate	÷
interchange	↭
alternate	∼
cross	╪
link or grasp	⌶
contact	×

Minimal Pairs
Approach : Separate

NARROW-MINDED /⊃B$_{>⊥}$ B$_{<⊥}$ ⊃⊂/

Two B hands: left hand, palm facing right and fingers pointing away from the signer; right hand, palm facing left and fingers pointing away from the signer. Hands, held at either side of the head, move towards each other.

BROAD-MINDED /⊃B$_{>⊥}$ B$_{<⊥}$ ÷/

Two B hands: left hand, palm facing right and fingers pointing away from the signer; right hand, palm facing left and fingers pointing away from the signer. Hands, held at either side of the head, move away from each other.

Interchange : To and Fro

SNOWBALL /∅ B̄$_{a>}$ × B̈$_{D⊥}$ ↭/

Two B̈ hands: left hand, palm facing up and fingers pointing right; right hand, palm facing down and fingers pointing away from the signer. Right hand is held on top of left hand in neutral space. Hands interchange.

VALUABLE /∅ B̄$_{a>}$ × B̈$_{D⊥}$ ⊥/

Two B̈ hands: left hand, palm facing up and fingers pointing right; right hand, palm facing down and fingers pointing away from the signer. Right hand is held on top of left hand in neutral space. Hands move to and fro.

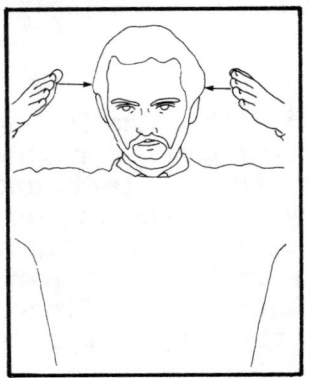
NARROW-MINDED

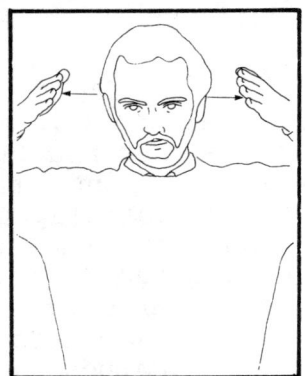
BROAD-MINDED

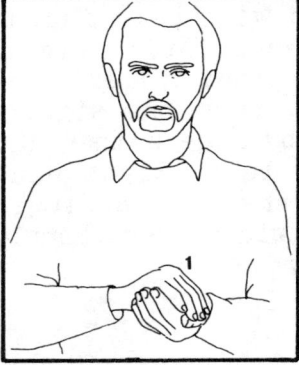
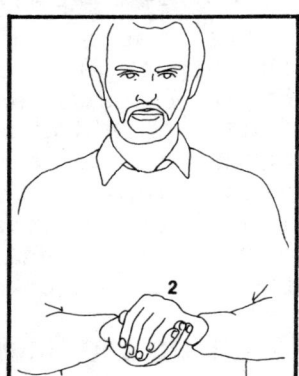
SNOWBALL 1 2

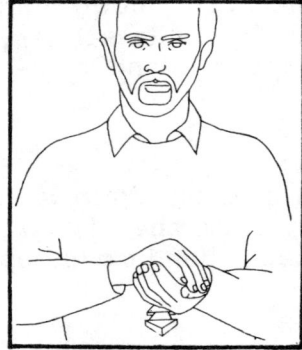
VALUABLE

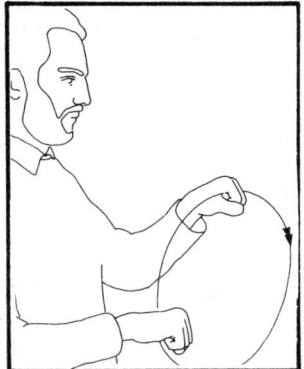
CYCLING

HORSE-RIDING (verb)

MISTAKE

OPPOSE

ENGINEER

HOW

Alternating : Non-Alternating

CYCLING /⌀A⌑⊥ ┐ A⌑⊥ $\overset{c}{\underset{v}{\cdot}}\sim\cdot$/

Two A hands, palms facing down and fingers pointing away from the signer, are held side by side in neutral space. Hands perform a repeated alternating forward circular action in the vertical right angles plane.

HORSE-RIDING /⌀A⌑⊥ ┐ A⌑⊥ $\overset{c}{\underset{v}{\cdot}}\cdot$/

Two A hands, palms facing down and fingers pointing away from the signer, are held side by side in neutral space. Hands perform a repeated simultaneous forward circular action in the vertical right angles plane.

Crossing : Separating

MISTAKE /⌀G_T> ┐ G_T< $\overset{+}{\,}$/

Two G hands: left hand, palm facing the signer and finger pointing right; right hand, palm facing the signer and finger pointing left. Hands, held side by side in neutral space, cross over each other.

OPPOSE /⌀G_T> ┐ G_T< $\div$/

Two G hands: left hand, palm facing the signer and finger pointing right; right hand, palm facing the signer and finger pointing left. Hands, held side by side in neutral space, separate from each other.

Interlinking : Contact

ENGINEER /⌀5̈_T> ┐ 5̈_T< $\overset{\scriptscriptstyle\mathrm{I}}{\,}$/

Two 5̈ hands: left hand, palm facing the signer and fingers pointing right; right hand, palm facing the signer and fingers pointing left. Hands are held side by side in neutral space. Fingers of one hand interlink with fingers of the other hand.

HOW /⌀5̈_T> ┐ 5̈_T< $^{\times}$/

Two 5̈ hands: left hand, palm facing the signer and fingers pointing right; right hand, palm facing the signer and fingers pointing left. Hands are held side by side in neutral space. Hands contact each other.

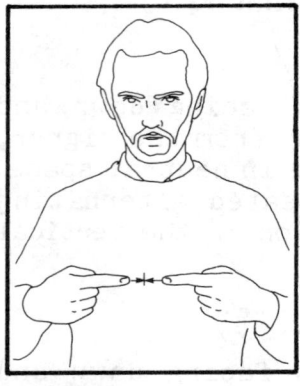
CONTACT

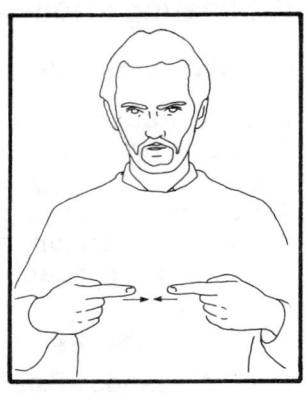
AGAINST

IN

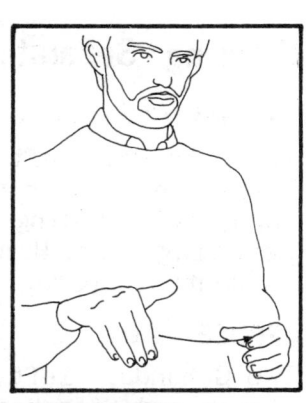
PARTICIPATE

Contact-Non-Contact

CONTACT /⌀G_T> G_T< ᵓᶜˣ/

Two G hands: left hand, palm facing the signer and finger pointing right; right hand, palm facing the signer and finger pointing left. Hands, held in neutral space, come towards each other and tips of index fingers touch.

AGAINST /⌀G_T> G_T< ᵓᶜ/

Two G hands: left hand, palm facing the signer and finger pointing right; right hand, palm facing the signer and finger pointing left. Hands, held in neutral space, move towards each other.

Examples of Entering

IN /C̄_>⊥ B̈_b⊥ °/

Manual tab C is held with palm facing right and fingers pointing away from the signer. Right B̈ hand, palm facing down and fingers pointing away from the signer, is held above left hand. Right fingers enter space between thumb and fingers of left hand.

PARTICIPATE /C_>⊥ ˌ B̈_b⊥ °/

Manual tab C is held with palm facing right and fingers pointing away from the signer. Right B̈ hand, palm facing down and fingers pointing away from the signer, is held beside left hand. Right hand moves to enter left C hand.

Manner

It seems useful to employ the general term 'manner' to cover the nature of the action performed by the dez as opposed to the spatial route taken by the dez. Thus the dez may perform a circular action (manner) on the vertical plane (direction). This is a somewhat artificial distinction but it may help to clarify the description. The account of manner presented here includes several new interpretations of established symbols, as well as several new symbols. It may, therefore, be useful to describe these innovations step by step.

Friedman presents nine choices under the heading of manner: three of these she refers to as macro movements, six she regards as micro movements:

Macro	straight
	twist
	circular
Micro	bend fingers
	bend knuckles
	bend wrist
	open
	close
	wiggle

Macro Movement-Circular

There are a considerable number of movement choices subsumed under the heading of circular movement. Our own experience of using the transcription system over the last few years, and particularly our attempts to teach it to others, has shown up some of the inconsistencies inherent in our original presentation. We have decided against making radical alterations to the transcription system here, but hope that the following account will clarify the range of choices and show how the symbols can be used in a consistent way to give precise information on the type of circular movement involved.

The difficulty in this area is that we are dealing with three separate planes of movement. Moreover, the anatomical labels for these planes (sagittal, coronal and lateral) are unfamiliar to most of us and therefore it is not altogether obvious what terminology to use. We hope the following labels will prove acceptable.

Of the three planes in which circular movement can occur, one is horizontal and two are vertical. If we imagine for a moment that our signs actually draw a circle in the air, then circles made on the horizontal plane would be parallel with the floor. Such circular movement involves both right to left and to and fro movement. As with the other planes, we can indicate the complete movement, by using symbols to illustrate the first two elements in the movement. The symbols ⊰ indicate that the first part of the movement is away from the signer and the second to the right. To complete the circle the hand must move towards the signer then to the left. This is of course an artificial separation, but as we shall see below, the use of such sets of symbols can be enough to distinguish types of circular movement.

There are two vertical planes in which circular movement can occur. The first we are labelling vertical-parallel. This means that the circle 'drawn' by the signer is parallel to the body. It is thus exploiting the up/down and side to side dimensions. The symbols ⊰ will show that the hand moves to the right and down, then to the left and up, to complete the circle.

The second vertical plane is labelled here vertical-right angles. This means that the circle drawn by the signer is at right angles to the body. It is thus exploiting the up/down and the to and fro dimensions. The symbols ⊽ will show that the hand first moves away from the signer and down, then towards the signer and up, to complete the circle.

There is one further complication: within each of these choices there is a further directional choice. Thus the movement may be either clockwise or anti-clockwise. This can be shown quite simply by using the symbol for leftwards first, in relation to the horizontal, and vertical-parallel planes, and using the symbol for towards the signer in the vertical-right angles plane.

In two-handed signs, slightly different conventions are used for two of the planes, the vertical parallel and the horizontal. Here is seems easier to use the symbols for separating, ÷, and converging, ⊃⊂, to clarify direction of movement. In ⊰̸ the hands move away, separate, move towards the body and come together again - this is the 'typical' pattern, with the right hand making a clockwise movement. To show the opposite movement in horizontal signs the symbol would be ⊰̸. Should the movement of both hands be in the same direction, this could be shown by leaving out the separating and converging symbols, and replacing them with a directional symbol, as in the single dez signs. In a two-handed sign, ⊰̸, would mean that both hands made a clockwise circular motion in the horizontal plane.

The following examples should help to clarify the distinctions proposed. However, it may be noted that we have not been able to find minimal pairs for all the distinctions, particularly as we are trying to illustrate both one-handed and two-handed signs. This may suggest that some of the choices, such as those within the vertical-parallel plane, are peripheral. However, they are included here for clarity. Where minimal pairs do not occur, the heading "Examples" is used. The overall distinction between the horizontal and vertical-parallel planes can be seen in the minimal pair WHERE and PLAY. No minimal pair has been noted which distinguishes the two vertical planes.

The overall distinction between straight movement and circular movement can be seen in the following minimal pairs:

Minimal Pairs

Up and Down : Circular

IDLE /∅λ̈ₐ⊥ ~·/

Right λ hand, palm facing up and finger pointing away from the signer, is held in neutral space. Hand moves up and down twice.

UNEMPLOYED /∅λ̈ₐ⊥ ⸚·/

Right λ hand, palm facing up and finger pointing away from the signer, is held in neutral space. Hand makes a repeated circular movement in the vertical-parallel plane.

IDLE

UNEMPLOYED

Separating : Circular Separating

FLAT /∅B_{D⊥} ıx B_{D⊥} ÷/

Two B hands, palms facing down and fingers pointing away from the signer, are held side by side and touching in neutral space. Hands move apart.

SWIM /∅B_{D⊥} ıx B_{D⊥} ⸚/

Two B hands, palms facing down and fingers pointing away from the signer, are held side by side and touching in neutral space. Hands make a separating circular movement in the horizontal plane.

FLAT

SWIM

Circular Motion: Horizontal

Single Dez Signs - Minimal Pair

STORY /∪G_T∧ ˣ⁄⁄ B̄ₐ> B_b⊥ $\frac{c}{x}$/

Right G hand, palm facing the signer and finger pointing up, is held touching mouth. Manual tab B is held with palm facing up and fingers pointing right. Right G hand moves down, changing to a B hand with palm facing down and fingers pointing away from the signer, to make contact with left palm, and moves in a clockwise circular motion, maintaining contact.

FORGIVE /∪G_T∧ ˣ⁄⁄ B̄ₐ> B_b⊥ $\frac{c}{x}$/

Right G hand, palm facing the signer and finger pointing up, is held touching mouth. Manual tab B is held with palm facing up and fingers pointing right. Right G hand moves down, changing to a B hand with palm facing down and fingers pointing away, to make contact with left palm, and moves in an anti-clockwise circular motion, maintaining contact.

STORY   FORGIVE

Double Dez Signs - Examples

SWIM /∅B_b⊥ ιx B_b⊥ $\frac{c}{÷}$/

Two B hands, palms facing down and fingers pointing away from the signer, are held side by side and touching in neutral space. Hands make a separating circular movement in the horizontal plane.

VIDEO TAPE /∅G̈_b⊥ G̈_b⊥ $\frac{c}{\div}$/

Two G̈ hands, palms facing down and fingers pointing away from the signer, are held in neutral space. Hands make a converging circular movement in the horizontal plane.

SWIM   VIDEO TAPE

Circular Motion: Vertical-Parallel

Single Dez Signs - Examples

EMBROIDER /F>⊥ ıx F<⊥ $\overset{e}{\underset{v}{\cdot}}$/

Manual tab F is held with palm facing right and fingers pointing away from the signer. Right F hand, palm facing left and fingers pointing away from the signer, is held to the side of, and touching, left hand. Right hand makes clockwise circular motion in the vertical-parallel plane, then touches left hand again. The action is repeated.

SUSPICIOUS /∩I_{T∧} $\overset{e}{\underset{v}{\cdot}}$/

Right I hand, palm facing the signer and finger pointing up, is held at right side of forehead. Hand makes anti-clockwise circular motion in the vertical-parallel plane.

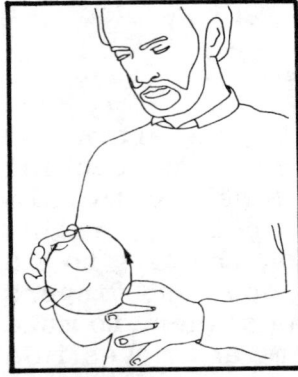
EMBROIDER

SUSPICIOUS

Double Dez Signs - Examples

PLAY /∅ B_{α⊥} B_{α⊥} $\overset{e}{\underset{v}{\cdot}}$/

Two B hands, palms facing up and fingers pointing away from the signer, are held in neutral space. Hands make a separating circular movement in the vertical-parallel plane.

COMPUTER /∅ G_{D⊥} G_{D⊥} $\overset{e}{\underset{v}{\cdot}}$/

Two G hands, palms facing down and fingers pointing away from the signer, are held in neutral space. Hands make converging circular motion in the vertical-parallel plane.

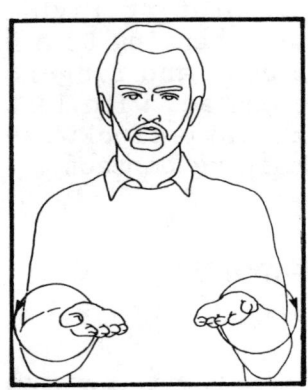
PLAY

COMPUTER

Circular Motion: Vertical-Right Angles

Single Dez Signs - Minimal Pair

NEXT YEAR (forward) /G_{T>} ıx G_{T<} $\overset{e\ x}{\underset{v}{\cdot}}$/

Manual tab G is held with palm facing the signer and finger pointing right. Right G hand, palm facing the signer and finger pointing left. Hands are held side by side with fingertips touching. Right index finger moves away from the signer and down in a circular movement, then touches left index finger again.

LAST YEAR (backward) /G_{T>} ıx G_{T<} $\overset{e\ x}{\underset{v}{\cdot}}$/

Manual tab G is held with palm facing the signer and finger pointing right. Right G hand, palm facing the signer and finger pointing left. Hands are held side by side with fingertips touching. Right index finger moves towards the signer and down in a circular movement, then touches left index finger again.

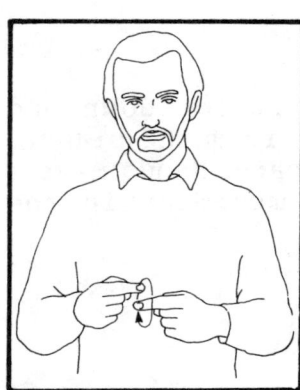
NEXT YEAR

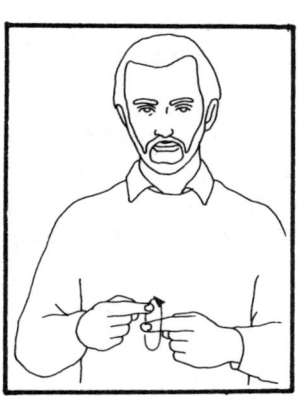
LAST YEAR

Double Dez Signs-Minimal Pair

HORSE-RIDING /∅A₅⊥ ı A₅⊥ $\frac{e}{v}$·/

Two A hands, palms facing down and fingers pointing away from the signer, are held side by side in neutral space. Hands perform a repeated simultaneous forward circular action in the vertical right angles plane.

ROWING /∅A₅⊥ ı A₅⊥ $\frac{e}{v}$·/

Two A hands, palms facing down and fingers pointing away from the signer, are held side by side in neutral space. Hands perform a repeated simultaneous backward circular motion in the vertical right angles plane.

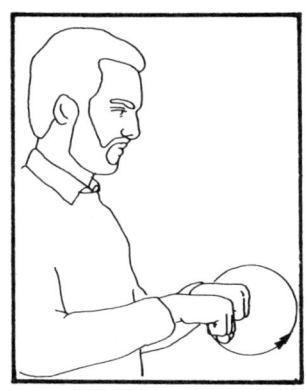

HORSE-RIDING   **ROWING**

Distinction between Planes
Horizontal Plane: Vertical-Parallel Plane

WHERE /∅B₀⊥ B₀⊥ $\frac{e}{\div}$/

Two B hands, palms facing up and fingers pointing away from the signer, are held in neutral space. Hands make a separating circular movement in the horizontal plane.

PLAY /∅B₀⊥ B₀⊥ $\frac{e}{\div}$/

Two B hands, palms facing up and fingers pointing away from the signer, are held in neutral space. Hands make a separating circular movement in the vertical-parallel plane.

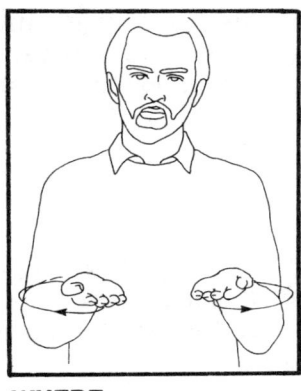 

WHERE   **PLAY**

Twisting

The other category in this group is twist. Stokoe establishes three options under the heading of rotary action: ɑ , supinating rotation, ie moving to the palm up position; ᴅ , pronating rotation, ie moving to the palm down position; and ω twisting movement. This final option, Stokoe describes as the combination of the supinating and rotating movements producing oscillation so that there is rapid change from one direction to the other (Stokoe, 1978, p52). In this account we have decided to use the twist symbol wherever there is a rotary action which does not involve a final position that is either fully supinated or fully pronated. A directional symbol placed below the twist symbol, ω, can be used for further clarification. In COLLEGE /⌒C<∧ $\frac{ψ}{\div}$/ the palm ori is initially palm left, the hand then twists so that the palm faces the signer. Where a short repeated action is used, the normal marks for short and repetition can be used. In COMMITTEE /⌒C<∧ $\frac{ω}{\div}$·/ the initial palm and finger ori is the same as for COLLEGE, but the movement is a very slight twist repeated several times. Clearly, it would be descriptively incorrect to use the symbols ɑ or ᴅ for either of these signs as the palm does not end either in the up or down position. It is probably most helpful to think of twist, ω , as the distinctive choice, and the other symbols as providing extra detailed information, eg twisting away from the signer or twisting up. Where twisting up or down is involved, we have decided to use ɑ or ɒ alone, to be more in keeping with existing practice. The following signs will illustrate how the symbols are used. The minimal pair ABOUT (area):ABOUT (approximate) shows the difference between circular and twisting action; the minimal pair NERVOUS:CROWD shows the difference between twisting and straight movement and the pair COLLEGE:COMMITTEE the difference between twist and twist repeated. TRANSLATE: DEPOSIT shows the distinction between twisting up and twisting down.

Circular: Twist

ABOUT (area) /ø5ᴅ⊥ $\frac{e\cdot}{\flat}$/

Right 5 hand, palm facing down and fingers pointing away from the signer, is held in neutral space. Hand performs repeated circular action on the horizontal plane.

ABOUT (approximate) /ø5ᴅ⊥ $\overset{\omega\cdot}{}$/

Right 5 hand, palm facing down and fingers pointing away from the signer, is held in neutral space. Hand performs repeated twisting action.

Twist: Away

NERVOUS /ø5ᴅ⊥ 5ᴅ⊥ $\overset{\omega\cdot}{}$/

Two 5 hands, palms facing down and fingers pointing away from the signer, are held in neutral space. Hands perform repeated twisting action.

CROWD /ø5ᴅ⊥ 5ᴅ⊥ $^\perp$/

Two 5 hands, palms facing down and fingers pointing away from the signer, are held in neutral space. Hands move away from the signer.

Twist Towards: Repeated Twist

COLLEGE /⌒C<∧ $\frac{\omega\tau}{\tau}$/

Right C hand, palm facing left and fingers pointing up, is held at the right side of the forehead. Hand twists so that palm ends facing the signer.

COMMITTEE /⌒C<∧ $\overset{\omega\cdot}{}$/

Right C hand, palm facing left and fingers pointing up, is held at the right side of the forehead. Hand performs slight repeated twisting action.

ABOUT (area)

ABOUT (approximate)

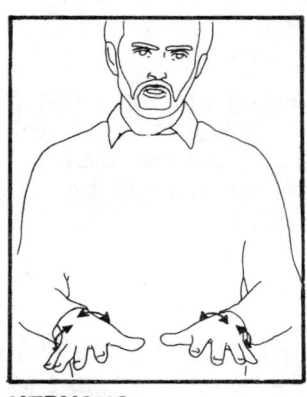
NERVOUS

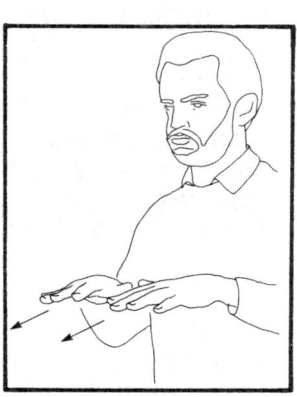
CROWD

COLLEGE

COMMITTEE

Twist Up:Twist Down

TRANSLATE /B̄a₎ Bb⊥ ˣᵃˣ/

Manual tab B is held with palm facing up and fingers pointing right. Right B hand, palm facing down and fingers pointing away from the signer. Right hand is placed on top of left hand then twists to palm up position and touches palm again.

DEPOSIT /B̄a₎ Ba⊥ ˣᵈˣ/

Manual tab B is held with palm facing up and fingers pointing right. Right B hand, palm facing up and fingers pointing away from the signer. Right hand is placed on top of left hand then twists to palm down position and touches palm again.

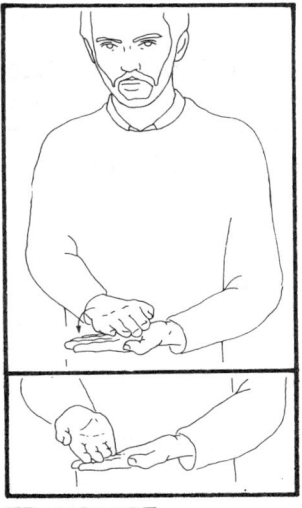
TRANSLATE

DEPOSIT

Bending

It may also be appropriate to regard one category of bending movement, bending at the elbow, under the general classification of macro movement. The other types, bending at the wrist, knuckles and fingers, are discussed below under micro movement. The problem with bending at the elbow is that many signs involve side to side or up and down action which could be interpreted as elbow bending but which can be described more easily under the directional headings already given. As elbow bending is rarely the prominent sig feature and as no minimal pairs have been noted which are distinguished only by this action, we have decided not to introduce a separate symbol into the system. However, the following examples, which have elbows prominent, use a definite bending action from the elbows. This information can normally be gleaned from the combined dez and sig symbols.

CRANE

POWERFUL

CRANE /B̄ᴅ₎ₓ √B̿b⊥ ?# [B̂]/

Manual tab B is held with palm facing down and fingers pointing right. Right B̿ hand, palm facing down and fingers pointing away from the signer. Right elbow is placed on back of left hand. Right elbow bends so that the arm moves upwards, and at the same time the hand closes to a B̂ hand.

POWERFUL /∅√Aa⊥ √Aa⊥ ?/

Two A hands, palms facing up and fingers pointing away from the signer, are held in neutral space. Elbows are prominent. Elbows bend so that both hands move upwards.

Micro Movements
Nodding, Waving, Flexing

The micro movements described by Friedman correspond to Stokoe's category of internal movements. Several different types of movements can be executed by the hands or fingers themselves. Stokoe distinguishes bending, wiggling, opening and closing. Friedman separates bending into the three separate actions of bending at the wrist, bending at the major knuckles and bending at the finger joints. However, she provides no separate symbols for these distinctions. Indeed, Friedman does not discuss the implications of her analysis for a transcription system. While initially we accepted Stokoe's single symbol η to represent all types of bending, it gradually became clear that this was descriptively confusing. By using three separate symbols, η to represent bending at the wrist, ɱ to represent bending at the major knuckles and ɱ to represent bending at the finger joints, we found it was possible to be much more explicit about the nature of the action.

Accordingly, it was decided to use these symbols in the transcriptions and similarly to use different words in the written description to indicate the three types of action:

η	nodding/bending	bending at wrist
ɱ	waving	bending at knuckles
ɱ	flexing	bending at finger joints

While the following signs will provide examples of how these symbols are used, it should be stressed that no minimal pairs have so far been found which are distinguished only by a bending action at the knuckles as opposed to bending at the wrist or finger joints. Once again we have been prepared to modify the transcription to suit the requirements of the learner.

YES /øA⊥∧ η̇/

Right A hand, palm facing away from the signer and fingers pointing up, is held in neutral space. Hand nods forward from wrist.

YES

WELCOME /øB̈ɑ⊥ B̈ɑ⊥ ɱ·/

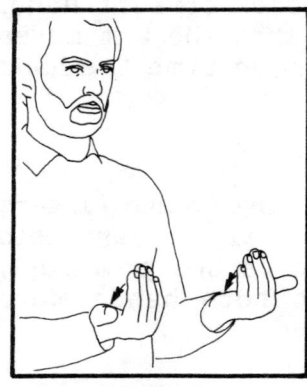

Two B̈ hands, palms facing up and fingers pointing away from the signer, are held in neutral space. Hands wave towards the signer in a repeated action.

WELCOME

GRUMPY /⊃5ₜ∧ ᵐ•/

Right 5 hand, palm facing the signer and fingers pointing up, is held in front of the face. Fingers perform a repeated flexing action.

The general distinction between bending and twisting action can be seen in the following minimal pair:

Minimal Pair
Bending:Twisting

GAVEL /∅Â♭⊥ ᵇ•/

Right Â hand, palm facing down and fingers pointing away from the signer, is held in neutral space. Hand bends downwards twice.

KEY /∅Â♭⊥ ᵗ/

Right Â hand, palm facing down and fingers pointing away from the signer, is held in neutral space. Hand twists to the right.

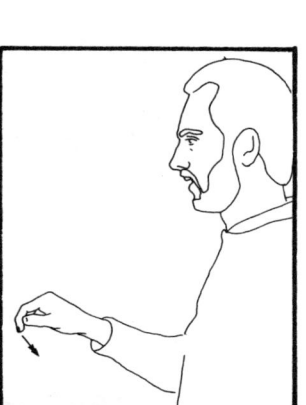

Wiggling

The action of flexing the fingers, ᵐ, is distinguished in this account from the action of wiggling, ᛉ. The latter involves a back and forth movement of the entire finger rather than any bending at the finger joints.

Minimal Pairs
Wiggling:Flexing

DIGITAL /∅5̈ₐ⊥ ᛉ/

Right 5̈ hand, palm facing up and fingers pointing away from the signer, is held in neutral space. Fingers perform wiggling action.

THROB /∅5̈ₐ⊥ ᵐ/

Right 5̈ hand, palm facing up and fingers pointing away from the signer, is held in neutral space. Fingers perform a flexing action.

Wiggling: Contact

FUNNY (Regional: Aberdeen) /⊔H<∧ ℛ/

Right H hand, palm facing left and fingers pointing up, is held at nose. Fingers wiggle in repeated action.

POSH /⊔H<∧ ˣ·/

Right H hand, palm facing left and fingers pointing up, is held at nose. Fingers contact nose in repeated action.

FUNNY (strange)   POSH

Crumbling

One additional symbol has been added to those representing internal action: ᴡ indicates crumbling action (cf Gestuno, WFD, 1975). Here the movement involves the rubbing of the thumb against the fingers as in the following signs.

SALT /∅Ĥ_D⊥ ᴡ/

Right Ĥ hand, palm and fingers pointing down, is held in neutral space. Thumb and fingers perform crumbling action.

DRY /∅B̂_α⊥ B̂_α⊥ ᴡ/

Two B̂ hands, palms facing up and fingers pointing away from the signer, are held in neutral space. Hands perform a crumbling action.

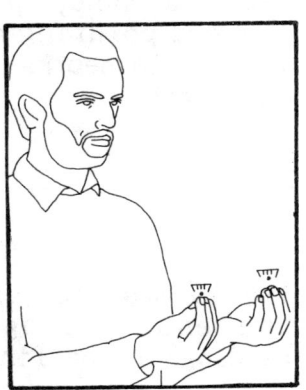

SALT   DRY

Minimal Pair

MONEY /∅Ĝ_α⊥ ᴡ/

Right Ĝ hand, palm facing up and finger pointing away from the signer, is held in neutral space. Thumb and finger perform crumbling action.

NEARLY /∅Ĝ_α⊥ ≈/

Right Ĝ hand, palm facing up and finger pointing away from the signer, is held in neutral space. Hand moves up and down in short sharp action.

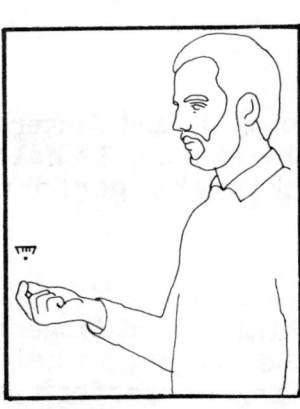
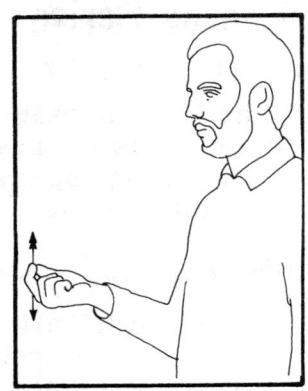

MONEY   NEARLY

Opening : Closing

Two closely related actions occurring as sig are the opening and closing actions. The exact nature of the action will depend on the initial handshape: 5 closes to A in HAVE; Ḡ closes to Ĝ in BIRD. In the first case the closing action involves movement of all fingers while in the second only thumb and first finger are involved. The opening and closing actions are frequently complementary rather than strictly distinctive in that, typically, closing action implies an initially open handshape while opening involves an initially closed handshape. However, the action of opening and the action of closing can each contrast significantly with other sign realisations, cf SUMMER:CLEVER and BOTTLE:CAN. The complementary nature of the closed:open opposition can be seen in the pair SLEEP:AWAKE.

Minimal Pairs

+Opening:-Opening

SUMMER /⌒Ȧ_{<∧} $\overset{\geq}{\underset{x}{\circ}}$ [Ḃ]/

Right Ȧ hand, palm facing left and fingers pointing up, is held with thumb touching left side of forehead. Hand moves to the right opening to a Ḃ hand.

CLEVER /⌒Ȧ_{<∧} $\overset{\geq}{x}$/

Right Ȧ hand, palm facing left and fingers pointing up, is held with thumb touching left side of forehead. Hand moves to the right, maintaining contact.

SUMMER 1

2

CLEVER

+Closing:-Closing

BOTTLE /C̄_{>⊥} × C_{<⊥} $\hat{\#}$[A]/

Manual tab C is held with palm facing right and fingers pointing away from the signer. Right C hand, palm facing left and fingers pointing away from the signer, is held on top of left hand. Right hand moves up and closes to an A hand.

CAN /C̄_{>⊥} × C_{<⊥} ⌃/

Manual tab C is held with palm facing right and fingers pointing away from the signer. Right C hand, palm facing left and fingers pointing away from the signer, is held on top of left hand. Right hand moves up.

BOTTLE

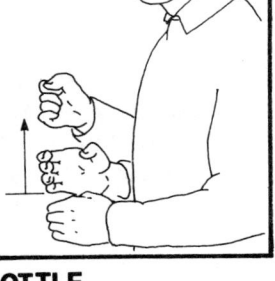

CAN (noun)

Closed : Open

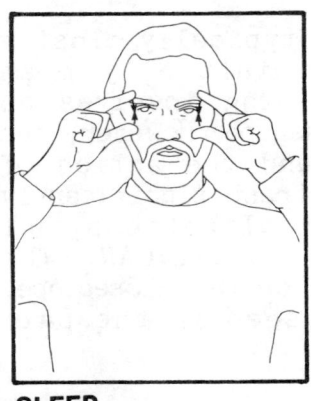
SLEEP

AWAKE

SLEEP /ᴗᵀG̅>ʌ G̅<ʌ ⋕[Ĝ Ĝ]/

Two G̅ hands: left hand, palm facing right and finger pointing up; right hand, palm facing left and finger pointing up. Hands, held at eyes, close to two Ĝ hands.

AWAKE /ᴗᵀĜ>ʌ Ĝ<ʌ ▫[G̅ G̅]/

Two Ĝ hands: left hand, palm facing right and finger pointing up; right hand, palm facing left and finger pointing up. Hands, held at eyes, open to two G̅ hands.

Repetition

In many signs, the same action is repeated. In some cases the action is performed twice, in others the action is repeated several times. A single dot • placed after the sig symbol shows that the action is repeated. Two dots indicate that the action is repeated several times. Repeated action can be distinctive as illustrated in the following minimal pair:

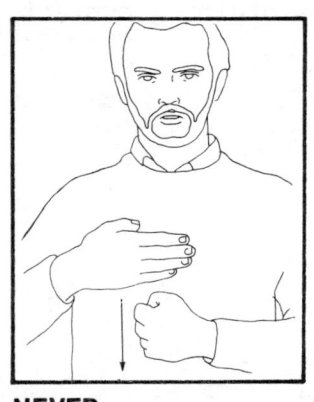
NEVER

CABBAGE

NEVER /Ā_T> ᵩ B_T< ⌄̇/

Manual tab A is held with palm facing the signer and fingers pointing right. Right B hand, palm facing the signer and fingers pointing left, is held in front of left hand. Right hand moves down so that palm brushes back of left hand.

CABBAGE /Ā_T> ᵩ B_T< ⌄̈/

Manual tab A is held with palm facing the signer and fingers pointing right. Right B hand, palm facing the signer and fingers pointing left, is held in front of left hand. Right hand moves down so that palm brushes back of left hand. The action is repeated.

Zero Movement

It has also been necessary to add one further symbol to the complete inventory of sig distinctions, this is the symbol ∅ indicating zero movement (cf Deuchar, 1978). Relatively few signs occur without any action whatsoever, although a considerable number simply involve contact without any other movement. Signs without contact and without movement typically occur in the neutral space area.

CALL

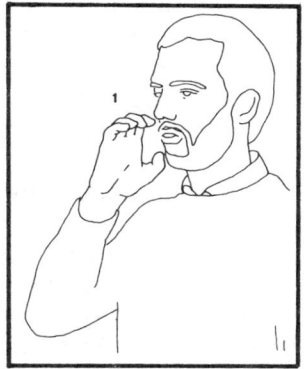

CONFIDENTIAL   **1**   **2**

OATH   **STOP**

Minimal Pairs
Zero: Closing

CALL /⋃C₍ₐ ∅/

Right C hand, palm facing left and fingers pointing up, is held at side of mouth.

CONFIDENTIAL /⋃C₍ₐ #[A]/

Right C hand, palm facing left and fingers pointing up, is held at side of mouth. Hand closes to an A hand.

Zero: Away

OATH /∅B⊥ₐ ∅/

Right B hand, palm facing away from the signer and fingers pointing up, is held in neutral space.

STOP /∅B⊥ₐ ⊥/

Right B hand, palm facing away from the signer and fingers pointing up, is held in neutral space. Hand moves away from the signer.

Short and Sharp Movement

As indicated earlier in the chapter, certain aspects of movement have received relatively little attention. Although the dynamics of movement have been studied more closely in recent years, these studies have mainly been made in relation to modulated or modified forms of signs, rather than their citation forms. As such forms are largely outside the scope of this presentation, we include here only two symbols which seem necessary to the transcription system for citation forms. Originally, following Stokoe, we used a single dot above the sig to indicate short and/or sharp movement. Here we have decided to separate these two aspects of movement as it is possible to have movements which are short but not sharp and vice versa. We are not, however, claiming that this distinction is phonemic. In signs such as HARD /⋃Ḡ₍ₐ ⊤̇ẋ/ and NEVER /Ā⊤₎ ₒB⊤₍ ẋ/ where there is a sharp movement, the dot above the sig is used as before. In signs such as EMBARRASS /⋂5⊤ₐ ⊤̊/ and WALES /∅W̄⊥ₐ ˚/ where there is a short movement, a small empty circle is used. In a few cases such as QUICK /Ḡ⊤₎ G₍⊥ ˚ẋ⋏/ and ORDER /⋃G₍ₐ ×⁰˂/ it may be necessary to use both symbols.

Placement of Symbols

As demonstrated both in Chapter 2 and in this chapter, appropriate placing of the sig symbols can indicate whether the movements involved in any one sign occur simultaneously or sequentially. However, several specific conventions relating to placement of the symbols should also be noted. The symbol for alternating, ~, is normally placed after all other symbols except the symbol for repetition. The symbol for repetition, •, can be distinguished from the symbol for sharp, •, by its placement: the repetition symbol is always placed in a final vertical column, while the symbol for sharp is always placed above the relevant sig symbol(s). Where an action is both short and sharp, the symbol for short, °, is normally placed first.

    ∿∼   up and down alternately

    ∿∼·   up and down alternately repeated

    T̊   towards sharp (dot placed above symbol)

    T·   towards repeated (dot placed at side of symbol)

    T̊   towards in a short sharp movement (short symbol placed first, sharp second; both placed above the sig symbol).

Finally, it should be noted that several problems still remain in relation to the interpretation of the sig symbols. In a relatively few cases there may be some ambiguity involved. In the sign CHECK /ʊᵉT̊<∧ˣ∥ØƷ<∧ ⇵̊/ sig symbols used are ⇵̊·. However, the ⇵ symbols refer to the overall direction, not to the direction of the twist, while the repetition symbol refers only to the twisting action. In other words, while the hand performs a repeated twisting action, it does not perform the movement away and to the right several times. One way of solving this problem is to make use of brackets with symbols occurring outside and inside the brackets. Thus the sig element for CHECK could be re-written as follows: (⚭)̊·. This would show that the short symbol only refers to the twisting action: the overall movement is quite long. Similarly, the directional symbols, ⇵, placed outside the brackets show that the overall direction of the action is away and to the right. The repetition symbol placed precisely after (⚭) shows that it is only this element which is repeated. If we wished to show that the whole action is repeated (ie the twisting hand moves away and to the right several times) we would need to make use of a further set of brackets, eg $\left[\begin{smallmatrix} (⚭)· \\ ⇵ \end{smallmatrix} \right]·$.

Obviously, such a solution makes the actual transcription quite complex. For this reason we have decided not to include it as a normal part of the transcription, although we offer the suggestion here as a possible solution to specific problems of interpretation. In practice, we have found that this type of example occurs relatively rarely.

CHAPTER SEVEN

Minor Parameters

It was suggested in Chapter 1 (pages 5-6) that as well as the major parameters of tab, dez and sig, several other aspects of sign production may be necessary for a full description of BSL signs. Klima and Bellugi (1979) distinguish the three minor parameters of orientation, hand arrangement and point of contact. They suggest that these parameters are minor in that they distinguish relatively few sets of minimal pairs as compared with the major parameters of tab, dez and sig. In this account of BSL signs, orientation may seem to fall somewhere in between the major:minor distinction in that orientation information is provided for every BSL sign. The number of minimal pairs distinguished by orientation alone is relatively small, compared with those distinguished by the major parameters, although as our work on BSL signs continues we are finding more examples of orientation minimal pairs than originally expected.

In Chapter 1 it was suggested that information relating to orientation, hand arrangement and point of contact would be necessary for a full description of the sign. In practice, it seems that if full informtion is given concerning orientation and hand arrangement, the exact point of contact can be predicted. Thus many of the point of contact problems noted by Friedman (1977) can be solved without devising a more elaborate framework of description.

As orientation already has a chapter to itself, this short chapter will provide information on how hand arrangement information is included in the transcriptions and will examine the question of whether point of contact should be regarded as a separate parameter.

Hand Arrangement

The options available within hand arrangement can be divided into two subsets: the first answers the question, 'How many hands are involved in the production of the sign?'; the second answers the question, 'When two hands are involved in the production of a sign, what is their relationship to each other at the onset of the sign's production?'

Number of Hands

It is possible to find minimal pairs of signs in BSL which are distinguished only by the use of two hands as opposed to one hand. In some cases the pairs are semantically related (IDLE:LAZY); in others there is no semantic link at all between the items (PARTY:PERHAPS).

It is important to note that the choice between one-handed or two-handed production may relate to grammatical, rather than lexical, structure. Thus some signs which have a citation form using only one hand, may have grammatically modulated forms using two hands. The sign LOOK which in its citation form uses one hand, /ᗡV₍ₐ ˣ⊥/, may be modulated to express the meaning 'they look at me'. The resulting form will make use of two V hands placed in front of the face, then twisting to point towards the face /⌒V_bL V_bL $\frac{\supset c}{\psi}$/. In other signs, the choice between the use of one hand or two seems to be related to emphasis and stress. CANNOT may be said to have a neutral form in which one hand is used /ØG_bL $\frac{\tau}{a}$/ and a strong form in which two hands are used /ØG_bL, G_bL $\frac{\tau}{a}$/. Similar examples include WITHOUT /ØB_bL, B_bL $\frac{\tau}{a}$/ and DON'T KNOW /⌒B_TA B_TA ˣ·ᵥ/. In most cases, the possibility of using a one-handed production or a two-handed sign, without changing the meaning, can only occur when the two-handed sign is fully symmetrical. Signs which involve an alternating movement, such as CYCLE /ØA_bL, A_bL $\frac{c}{\psi}$~/ or an interchanging movement, such as MAKE /ØB̂_a>, B̂_b< ˣᶜᵒˣ/ are unlikely to be produced as one-handed signs.

Minimal Pairs

IDLE /Ø ƛ̈_aL ~·/

Right ƛ hand, palm facing up and finger pointing away from the signer, is held in neutral space. Hand moves up and down twice.

LAZY /Ø ƛ̈_aL ƛ_aL ~·/

Two ƛ hands, palms facing up and fingers pointing away from the signer, are held in neutral space. Hands move up and down twice.

IDLE

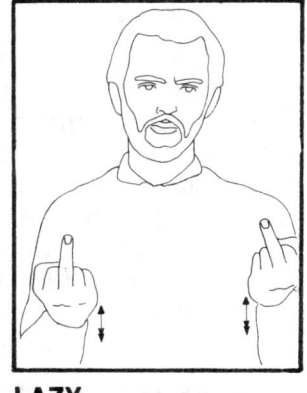
LAZY

PERHAPS /Ø Y_<ʌ ᵠ·/

Right Y hand, palm facing left and fingers pointing up, is held in neutral space. Hand twists in repeated action.

PARTY /Ø Y_>ʌ Y_<ʌ ᵠ·/

Two Y hands: left hand, palm facing right and fingers pointing up; right hand, palm facing left and fingers pointing up. Hands, held in neutral space, perform a repeated twisting action.

PERHAPS

PARTY

BLINK /ᗡ Ḡ_<ʌ #[Ĝ]·/

Right Ḡ hand, palm facing left and finger pointing up, is held at right eye. Hand closes to a Ĝ hand. The action is repeated.

SLEEPY /ᗡ Ḡ_>ʌ Ḡ_<ʌ #[ĜĜ]·/

Two Ḡ hands: left hand, palm facing right and finger pointing up; right hand, palm facing left and finger pointing up. Hands, held at eyes, close to Ĝ hands. The action is repeated.

BLINK

SLEEPY

Arrangement

In Chapter 2 (pages 31-34) several choices were presented indicating the relationship of one hand to the other in two-handed signs. The symbols used are those designated by Stokoe as interaction symbols, ie showing the way in which the two hands interact with each other. A clear distinction is made here between the use of these symbols to indicate hand arrangement and their use to express movement choices within the sig parameter. As already illustrated, the hand arrangement symbols are normally placed at the same level as the orientation symbols, ie as subscripts. The contrast between the use of these symbols for hand arrangement and their use for sig can be shown in a pair such as RELEASE /∅F$_{>⊥}$ ⅈF$_{<∧}$ ÷/ and JOIN /∅F$_{>⊥}$ ⅈF$_{<∧}$ ^{ⅈ}/. In RELEASE the interaction symbol ⅈ is used as a hand arrangement subscript to indicate that at the onset of the sign the two F hands are linked together. The movement, symbolised by ÷, involves the two hands separating. In JOIN the two hands are held in neutral space and then come together in a linking action, so here ⅈ is used as a superscript indicating the sig.

Here hand arrangement information is seen as essential phonological information capable, by itself, of distinguishing one sign from another. However, as with orientation, support for all the specific choices within hand arrangement is rather more difficult to provide. It should be stressed that the criteria used throughout this book for the establishment of minimal pairs are rather more demanding than in other comparable analyses. Having built orientation into the system, a pair of signs must have identical realisations in three out of four parameters rather than in two out of three in a tri-aspectual analysis. As the orientation parameter actually involves two choices, palm and finger orientation, minimal pairs are typically identical in four out of five choices, although when orientation itself is the distinguishing factor, the two orientation aspects may differ. If hand arrangement is also included then the figure rises to five identical realisations out of six. Despite the demands of such a system it is possible to find minimal pairs to support the main choices within hand arrangement, but at least two other choices are somewhat peripheral. The hand arrangement choices used within this account are:

    side by side   ı

    contact between the hands   ×

    one on top of the other   —

    one behind the other   ọ

    interlinking   ⅈ

    one inside the other (entering)   ⊙

    (see pages 31-34)

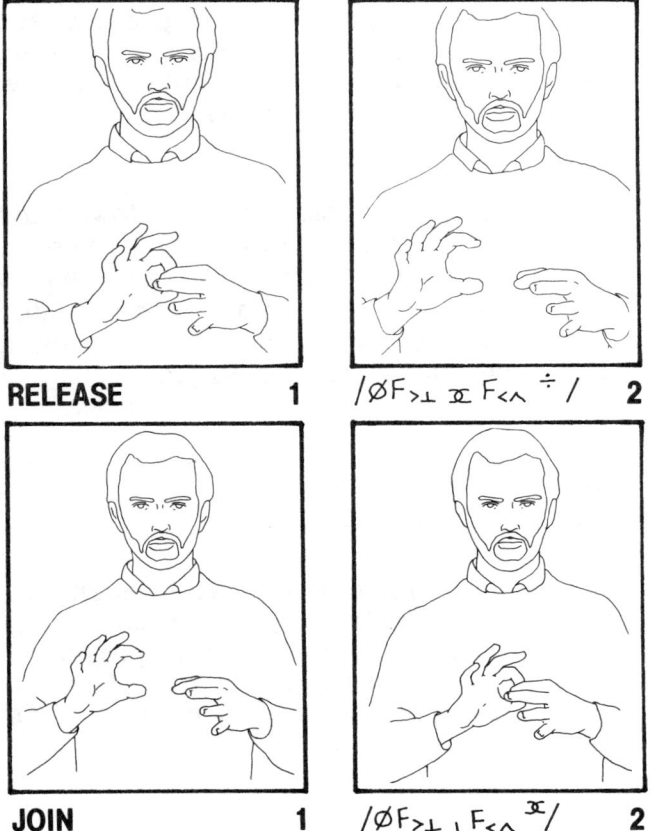

RELEASE   1   /∅F$_{>⊥}$ ⅈF$_{<∧}$ ÷/   2

JOIN   1   /∅F$_{>⊥}$ ⅈF$_{<∧}$ ^{ⅈ}/   2

It will be noted that one change from Words in Hand 1 is the addition of a hand arrangement choice for contact between the hands. This is shown by the contact symbol × placed as a central subscript. This is often used with another hand arrangement symbol such as side by side, ı, or one on top of the other, —, so that the point of contact is more obvious. The use of the contact symbol in this way allows us to give more precise information on the way in which the hands relate to each other at the start of the sign. It also allows the contact symbol in sig to remain where this is clearly indicating contact as part of the action of the sign. In double dez signs, such as PRACTISE /ØO$_{>⊥}$ ıx O$_{<⊥}$ $^{I.}$/ and FOLLOW /ØG$_{D⊥}$×G$_{D⊥}$ ϙ $^{⊥}$/ the hand arrangement information shows that the hands remain the same throughout the production of the sign. In PRACTISE, the hands are side by side with fingers touching throughout the sign; in FOLLOW the right hand is behind the left with right finger touching the back of the left hand throughout the sign. If the hands do not remain together this can be shown by the sig symbols, particularly the separating symbol ÷.

In <u>Words in Hand 1</u> we commented that placing this contact symbol under hand arrangement may artificially place initial contact between the hands in a separate category from the types of contact established in Chapter 6. However, it does seem clear that there is a difference between signs such as FOLLOW where the action is 'moving away from the signer' and AGREE /ØÂ$_{>⊥}$ ı Â$_{<⊥}$ $^{×}$/ where the action involves a contact. This new analysis does mean that pairs such as PARALLEL /ØG$_{D⊥}$ ı G$_{D⊥}$ $^{⊥}$/ and FOLLOW /ØG$_{D⊥}$×G$_{D⊥}$ ϙ $^{⊥}$/ are distinguished by hand arrangement alone.

The two peripheral choices within hand arrangement are interlinking and entering. Usually the fact that either of these arrangements is involved at the onset of a sign limits the type of action that can occur. Hence, no 'full' minimal pairs of the type mentioned above can be noted for these two choices, although a pair such as RELEASE:JOIN shows the descriptive necessity for retaining interlinking as a hand arrangement option. The following minimal pairs provide support for the other main options under hand arrangement.

Minimal Pair

PARALLEL /ØG$_{D⊥}$ ı G$_{D⊥}$ $^{⊥}$/

Two G hands, palms facing down and fingers pointing away from the signer, are held side by side in neutral space. Hands move away from the signer.

FOLLOW /ØG$_{D⊥}$ × G$_{D⊥}$ ϙ $^{⊥}$/

Two G hands, palms facing down and fingers pointing away from the signer, are held in neutral space. Right hand is held behind left hand with right index finger contacting back of left hand. Hands move away from the signer.

PARALLEL

FOLLOW

Side by Side : Neutral

WITH /Ø5$_{α>}$ ı 5$_{α<}$ ⁀[B̂ B̂]×/

Two 5 hands: left hand, palm facing up and fingers pointing right; right hand, palm facing up and fingers pointing left. Hands, held side by side in neutral space, come together closing to B̂ hands and touch.

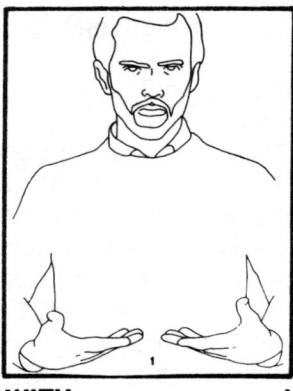

WITH   **1**

2

TOGETHER 1 2

TOGETHER /∅5ₐ˲ 5ₐ˱ ⁾ᶜ#[B̂B̂]ˣ/

Two 5 hands: left hand, palm facing up and fingers pointing right; right hand, palm facing up and fingers pointing left. Hands, held in neutral space, come together closing to B̂ hands and touch.

One above the other: One behind the other

PANTOMIME /B̄ᴛ˲ Bᴛ˱ ˣ˙/

Manual tab B is held with palm facing the signer and fingers pointing right. Right B hand, palm facing the signer and fingers pointing left, is held above left hand. Right hand contacts left hand twice.

MORE /Bᴛ˲ ₉ Bᴛ˱ ˣ˙/

Manual tab B is held with palm facing the signer and fingers pointing right. Right B hand, palm facing the signer and fingers pointing left, is held in front of left hand. Right hand contacts left hand twice.

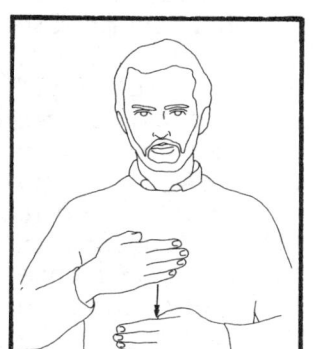 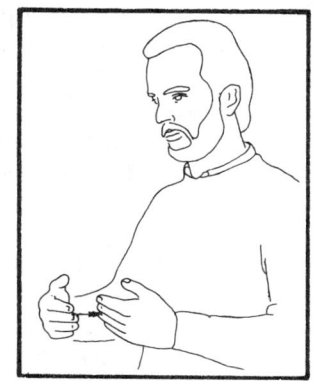

PANTOMIME   **MORE**

As already indicated in relation to contacting, in some cases it may be necessary to use two hand arrangement symbols simultaneously: CHINWAG /∅5̄˲∧ˎ5˱∧ ²˙/ makes use of two 5 hands which are held close together but with the right hand above the left. In ARRIVE /B̄ₐ˩ B̈ᵦ˩ ₉ ⌵ˣ/ the right hand is held above and behind the manual tab B.

Finally, it should be noted that no special symbol is used for what may be termed neutral hand arrangement. This is where the two hands are placed in the expected way in relation to each other, given the choice of tab. If the tab is the mouth then the hands will be closer together than if the tab was the chest. It is not necessary to add side by side, even though the hands may be as close together at the mouth as when they are side by side in neutral space. Hand arrangement is thus dependent, to some extent, upon the realisations of the major parameters, especially tab.

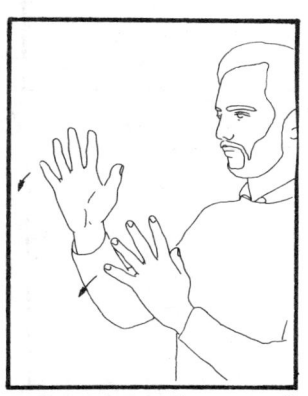 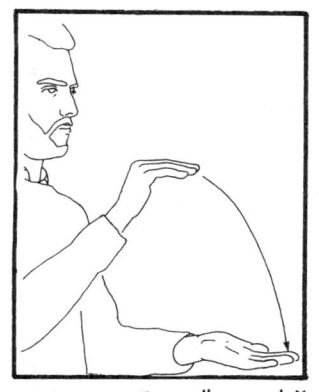

CHINWAG /∅5̄˲∧ˎ5˱∧ ²˙/   **ARRIVE** /B̄ₐ˩ B̈ᵦ˩ ₉ ⌵ˣ/

Point of Contact

Klima and Bellugi (1979) have posited a third minor parameter, point of contact, which provides choices as to the exact contacting region of the active dez hand(s). If we take a handshape such as Å, the actual part of the hand which may contact the other hand, or a body tab, may vary: in PROBLEM /B₍>⊥₎,Å₍bʟ₎ˣ·/ and KNOW /⌒Å₍<∧₎ˣ·/ the tip of the extended thumb acts as the point of contact. In AGREE /ØÅ₍>⊥₎,Å₍<⊥₎ˣ / and FRIEND /ØÅ₍>⊥₎,Å₍<⊥₎ˣ·/ the contact is between the bent fingers.

The term point of contact is a somewhat unfortunate one in that it is used by some authors to refer not only to the specific part of the active dez which makes contact with the tab, but also to the exact position on the tab which is contacted. Thus in PROBLEM there would be two 'point of contact' difficulties: what does the contacting and exactly where does it touch? The answers here are, the tip of the thumb does the contacting and the place it touches is the centre of the left palm. In order to avoid confusion, we have decided to use <u>point of contact</u> solely for the first type, ie the part of the active dez which makes the contact. The term <u>place of contact</u> refers to the exact position on the manual tab or body where the contact is made. In KNOW the point of contact is the tip of the thumb, the place of contact is the right side of the forehead.

Klima and Bellugi (1979) provide only one example to support their claim that point of contact should be treated as a minor parameter. This is the ASL minimal pair EVERDAY:GIRL. The authors suggest that these two signs are distinguished "by their contacting regions: thumb tip in GIRL (which calls for the Å variant), palm side of the hand in EVERYDAY" (Klima and Bellugi, 1979, p46). If we transcribe these ASL signs using our notation system, ie GIRL /3Å₍⊥∧₎ˣ⊥/ and EVERYDAY /3A₍<∧₎ˣ⊥/, two points become immediately apparent: the difference in the dez configuration and the difference in orientation. It so happens that in BSL, A and Å are separate phonemes while in most descriptions of ASL, Å is regarded as an allophone of A. However, the other factor is the one that is important here, namely that the orientation realisations are different in the two signs. In fact, after an examination of a large group of BSL

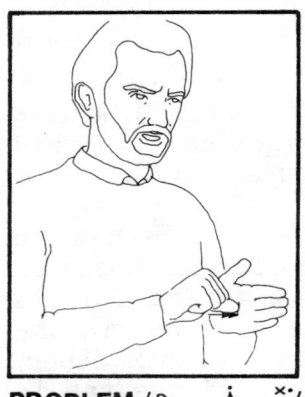
PROBLEM /B₍>⊥₎,Å₍bʟ₎ˣ·/

KNOW /⌒Å₍<∧₎ˣ·/

AGREE /ØÅ₍>⊥₎,Å₍<⊥₎ˣ /

FRIEND /ØÅ₍>⊥₎,Å₍<⊥₎ˣ·/

EVERYDAY(ASL) /3A₍<∧₎ˣ⊥/

GIRL(ASL) /3Å₍⊥∧₎ˣ⊥/

DANGER /⌒B₍<∧₎ᵀˣ/

DANGER(Learner's error)

signs it has become clear that in the majority of cases, point of contact can be predicted, given the realisations of the other parameters. In this regard, orientation and hand arrangement information may be crucially important.

Without orientation information there is no way of knowing that point of contact in DANGER /^B<ᴧᵀˣ/ is the index finger edge of the B hand. Similarly, without orientation and hand arrangement information it would be impossible to predict that point of contact in FULL /B_b> B_bᴧ ^ˣ/ is the back of the B hand. Obviously, in all these cases, we can make a prediction as to point of contact given the realisations of all the other parameters: each is important. It is too tempting to suggest that one, say the dez realisation, is crucial, but even this would be to over-simplify the way in which the parameters interact in sign production. It is also important to stress here, that the claim that point of contact can generally be predicted from the realisations of the other parameters, does not imply that it is thereby possible to be absolutely precise. The precise point of contact in DANGER is normally the index finger: if, given the above transcription, the learner actually uses a different point on the same edge of the hand, eg thumb rather than index finger, the resulting sign might appear slightly odd, but there would be no difference in meaning. In other words, this difference would be phonetic rather than phonemic.

It may seem then that there is very little evidence to support the claim that point of contact should be regarded as a separate parameter. In BSL we have so far found only one example of a minimal pair in which the only distinguishing feature is point of contact. In fact, given the other transcription changes introduced in this second edition, this is not a true minimal pair. According to the old system ROOF and PRAY had exactly the same transcription /∅B>ᴧ ı B<ᴧˣ/. In our new system the contact symbol is placed centrally for PRAY, as it is part of the hand arrangement and the sig is zero movement. In ROOF the contact is part of the sig. However, it is true that the

ROOF /∅B_bᴧ ı B_bᴧ ˣ/   **PRAY** /∅B>ᴧ ıx B<ᴧ ∅/

actual point of contact in such signs can be confusing, because the orientation choices are not precise enough. In <u>Words in Hand 1</u>, orientation was shown as the same for both signs even though in ROOF the hands are held at an angle and contact is at the fingertips, while in PRAY the hands are held straight and the contact is between the full inner surfaces of the hands.

One way of providing a more accurate description of the orientation of signs such as ROOF and BOAT is to transcribe these signs using opposing palm and finger orientation. In BOAT, palm orientation would be towards the signer, and finger orientation away from the signer, /∅B_Tㅗ ıx B_Tㅗ ㅗ/ and in ROOF, palm orientation would be down and finger orientation would be up, /∅B_bᴧ ı B_bᴧ ˣ/. While this seems illogical and physically impossible, it is not completely so, as the hands can arch away or up if we attempt to produce the required orientation. However, even if it is seen as illogical, there is no reason why we should not establish the convention that opposing palm and finger orientation mean 'diagonal' as in ROOF and BOAT. This, then, is exactly what we propose to clarify the distinction between ROOF and PRAY. The transcription would be ROOF /∅B_bᴧ ı B_bᴧ ˣ/ and PRAY /∅B>ᴧ ıx B<ᴧ ∅/.

Although it is possible to find other examples where the transcription is not precise enough to ensure correct production by a learner, we have so far not found any minimal pair which is distinguished by point of contact alone. We would expect that future work may lead to the discovery of a few other examples, but our evidence suggests that it is highly unlikely that it would ever be possible to find evidence to support specific choices within a point of contact parameter. For this reason, point of contact information is here regarded as essentially phonetic and predictable from the other parametric realisations. It is only 'built into the system' insofar as the choices from the other parameters should allow us to make accurate point of contact choices.

Of course, it is recognised that for specific purposes it may be useful to have some way of indicating more precise point of contact information, whether in the learning situation or in certain types of linguistic or phonetic analysis. Some problems we have noted may illustrate the needs within the context of teaching and learning BSL. The signs GERMANY /⌒G<ʌˣ/ and SILENT /ᴜG<ʌˣ/ both make use of the G hand contacting a face tab: the forehead in GERMANY and the mouth in SILENT. All of the other information in the two transcriptions is identical, yet in GERMANY it is the section of the hand between the wrist and thumb which contacts the forehead, while in SILENT it is the outer edge of the index finger which contacts the mouth. In the latter case, the learner may be guided by iconic clues and the physical awkwardness of producing the sign any other way, but in GERMANY iconicity is less obvious and index finger contact could easily be used by mistake.

SILENT /ᴜG<ʌˣ/   **GERMANY** /⌒G<ʌˣ/

Margaret Carter (Carter and Maddix, 1980), in association with the Bristol Sign Language Group, has developed a set of notation conventions which allow extra details to be presented within the transcription. The same symbols can be used to indicate both place of contact on the manual tab and point of contact of the active dez. Thus, by adding ⊔ before the manual tab B, in BUTTER, it can be shown that the place of contact is the palm, while adding ⊞ before the H dez, can show that the length of the first two fingers is used. Using our own transcription conventions plus the additions for contact, the notation would become /⊔Bɑ⊥⊞H⊤<ˣ·/. Similarly, in the sign FILM it is possible to show that it is the thumb edge of the hand ⌐ and the wrist below the palm ⊣ which come into contact, /⌐Bᴅ>⊣5⊥ʌ♀ ½ /. Within the Carter-Maddix system, hand arrangement details would not necessarily be shown. In most cases the hand arrangement would be clear from the point of contact information. The symbols used by Carter and Maddix are as follows:

Point on Hand	Symbol
Individual fingertips:	a e i o u
Base of individual fingers:	a̱ e̱ i̱ o̱ u̱
Tips of fingers: (one or more)	⊞
Length of fingers: (one or more)	⊞
Edge of hand:	
thumb	⌐
little finger	⌐
Surface of hand:	
palm	⊔
back	⊓

Wrist:

   below palm   ⊣

   below back of hand   ⊢

Elbow: +

Carter and Maddix also use other letters of the British manual alphabet to notate borrowed signs such as KITCHEN which would become simply /k·/ (ie the letter K repeated) or MOTHER which would be /m·/. Signs other than borrowings can also use manual alphabet letters to clarify contact. Thus Y is used in BUTTERFLY to show that contact is at the position where the letter Y is produced. The Carter-Maddix transcription is /∅ᵞ55 ⊤̃²̞/ while our own transcription, without point of contact symbols is /∅ Ḃ_{T>} ₓ Ḃ_{T<} ᵐ/. Using the point of contact addition, our transcription becomes /∅ᵞ Ḃ_{T>} ₓ Ḃ_{T<} ᵐ/.

It will probably be apparent that when we mix the two systems we sometimes have superfluous or redundant information. This is because to some extent we have taken different routes to solving the same set of problems. Similarly, Friedman (1977) proposes that:

> *"for signs in which the hands (or hand) make contact with the body (contact signs), the orientation specification designates the point of contact - that part of the hand that touches the body."*
>
> *(Friedman, 1977, p46)*

Friedman suggests this solution as an alternative to trying to account for all possible (non-distinctive) variations of the hands' spatial orientation. However, on our present evidence, building point of contact into the system in this way is descriptively more complex and 'costly' in terms of symbols. Friedman isolates five contrasting points of contact: fingertip, thumb-tip, palm, side and dorsal, but notes that these points have to be defined for each handshape. Thus, fingertip for ४ is the tip of the middle finger, for D(G_d), the tips of the thumb and fingers in contact, and in F, the tips of the thumb and index finger. The interpretations appear to be based on point of contact constraints already noted within the system, eg Friedman comments that the tip of the extended index finger never occurs as point of contact with D. Some of the constraints are physical: fingertip contact is impossible with A because the typical A used in ASL has the fingertips pressed against the palm: fingertip contact would presumably be possible with the closed fist of CSL which typically has the fingers bent once, not twice (see Klima and Bellugi, 1979, p161).

Clearly it is important to be able to characterise the phonological system fully by noting constraints on the point of contact system. Thus, as already noted (pages 5-6), Klima and Bellugi (1979) have compared the way in which the F handshape is used in ASL and CSL: in the former, contact signs always use the thumb and index finger, in CSL, the extended three fingers are typically used for contact. Therefore, one important difference between the two systems lies not in the choice of handshape, but in how that handshape is used within the system. Friedman presents a table (page 48) showing occurring, non-occurring and impossible points of contact for ASL handshapes. Some of the specific constraints have been questioned by American researchers who claim that there are ASL signs which exhibit contact points labelled as either non-occurring or impossible by Friedman. It is not possible for us to comment in detail on this matter in ASL, and although we have already gathered a considerable amount of information on the structure of BSL signs, it does seem premature at this stage to make definitive statements about permitted points of contact. By using the Carter-Maddix system we are able to provide point of contact information without making any assumptions about existing constraints. As we build up larger and larger files of signs it should be possible to be more precise about the point of contact constraints. However, the following comments should provide some indication of our present evidence relating to point of contact restrictions.

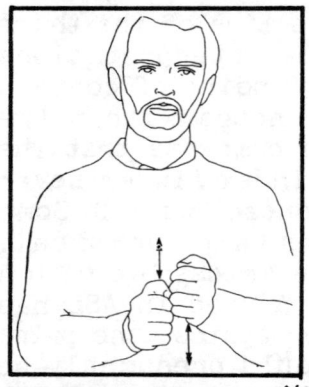 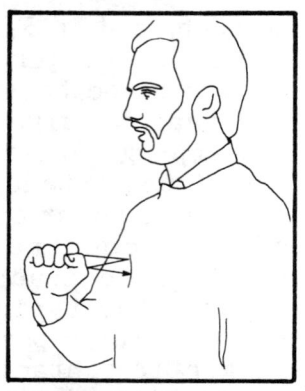  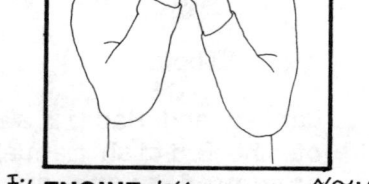

BROTHER /ØA₍>⊥₎ ıx A₍<⊥₎ x̃·~/ **COUGH** /⌐ ⌐A₍<∧₎ x·/ **CABINET-MAKER** /Ḡ₍>⊥₎ A₍<⊥₎ x̄·/ **ENGINE** /ØA_{T∧} ıx A_{T∧} x̃·~/

Several handshapes, particularly but not exclusively, the unmarked handshapes, exhibit a wide range of contact points. This range can be seen for A in the following signs: BROTHER /ØA₍>⊥₎ ıx A₍<⊥₎ x̃·~/ has contact between the middle finger joints of the two hands; COUGH /⌐ ⌐A₍<∧₎ x·/ has thumb/index finger edge contact; CABINET-MAKER /Ḡ₍>⊥₎ A₍<⊥₎ x̄·/ has little finger edge contact; PISTON ENGINE /ØA_{T∧} ıx A_{T∧} x̃·~/ has palm/little finger edge contact while FOOTBALL /B_{b⊥} A_{>v} ?x/ has back of hand contact. Other handshapes such as B, G, 5, and V also exhibit a fairly wide range of contact points. Much more limited are F, which only has finger and thumb tip contact, and ㅂ which typically has middle finger contact. Nevertheless, at least one sign has been noted using the closed allophone 8̂, ie LEFT /Ø8̂₍>⊥₎ₓ 8̂₍<⊥₎ ㅂ[55]/, in which contact is between the thumb edge of the left hand and the little finger edge of the right hand. In handshapes such as Y, and 井 we have not noted any signs which have contact by the little finger alone. Some points of contact, said to be non-occurring but possible in ASL, do in fact occur in BSL. Examples include dorsal contact for 井 as in DEVIL /⌒井_{b⊥} ?x/ and fingertip contact for M (W_m) as in MAD /⌒Ẅ_{m T∧} x·/. The 井̂ variant is often used specifically when point of contact is the closed middle finger and thumb. Examples include SHY /3井̂₍<∧₎ ᵉₓ/ and SHAME /3井̂₍<∧₎ x⊥/.

Whatever the specific point of contact constraints turn out to be within BSL phonology, it is worth stressing again that within the phonemic transcription system outlined here, explicit point of contact information is not required. The incorporation of hand arrangement and orientation information on a systematic basis allows for the simplest and most adequate description of the vast majority of BSL signs.

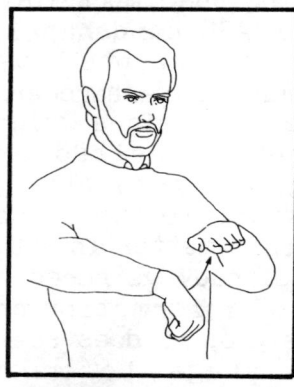

FOOTBALL /B_{b⊥} A_{>v} ?x/

  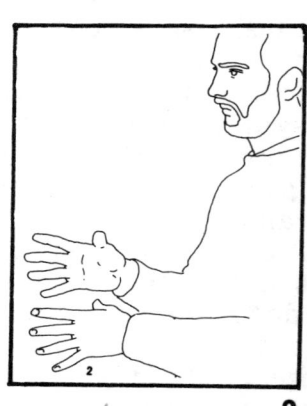 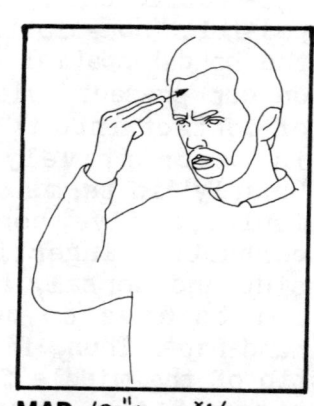

DEVIL /⌒井_{b⊥} ?x/ **LEFT** /Ø8̂₍>⊥₎ₓ 8̂₍<⊥₎ ㅂ[55]/1 2 **MAD** /⌒Ẅ_{m T∧} x·/

CHAPTER EIGHT

Description and Use

Alternative Descriptions

The account of BSL sign structure presented in this book is based on a number of assumptions, several of which are controversial. Clearly, there are alternative descriptions which may capture the nature of the linguistic system more fully than in this account. Here we wish to indicate some of the problems in arriving at an analysis and some of the solutions which we have considered but rejected.

Sign Language Phonology

Probably the most fundamental issue concerns the analogy between sign formation and phonology in spoken language. Is it really possible to find sign language equivalents of phonological constructs such as phonemes and allophones? Stokoe himself suggests that the analogy is not so much between sign formation and phonology as between:

> *"methods of procedure with data in two contrasting modes of transmission and perception. Indeed it is not analogy but identity of method."*
>
> *(Stokoe, 1979, p181)*

Our own approach largely accords with this in that we have also adopted a structuralist minimal pair analysis in order to identify distinctive contrasts and hence distinctive elements. Nevertheless, we have inevitably made assumptions concerning the sign language equivalents of phonemes, allophones, morphemes and possibly even syllables. To suggest that these could be direct or exact equivalents would be to deny the special characteristics of the visual-gestural medium, in particular the feature of simultaneity in production. All the work carried out on sign languages over the last twenty years has directed us towards the central insight that the language medium imposes special constraints and possibilities upon the organisation of the linguistic system. If, despite the special characteristics of the visual-gestural medium, we have extended such terms as phonology and phoneme to sign language description, we must make explicit the nature of the comparison.

In this account, the phonemes of the language are the significant realisations of each parameter. These phonemes are of different types depending upon the parameter (eg tab phonemes, dez phonemes), but they are each capable of distinguishing minimal pairs of lexical items. It has been suggested that:

> *"the equivalent of a phoneme is not an individual tab, sig or dez realisation, but an entire sign ... tab, dez and sig realisations can be compared with specific places or manners of articulation."*
>
> *(Joachim Mugdan, personal communication)*

However, such an equivalence between sign and phoneme would blur the distinction between phonology and morphology. Indeed, Kegl (1979) in her analysis of ASL verbs and the role of classifiers (see page 185) asked, "Do we have a system where the phonological and morphological units are the same?" On the evidence so far available for BSL the answer is "No." (See further below.) The formational elements of BSL can combine in different, but not purely random, ways to produce BSL morphemes. These elements combine simultaneously rather than sequentially yet it is clearly possible to break down the morphological units of BSL into essential components. It is worth noting that despite the important emphasis on simultaneous production, signs do occur in time as well as space and thus do have a beginning, a middle and an end. Therefore, a feature such as 'contact' may occur throughout a sign's production or only at specific points, eg the beginning or the end. Of course, at whatever point we choose we can 'freeze' a sign in space and time, yet still note the realisations of the specific parameters: the hand will have a specific configuration and a particular orientation, it will be held in a specific position and be in the course of executing a particular movement. It is quite possible to observe and describe such components of BSL signs.

Discrete Elements

Klima and Bellugi (1979) have shown that it is possible to get some clues as to the internal structure of signs and how they are processed by examining sign errors. Just as we can note and even predict errors in spoken language production, so we can note and learn from errors in sign language production. As Fromkin (1971) remarks:

> *"What is apparent in the analysis and conclusions of all linguists and psychologists dealing with speech, is that despite the semi-continuous nature of the speech signal, there are discrete units at some levels of performance which can be substituted, omitted, transposed or added . . ."*

(Fromkin, 1971, p29)

There has been some resistance within sign language research to the notion of discrete elements, but the recognition of such elements does not imply sequential analysis. If we use 'discrete' to refer to elements which can be separated out from the substance of the sign for the purpose of analysis or which can be omitted or substituted in actual production, then indeed the primes of BSL signs are discrete elements. Some of the most fascinating research into early sign language acquisition by infants has shown how children replace one significant element with another (McIntire, 1974, 1977; Boyes-Braem, 1973). This work shows that children may substitute unmarked handshapes such as B or 5 for marked handshapes. In experiments with adult signers, substitutions in the form of anticipations and preservations have also been noted by Klima and Bellugi. Their detailed evidence provides considerable support for the independence of the major parameters and the discreteness of the individual primes. (See Klima and Bellugi, 1979, Ch5).

Feature Analysis
Handshapes

Of course, the concentration on the individual realisations of each parameter has one important negative result: it ignores the phonetic relationships which exist among such items. Particular dez realisations may have shared features while differing in other important respects. B and 5 are both fully open in that the fingers are fully extended, but they differ in that B has the fingers held together while 5 has the fingers spread, ie held apart. The feature 'spread' also distinguishes H and V, yet it is non-distinctive in F, where both spread and together forms occur in free variation. Distinctive feature analysis has played an important part in phonological theory in recent linguistic history. Once we examine phonemes with reference to sets of phonetic properties or features, it is possible to note that primes which share the same phonetic features often undergo the same phonological processes. American researchers in particular have developed distinctive feature analyses for the major parameters of ASL. Although most would agree that completely adequate analyses have not yet been arrived at, many of the features isolated appear relevant to cross-linguistic studies. It is certainly important to develop feature analyses which can allow comparisons among sign languages as well as examination of specific sign languages.

Feature analyses of handshape include those developed by Kegl and Wilbur (1976); Lane, Boyes-Braem and Bellugi (1976); and Boyes-Braem (1981). Boyes-Braem proposes the use of 'significant' rather than 'distinctive' features for her handshape features, in that they are not detailed phonetic features, but in other ways significant (see below). The features presented in Klima and Bellugi (1979) are:

Compact   no fingers extended

Broad   three or more fingers extended

Ulnar   at least the little finger extended

Full   all four fingers extended

Concave   at least two fingers bent

Dual   two fingers extended

Index   index finger alone extended

Radial   at least the thumb extended

Touch   at least one fingertip touching thumb

Spread   two or more fingers spread

Cross   two fingers overlapping.

A handshape such as Y would be:

- Compact
- Broad
+ Ulnar
+ Radial

The handshape I would be:

- Compact
- Broad
+ Ulnar
- Radial

Hence the distinction between the two handshapes can be described in terms of the presence or absence of the feature 'Radial'. Klima and Bellugi arrived at their particular feature analysis by moving from psychological data towards the linguistic model. They used the results of perception experiments which involved presenting handshapes of ASL under conditions of visual masking. The choice of specific features was guided by the results of these experiments which showed particular patterns of confusion. (For critical discussion see Todd, 1980.)

A particularly important piece of work on feature analysis in relation to ASL has been produced by Penny Boyes-Braem (Boyes-Braem, 1981). The author argues that:

> *"the formal or signifying components of the handshape parameter ... have some sort of connection with the meaning they signify."*
>
> *(Boyes-Braem, 1981, p219)*

One of the many examples cited is the use of the B handshape for the language-specific paradigm meaning 'paper'. The handshape has the features + Linear, + Surface, + Full,

> *"which together give the representation of a broad flat surface."*
>
> *(Boyes-Braem, 1981, p219)*

This work is complemented by that of Betsy McDonald (McDonald, 1982) who also provides a feature analysis of handshapes and shows how these are used in what have been termed 'classifiers'. McDonald is particularly interested in the productive power of these handshapes in the creation of new signs. Both authors see the real world, everyday use of the hands, in activities such as handling and touching, exploited within the structure of ASL signs. As Boyes-Braem comments, it is remarkable that, working independently, the two researchers should have come up with such complementary theses. Their analyses appear to give support to the notion of 'creative conflict' in sign language (Edinburgh BSL Project, 1983). While new signs may be derived from iconic and/or metaphoric bases, such forms are modified by the particular set of handshapes in the language. While Boyes-Braem demonstrates the match between an underlying concept and a visual metaphor, she notes that:

> *"the language is still bound to the limited set of handshape features available to it for representing that metaphor."*
>
> *(Boyes-Braem, 1981, p220)*

Exactly how analyses of this type relate to the account of BSL signs presented here remains something of an open question. In our more recent work in these areas, we have tried to demonstrate that such analyses show the limitations of a purely phonemic approach, but do not render it invalid. It certainly seems that the 'explanatory' power of these other analyses is impressive, especially in relation to the development of new lexical items. However, whether signs are 'motivated' iconically or metaphorically, or whether they are purely arbitrary, the system presented here can offer a basis for description. Moreover, while the type of motivation so clearly demonstrated by Boyes-Braem, McDonald and other researchers, such as Bergman (1982), obviously exists in BSL, we continue to note a large number of arbitrary signs. In some cases we may be missing the clues to metaphorical derivations, in other cases an 'arbitrary' label is clearly appropriate.

Position

Distinctive feature analyses for the other parameters have also been developed but on the whole they are less satisfactory than those developed for handshape. Kegl and Wilbur (1976) establish the following features for the tab parameter:

> Head
> Trunk
> Hand
> Extreme
> Central
> Top
> Bottom
> Lateral
> Dorsal

The fact that the physical locations are so variable means that some features simply act as place labels, eg trunk, head and hand. However, the inclusion of such features as 'extreme', 'central' and 'lateral' is important: work on historical change in ASL shows that physical and geometrical characteristics of the body are particularly important in relation to patterns of formational change. ASL signs previously made on the periphery of the trunk location (+ Extreme) such as LIKE and PLEASE are now made nearer to the line of bilateral symmetry (+ Central). Wilbur (1979, p61) also notes the importance of the features 'ipsilateral' and 'contralateral', possibly expressible as

+/- Ipsilateral. BSL DANGER /⌒B₍∧ ᵀˣ/ has ipsilateral contact while WHY /⌐¬G♭₍ˣ/ has contralateral contact.

Movement

The analysis of movement within sign structure is perhaps the most daunting of all the tasks facing the researcher. It is clear that the description of movement presented in Chapter 6 is much closer to a feature analysis than a true phonemic analysis. Frequently several sig symbols are required within the transcription, each representing some feature of movement: the combination of these features produces the significant movement. Although it has been possible to extricate specific features and provide minimal pairs to show how these alone can distinguish pairs of otherwise similar signs, we have not begun to compute the permitted combinations of sig features. In their discussion of the formational components of morphological processes, Klima and Bellugi (1979) have extended previous approaches to the analysis of movement. One important aspect of their description is the inclusion of six dimensions relating specifically to the temporal aspects of movement: onset/offset manner, rate, tension, evenness, size and contouring. Such features may also be important at the phonological level. The two BSL signs EGG /Ō₍⊥ ׀ Hα⊥ ˢ̰/ and CREAM /Ō₍⊥ ׀ Hα⊥ ˢ̱/ differ only in the speed of the movement: EGG involves a fast movement; CREAM uses the same action but at a slower rate

Transcription

In Words in Hand 1 (p232) we noted that by deciding not to attempt a feature analysis of the different parameters, we had missed some opportunities for showing the relationships among different realisations of these parameters. Although, once again, the analysis presented here is phonemic, we have attempted some rationalisation of the transcription symbols to allow some similarity of labelling. The major changes, ie those within the handshape parameter, are discussed in detail in Chapter 4. All of the inconsistencies we ourselves noted (Words in Hand 1, pp232-3) have now been changed, and we hope remedied, in this second edition. Examples include the use of different diacritics to indicate the different types of bending (knuckles and fingers) and the change in the names given to related handshapes, so that X and L are now treated as types of G. We have also taken up the suggestions made by a number of readers, including our colleagues John Fisher (Scotland), Joachim Mugdan (West Germany) and Brita Bergman (Sweden), of regarding the angled formations of handshapes such as G, I, ⅄ and V as allophonic variants, labelled by appropriate diacritics.

Certain other problems remain within the transcription system, although these relate as much to the basic analysis as to the actual labelling difficulties. Throughout Words in Hand 1 we attempted to support our analysis with illustrative examples and minimal pairs. Where a posited phoneme seemed dubious or peripheral, we tried to indicate that this was so and to give reasons for our hesitation. For the most part, decisions made then have stood up to our subsequent analysis of many more BSL signs. Those changes in status which have been made in this edition, eg giving phonemic status to Ĥ and Ĝ, have been made only after detailed examination of examples. Of course, awkward examples do remain. We are no further forward in deciding upon the appropriate allocation of the allophone Ψ̇ (see Words in Hand 1, pp223-4) simply because it occurs so rarely. Those handshapes which occur primarily in initial dez signs, even if they are not recognised as such by users, also provide problems of status. Both R and Ψ are of dubious phonemic status because pairs cited show contrast between initial dez signs and non-initial dez signs. There are two ways of looking at such examples. On the one hand they can be regarded as simply ordinary signs within the language, whatever their derivation. On the other, they can be regarded as constituting a separate group of English influenced signs. Of the two examples, R is by far the more problematic in that it occurs almost entirely in initial dez signs. Ψ is much wider in scope and although we were able to note a range of apparent minimal pairs which made use of non-initial dez signs, many of these turned out, on closer examination, to have essential non-manual features. Thus both KISS /◡ Ψ̂_TA ᵀˣ/ and DUMMY /◡ Ψ̂_TA ᵀˣ/ seemed at first to contrast minimally with EAT /◡ O_TA ᵀˣ/ , but in KISS the lips make a kissing action and in DUMMY the lips 'hold' the fingers as in the sucking of a dummy. It is indeed debatable whether the sig should be contact or entering. Despite the low occurrence of non-initial dez signs we have retained phonemic status for R and Ψ. This is precisely because within particular communities, these handshapes alone distinguish pairs of otherwise identical signs. In many cases the initialised aspect is not consciously recognised by the users and therefore, for the signer there is not necessarily a difference in kind between these and other signs.

Non-Manual Activity

Throughout our account of BSL signs we have concentrated on manual signs. This seems a legitimate strategy and in no way implies that non-manual aspects of sign production are less important. As indicated at the end of Chapter 5 (page 137), Stokoe has suggested that a tri-aspectual analysis may allow for generalisations about sign structure to be made whether the signs concerned are manual or non-manual:

> *"What the signer of ASL produces and the addressee of ASL sees as "a sign" is a unit of physical action. It may be seen under three aspects - artifacts of the analyst's willingness to ignore the other two while concentrating on one. The three aspects are:*
>
> *DEZ, what acts*
> *SIG, the action*
> *TAB, the location of the action.*
>
> *It is clear that this revised tri-aspectual analysis does not exclude non-manual active elements in the formation of ASL signs. Also it is clear that for some signs, specifying all three aspects will be redundant."*

(Stokoe, 1978b, p139)

While the advantages of having a descriptive system which can account for non-manual and manual features are enormous, practically the problems involved are also immense. As Stokoe himself says:

> *"It is the remarkable mobility of hands and arms that make it necessary to specify tab aspect for (some) manually performed signs."*

(Stokoe, 1978b, p140)

In Words in Hand 1 we suggested that this very mobility forced us to treat the hands in a different way from other sign language articulators, such as head, eyes, mouth and shoulders. We claimed that the kind of 'actions' we can perform with the eyes are quite different from those we can perform with the hands. Coping with such variations as blowing out/sucking in of the cheeks, eyebrow raising, tongue position, head nodding and shoulder angle within one descriptive system designed initially for manual signs, seemed at that stage unlikely. However, our subsequent, more detailed work on non-manual features and on a coding system to transcribe these features has forced us to eat at least some of those words! Certainly we have had to create a new way of transcribing non-manual features, but we have done this by exploiting existing symbols within the Stokoe Notation System, particularly the sig symbols. Appropriate placing of these symbols on a simple facial circle can allow us to represent such information as 'eyes to the left', 'mouth open', 'mouth opening', 'cheeks sucked in', 'cheeks puffed out', etc. This is not the place to describe this new system in detail (a full account is in preparation) but to give a hint of the nature of the system, we have transcribed both the manual and non-manual elements of those signs on pages 187 and 188 which have inherent non-manual features.

In Chapter 1 (page 2), the obligatory use of non-manual features to accompany certain manual actions is compared with the use of pitch to distinguish otherwise identical strings of sound segments in some spoken languages. It is worth noting that pitch is an aspect of the production of all sounds. The actual pitch may vary from production to production; in some languages relative pitch may be distinctive at the sentence level, in other languages it may be significant at both word and sentence levels. To judge the basis of the comparison between pitch and non-manual features, we must decide whether non-manual features constitute an inherent element of all sign utterances, just as pitch is an inherent element of all spoken utterances. Certainly non-manual features always co-exist with manual features: the signer has his head in a particular position, uses a specific gaze, etc. The question is whether these actions are any more significant than, let's say, whether one foot is in front of the other. It is clear from research on other sign languages that even where choices made by the signer seem to the outsider either neutral or irrelevant, deaf signers themselves are highly sensitive to extremely slight changes of body movement. Not all such movement is linguistic and it is the task of the researcher to specify the significant types of action.

If we think of signing as a multi-channel activity, involving sometimes complex interaction between manual and non-manual features, then direct comparison between pitch and non-manual elements may seem a little more problematic. Baker and Padden (1978) specify five different channels

> the hands and arms
> the head
> the face
> the eyes
> the total body orientation or posture

and label the individual behaviours within these channels, 'components'. The Baker and Padden account is primarily concerned with discourse and the grammatical function of non-manual features, such as pronominal reference, negation, questions and relative clauses (see also Liddell, 1978 and 1980). However, the authors also note that

IMAGINE /⌒B̂ₜ∧ $\stackrel{e}{\xi}$/   **DREAM** /⌒B̂ₜ∧ $\stackrel{e}{\xi}$/

  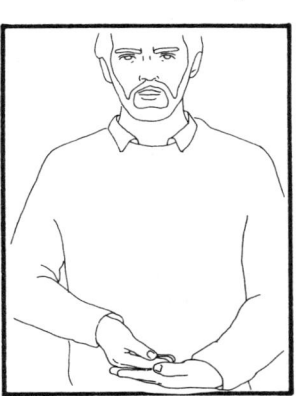 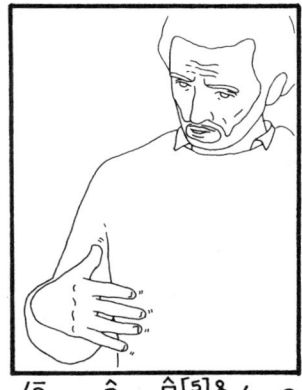

EXPENSIVE   1   /B̄ₐ₌ₓ B̂₍ᵥ ê[s]ʔ/   2   **HOW MUCH**   1   /B̄ₐ₌ₓ B̂₍ᵥ ê[s]˟/   2

certain ASL signs have compulsory non-manual components: ASL SEARCH /CC^e/ requires searching movements of the eyes. Specific non-manual features may be required concomitants of BSL manual signs: IMAGINE /⌒B̄_{T∧}ᶟ/ and DREAM /⌒B̄_{T∧}ᶟ/ both use exactly the same manual activity but differ in that DREAM must be performed with the eyes closed. EXPENSIVE /B̄_{a>}×B̂_{<v} ᵈ⁽⁵⁾ᶻ/ and HOW MUCH /B̄_{a>}×B̂_{<v} ᵈ⁽⁵⁾ᴿ/ are very similar in their manual elements, yet differ in their realisations of the non-manual channels. EXPENSIVE typically includes sucking in of the cheeks and rounded lips, HOW MUCH demands the use of a questioning pattern, eg raised eyebrows, head forward. Further examples of signs which include inherent non-manual elements can be found in SIGN (Edinburgh BSL Project, 1983). The notion that several different channels are involved in sign production seems to imply a difference in the nature of each channel. Some researchers (Hansen, 1980; Bergman and Hansen, 1980) use different terminology to cover the same phenomena and specify seven separate articulators which may be employed in the production of a signed utterance: left hand, right hand, head, face, mouth, eyes and body. A description in terms of the simultaneous co-ordination of a range of articulators within sign production probably allows a closer analogy between the spoken utterance and the signed utterance. The different articulators together provide the 'physical action' which is lexically or grammatically meaningful.

Current Developments

We have already mentioned several recent developments in relation to the phonological analysis of BSL signs. Much of the work done on the temporal and dynamic aspects of sign production has been in relation to compounds (Klima and Bellugi, 1979). Recent work by Scott Liddell (Liddell, 1983) is also focusing on compounds, but is giving more attention to the notion of syllable structure in ASL signs. Liddell suggests that signs are analysable into movement and hold segments and proposes a number of syllable types for ASL. He is also attempting to show how these syllables can change in a predictable way when they occur as the first element in compound signs.

Such developments show the enormous potential for future work on BSL phonology. In our own work we are looking at both the 'chunking' of BSL utterances and the ways in which signs and sign utterances can be modified to give differing focus and emphasis to different parts of the message. As in other work quoted earlier, this demands moving beyond what is strictly speaking phonology and into the realms of morphology, syntax and 'text'.

Signs in Use

Throughout this book, the examples quoted have been so-called citation forms. The citation form of a sign is an idealised representation encompassing the essential ingredients of that sign's production. In actual use the sign may be altered to such an extent that one of the ingredients is either lost completely or substantially changed in form. Such changes may be the result of phonological, morphological or syntactic processes.

Phonological Processes

In spoken language it is well-known that when morphemes come together within words, compounds or even sentences, changes may occur in the realisations of the phonemes involved. Typical processes include assimilation, deletion and addition. Probably the most frequent and important is assimilation where a particular element takes on features from a neighbouring element. Such changes may be 'progressive' in that one element takes on features of a prior element; 'regressive' in that an element is affected by what comes after it or 'mutual' in that two elements affect each other. Wilbur (1979) provides examples from ASL: in the ASL utterance WE REFUSE the handshape used for WE is changed from H to A in anticipation of the A handshape in REFUSE (regressive assimilation). Similar examples have been noted in our analyses of BSL video tapes, although at this stage we do not know which changes reflect regular and systematic phonological processes and which are merely idiosyncratic examples. Present evidence certainly shows that the manual tab is particularly susceptible to assimilation; if two signs having manual tabs occur in sequence the second sign may use the manual tab already produced. This is especially true if the tab is one of the most frequent unmarked handshapes, such as A, B and 5.

In other cases, one component of a sign may be completely deleted. An utterance such as I REMEMBER in its 'full' form would involve the following sequence: /⌐⌐⌐Ğ⊤< ˣ/^G<^ ˣ//Ā□>A▫⊥ ˅ˣ/.

I

REMEMBER

The first two morphemes require the same handshape placed in different positions - the sig in each case is simply contact with the body. Typically one of these morphemes is omitted entirely so that either the trunk or head is used as tab; the G hand then changes to A for the second part of the compound REMEMBER. If the trunk is chosen as tab the hand may move upwards slightly, in the direction of the head, before making the downward movement to meet the left hand. In many signs, the contact element of the sig is omitted: the dez moves towards the tab but contact does not actually occur.

In speech certain phonetic devices such as 'glides' and 'liaisons' (eg linking 'r') can be added to allow smooth transition from one unit to another. Our impression at this stage is that in BSL there are typical movement glides, usually made with a neutral handshape, which allow the signer to proceed without the signing taking on a disjointed appearance. As with the other processes mentioned here, there is very little research available as yet. However, work is progressing and the information gleaned may be particularly helpful to learners who find difficulty in comprehending signs in use.

We have also noted that in actual production, 'target' locations may be 'missed' without causing any interpretation problems for the addressee. Thus, DEAF /ᵔH<^ ˣ / which in its citation form has contact on the ear, may be produced with contact on the cheek. As far as we know, there is no sign with exactly the same handshape and movement occurring on the cheek, hence the possibility of blurring or neutralising the distinction in this particular case. It is interesting that such neutralisation occurs despite the apparent iconic origins of the sign.

Similarly, DON'T KNOW /^B⊤^ˣ˖/ is made with contact on the forehead. Examples have been noted which not only omit the contact but involve the hand approaching the mid-face or nose rather than the forehead. It is interesting to note that in some cases the head moves back in a form of emphasis. Again, at this stage, we do not know exactly which phonological distinctions can be neutralised in which environments, but there is enough evidence to show that neutralisation does occur.

DEAF /ᵔH<^ ˣ/   1

DEAF   2

DON'T KNOW /^B⊤^ˣ˖/1

DON'T KNOW   2

Morphological Processes

The ways in which the individual morphemes of a language can be modified to express changes in meaning vary from language to language.

Mechanisms include adding meaningful elements or affixes, changing vowel or consonant segments, reduplication, and tone or stress alterations. Such changes may have grammatical function, to express grammatical categories such as number or tense, or lexical function, to modify the lexical content of a vocabulary item, eg 'meaning' - 'meaningful'; 'meaning' - 'meaningless'. There are clearly recognisable morphological processes of both types in BSL but sequential processes such as affixation are much less prevalent than in spoken languages. The simultaneity characteristic of sign production influences the choice of internal changes which exploit the dimensions of both space and time. Meaningful patterns occur which involve changing one or more of the realisations of the major parameters. The following examples illustrate the varying form and function of grammatical morphological processes in BSL.

A change in handshape may be used to incorporate information about 'number' into the form of the sign. NEXT YEAR /$G_{T>}$ ıx $G_{T<}$ $\frac{e}{v}$/ makes use of the G handshape as dez. This can be 'modulated' or 'inflected' to mean "in two years time" or "in three years time" by changing the handshape to V or W.

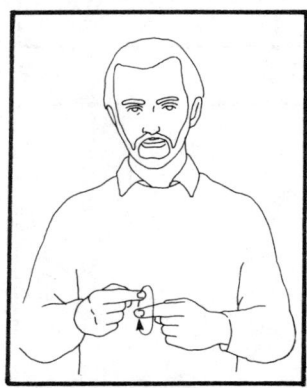
NEXT YEAR

TWO YEARS TIME

THREE YEARS TIME

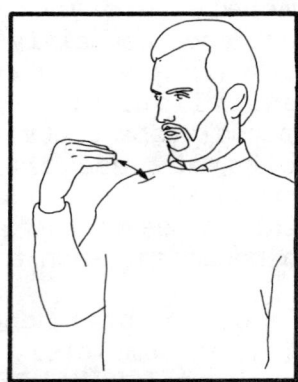
REMIND ME

REMIND YOU

REMIND HIM

Similarly, LAST WEEK /√$\bar{B}_{D>}$×$G_{<⊥}$ $\frac{s}{v}$/ can be changed to mean "two weeks ago", "in five weeks time", etc. Changes in position and orientation often combine to produce a meaningful change within a sign morpheme. REMIND may be performed with palm facing the signer and contact on the shoulder /⌐¬$\ddot{B}_{T∧}$ ×·/, REMIND ME; with palm facing away in neutral space, REMIND YOU; or with palm facing right in neutral space, REMIND HIM. The information about the object of the verb has been incorporated into the sign itself. The citation form of LOOK is /ʊ$V_{<∧}$ ×⊥/ but the position, orientation and movement of the V hand may be systematically changed to incorporate information of various types: subject/object information can be included in examples such as I LOOK AT YOU (plural), HE LOOKS AT ME, THEY LOOK AT EACH OTHER. Information on manner can also be included, eg I LOOK UP, I LOOK AROUND. In all of these cases the sign would be accompanied by non-manual features, thus LOOK UP involves the action of looking upwards.

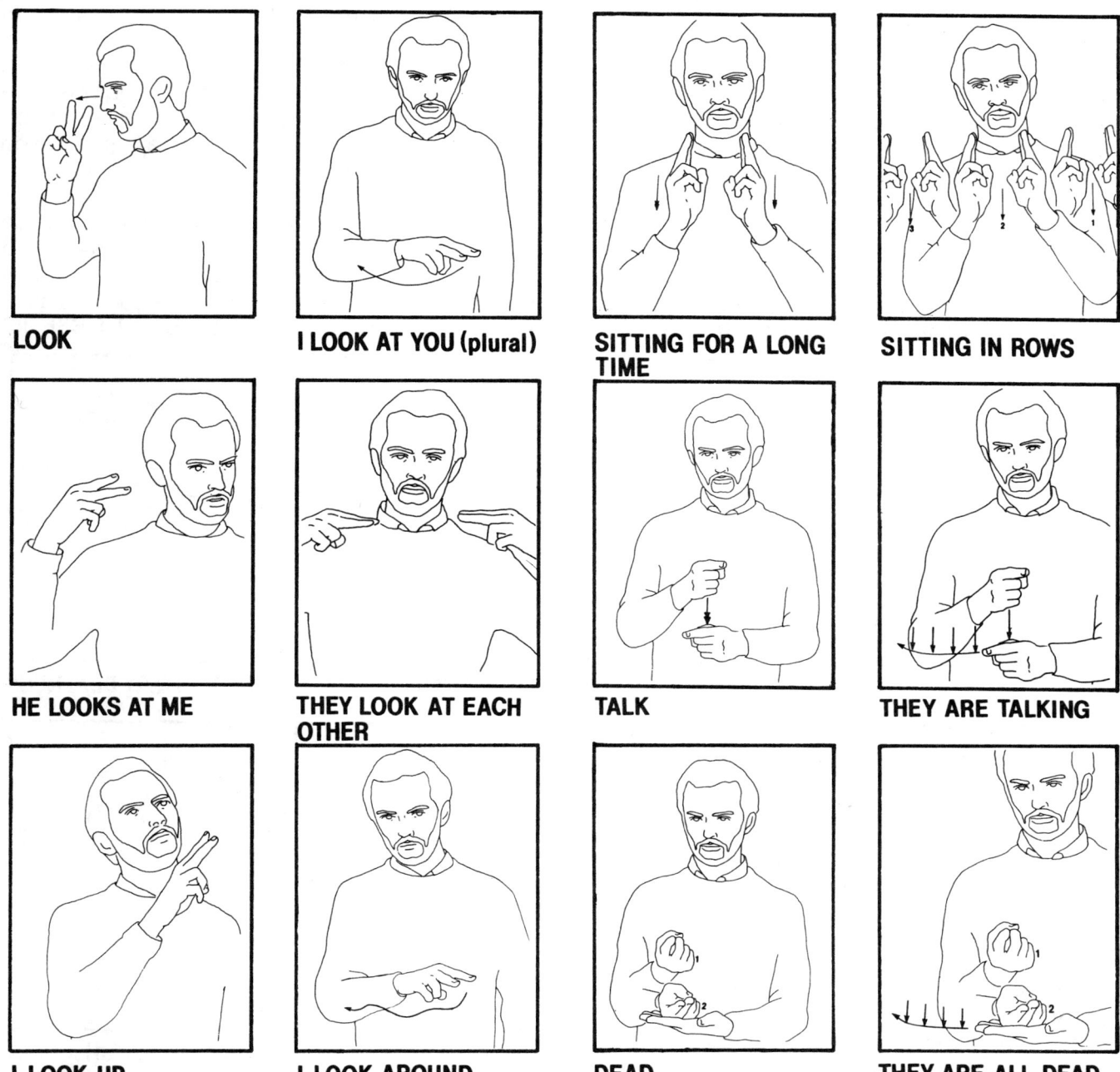

LOOK | I LOOK AT YOU (plural) | SITTING FOR A LONG TIME | SITTING IN ROWS
HE LOOKS AT ME | THEY LOOK AT EACH OTHER | TALK | THEY ARE TALKING
I LOOK UP | I LOOK AROUND | DEAD | THEY ARE ALL DEAD

Movement may be used to express number, manner, aspect and other grammatical categories. SIT /∅H₍₎∧ ᵢ H₍∧ ⁰ / in its base form is produced in neutral space with one sharp downward movement. A repeated downward movement can mean "sitting for a long time" while the use of repeated downward movements from left to right means "sitting in rows".

Similarly, TALK has as its base form /Ḡ₍ₜ₎ G₍₎ ˣ˙/ but this may be modulated by making the hands move round in an arc to indicate "they are talking". One of the signs for DEAD is /B̄ₐ₎ Ḧₐ⊥ ˘ˣ[ᵛ]/ which can be modulated by repetition and movement to mean "they are all dead".

Klima and Bellugi (1979) have noted that movement is particularly important for the expression of 'aspectual' information in ASL. The grammatical category of aspect relates to "the internal constituency of the situation" (Comrie, 1976), therefore, an action may be view as completed, on-going, happening again and again, just beginning and so on. It seems that, on present information, ASL has a larger number of aspectual modulations than any known spoken language. BSL signs may also be systematically altered to express aspect, and in some contexts such modulations are obligatory. The sequence HE COMES EVERY DAY typically involves the verb COME modulated by repeated short movements (as in 1), while HE NEVER COMES involves a single, longer and sharper movement (as in 2).

although the phonemic realisations exploited are already part of the language. However, the coinage DIGITAL WATCH has also been noted: here the position is changed so that the right hand is placed in the normal position for WRIST WATCH.

Some negative markers may be compared to the use of 'un-', 'non-', 'dis-' and '-less' affixes in English as in "uninteresting", "non-smoker", "disloyal" and "speechless". In BSL NO

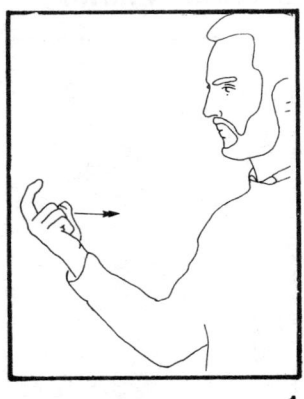 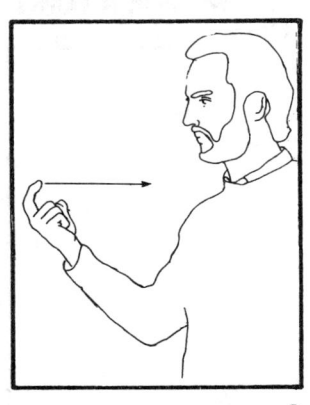

1   **2**

HEREDITARY   **HEREDITARY DEAFNESS**

Lexical morphological changes may include derivation of one word-class from another, eg deriving of nouns from verbs or verbs from nouns. Thus, the English verbs "to bottle" and "to catalogue" derive from the nouns "bottle" and "catalogue", while the nouns "bore" and "hand-out" derive from the verbs "to bore" and "to hand out". In order to show the derivational processes involved it is necessary to see whether the language distinguishes nouns and verbs in a systematic way. Research on ASL (Supalla and Newport, 1978) shows that such systematic differences can be found and regular derivational processes noted. Comparable processes in BSL are still being studied but it is clear that productive word-formation processes are available in BSL either by exploiting realisations of the parameters or by bringing together existing items in the language. The sign HEREDITARY /⌀H̄ᵦ>×Hᴅ⊥ ˇ/ is normally made in neutral space. By changing the position to the ear tab, it is possible to change the meaning to HEREDITARY DEAFNESS. The new sign DIGITAL /⌀5̈ₐ⊥ ˣ/ appears to have an iconic basis,

 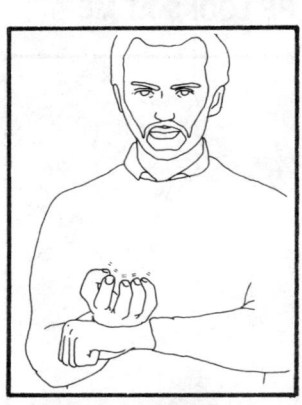

DIGITAL   **DIGITAL WATCH**

GOOD, the normal production of GOOD is changed by adding a side to side bending movement and opening the hand to a 5 hand. NOT KEEN /⌣Ȧ⊥∧ ˣᵊ[ᵊ]/ is rather different in that there is no direct relationship between this sign and the positive form KEEN /[]Ëᴛ>Ëᴛ< ˣ~/. The use of negative incorporation in BSL throws open the question of whether such internal changes should be regarded as examples of lexical or grammatical morphological processes. Compounding seems just as prevalent in BSL as in other sign languages./⌒G<∧ˣᵛ∥⌀G̈ₐ>×G̈ᴅ⊥ ᵎ/ is made up of two recognisable signs

NO GOOD

NOT KEEN

I WILL ALWAYS REMEMBER

CHECK

THINK and CONTINUE. The compound sign means something like "I will always remember" or "I'll never forget". The compound /ɪsᵉʮ˖<ᴧˣ⫽ ØY<ᴧ ʮ˙/ meaning CHECK, is rather more difficult to explain. Indeed, its status as a compound may be questioned as the first element is not identical with any one BSL sign: it is similar to SEE in that the index finger touches the face below the eye, but the handshape is ʮ rather than G. This may simply be a further example of a regressive change as the handshape takes some of the features of the following handshape, namely the extension of thumb and little finger. The second element is comparable to PERHAPS /ØY<ᴧ ʮ˙/ although, as we might expect, there are modifications of the movement. Klima and Bellugi (1979) have also noted particular patterns of movement, as well as changes of duration and rhythm in ASL compound signs.

A rather specialised category of morphological change in BSL involves the use of classifiers. As Lyons (1977, Vol 2, p460) notes, classifiers have received relatively little attention from linguists because, although they occur in many languages of the world, they are not used in the more familiar Indo-European family of languages. Allan (1977) provides an account of classifier languages based on data from over fifty languages. Typically, classifiers are words or markers which identify items as belonging to particular classes or sets. These may be 'natural' groupings such as "animal", "bird" and "person" or groupings dependent upon shared physical or functional properties. The physical property of shape is a common principle of organisation. Work on other sign languages has shown the use of specific handshapes to provide 'classifying' information. Classifying handshapes also exist in BSL, although, as we might predict, the list of classifying handshapes is not the same for all sign languages. Those so far noted in BSL include:

- G   person
- 5   people
- B   flat object
- A   mass, round objects
- V   legs
- C   curved object/edge

Classifying handshapes can function in a number of different ways within the language: as elements of lexical items including nouns and verbs, and as 'pro-forms', particularly pronouns. Lexical items using such forms include MEET /ØG>ᴧ₁G<ᴧ²ᶜˣ/, DOOR /Bᴛ> ꜀ Bᴛ< ²/ and WALK /ØV̈ᴅ⊥ ¹/. One of the most frequently used in BSL is the one for PEOPLE: the following illustrations show the varying ways in which the 'classifier' can be modified to produce particular lexical items and realise specific grammatical functions. (See <u>SIGN</u>, Edinburgh BSL Project, 1983, for further discussion and examples.)

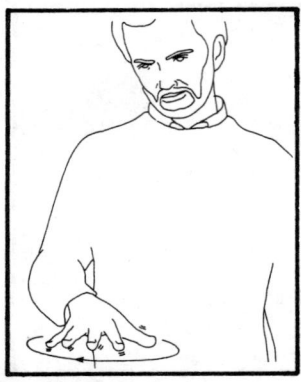
MINGLING

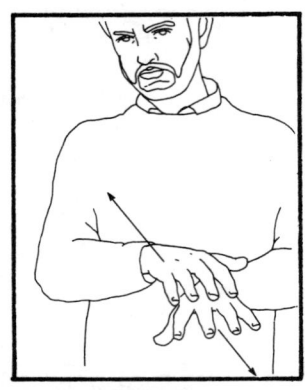
LARGE QUEUE

AUDIENCE

PEOPLE FILING

PEOPLE ENTERING

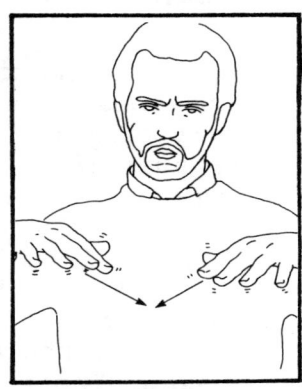
PEOPLE RUSHING

Syntactic Processes

The production of individual signs can be modified not only through morphological processes but also through the operation of syntactic processes. The nature of syntax in BSL is affected by two important characteristics of sign languages: spatiality and simultaneity. By placing signs at particular points in space and setting up relations between these points it is possible to indicate such important syntactic information as subject-object relations, noun modifications and pronominal reference. Clearly morphological and syntactic mechanisms interact to provide the complete grammatical information. Thus, a signer may position a particular item such as CHURCH /$\emptyset \bar{A}_{>\perp} \times A_{<\perp}{}^\sim$/ to the left and then use modulated signs to show people entering the church, leaving the church, etc. The fact that the signer can do several things at once also allows syntactic relations to be expressed in quite different ways in sign language. The accompanying illustration shows the simultaneous production of the sign CENTRE and the sign PEOPLE. The PEOPLE classifier is modulated to show people coming towards the centre from different directions. CENTRE /$\bar{8}_{a\perp} B_{\triangleright <}{}^{x\cdot}$/ is normally a two-handed sign, but as the full sign has already been articulated in the previous part of the utterance there is no problem at all of interpretation. Such repetition of a sign or part of a sign is a very common device. In a similar example, the signer first produced the two handed sign TERRIBLE /$\emptyset I_{\perp \wedge} I_{\perp \wedge}{}^{\dagger}$/ then, keeping the left hand in the same position, articulated the sign FORGET /$\wedge \hat{8}_{\perp \wedge}{}^{\dot{a}[5]}$/. Such simultaneous production which would be quite impossible in spoken language, does involve some modification of the citation form of TERRIBLE, ie the use of a one-handed, instead of a two-handed, variant.

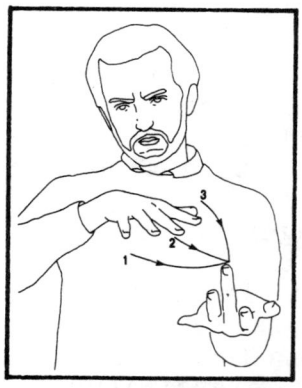
PEOPLE CAME TO THE CENTRE FROM ALL OVER

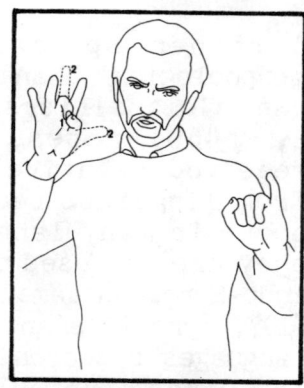
IT WAS TERRIBLE, I FORGOT

Transcribing BSL Utterances

The transcription system presented in this book is flexible enough to cope with most of the variations in sign production mentioned above. The inclusion of orientation is particularly important for the expression of syntactic and morphological information. This system should also allow relatively easy recording of signs which have no simple or direct English equivalents. These signs are sometimes referred to as 'idioms', but, as many researchers have indicated, the use of this term may distort the nature of these items. In our own work on a large corpus of BSL we originally used the term 'idiom' as a 'convenience' label for items which presented special problems of translation. While accepting that these items were not 'idioms' in the sense that "It's raining cats and dogs" is an idiom in English, it seemed reasonable to use the term for forms which were 'unique' to the language. However, as we work through the examples in our corpus, we realise that many of these so-called idioms have forms and functions directly comparable to other BSL signs and we realised that the use of the term idiom seriously distorts the nature of these items. Many are lexical items demanding the simultaneous use of non-manual features: such features are often difficult for non-signers to interpret, hence the inaccessibility of these signs to the hearing community. Others are relatively simple manual signs: indeed, we have been surprised to discover that many are single morpheme signs, although our initial impression was that compound signs featured largely in this group. Those signs which appear to have a grammatical function are often difficult simply because that function is not yet fully understood either by the researcher or the learner. Clearly such 'difficulties' exist only for those on the outside: those using such signs do so with ease although it may not always be possible for deaf people to be explicit about how these signs function in the language.

The following examples will show how signs which may demand a whole phrase or clause as a gloss, nevertheless incorporate typical features of BSL sign production. The first example /⌐˩G̈_{T<} ²̽/ is relatively simple in form in that it is a one-handed sign demanding body contact. The meaning is close to "happening again and again" or "persistent". The next example /ØO_{>∧ ı} O_{<∧} ⁾/ is also relatively simple in terms of manual structure but it normally includes a non-manual feature in the form of blowing out of the cheeks. This sign seems to be used most frequently with the verb "see" to mean "not (see) for a long time" in an utterance such as "I haven't seen him for ages". Although it has also been noted with other verbs such as "come", present evidence suggests that it typically co-occurs with "see".

The sign /[˩B̈_{D<} ²̂ ⅔ [ê]/ is manually 'complex' in the sense used in Chapter 4, ie because of the closing action of the sig, two handshapes are involved, although it is a one-handed sign. In typical production, the mouth is open at the onset of the sign and then closes in an action which 'matches' the closing action of the hand. Again this is a lexical sign which seems to have adverbial function and can be glossed as "for a short time" or "briefly" as in "I could only stay for a short time". /ØḦ_{a⊥ x} Ḧ_{b⊥} ?[ᴴᴴ]/ is a two-handed symmetrical sign with obligatory non-manual features of mouth opening and eye opening. This is an expression of amazement and could be translated as "flabbergasted", "incredible", etc, depending upon context.

The final two signs are difficult, not so much because of any complexity in form, but because they demand more explicit statements on how they function in the language. /Ø5_{D⊥} ᴿ·/, which is particularly simple in form, takes on functions comparable to those assumed by the verb "to be" in English. It appears

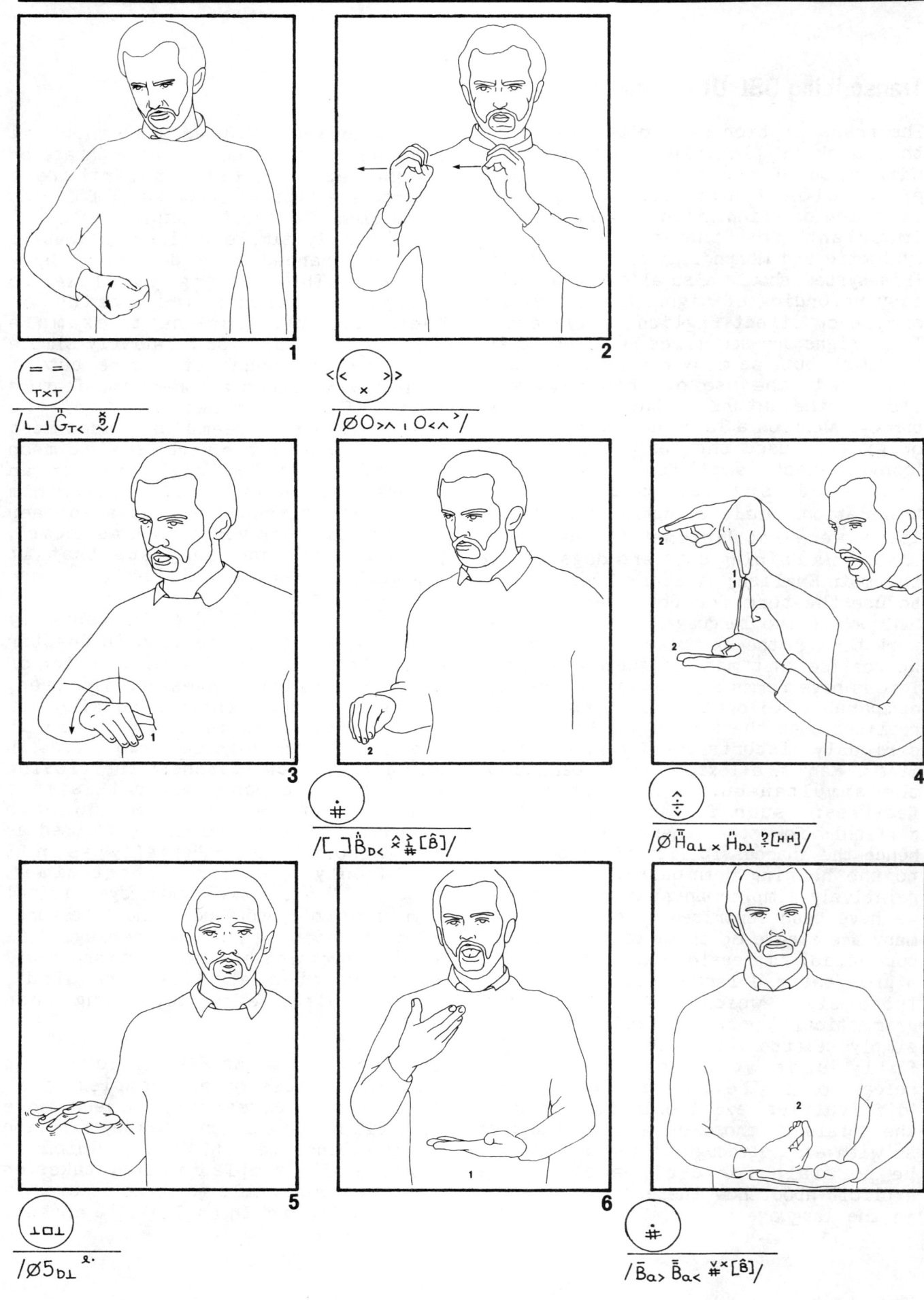

to act as a marker of predication or 'existence' in an utterance like "There was an old man in the corner". (See Lawson, 1983 and Hughes, Colville and Brennan, 1984.) /B̄a> B̄a< ⚡×[ĉ]/ is complex in both form and function. In production it combines manual and non-manual elements. As with /⌐⌐B̈ᴅ< ẑ¼[ĉ]/ above there is a closing action of the mouth which seems to mirror the closing manual action. It is used in such sentences as "We should have been killed but we weren't", "I should have saved a lot of money but I didn't".

The notation system allows such signs to be transcribed without reference to possibly distorting English glosses. This makes possible a closer examination of the range of linguistic environments in which the signs occur and hence a more accurate statement of their function within the language. Once we are able to look at the system in its own terms, we can discover those patterns of organisation which make British Sign Language a highly productive and efficient linguistic system.

Notes

References

ABERCROMBIE, D
1965
STUDIES IN PHONETICS AND LINGUISTICS. London: Oxford University Press.

ALLAN, K
1977
"Classifiers"   LANGUAGE 53:285-311.

BAKER, C
1980
"On the Terms Non-Verbal and Verbal" in PAPERS FROM THE FIRST INTERNATIONAL SYMPOSIUM ON SIGN LANGUAGE RESEARCH. Stockholm: Swedish National Association of the Deaf.

BAKER, C & PADDEN, C
1978
"Focusing on the Non-Manual Components of American Sign Language" in P Siple (ed) UNDERSTANDING LANGUAGE THROUGH SIGN LANGUAGE RESEARCH. London and New York: Academic Press.

BATTISON, R M
1973
"3-D and Digit Vision: Phonology in American Sign Language" Paper at 3rd Annual California Linguistics Conference, Stanford.

1974
"Phonological Deletion in American Sign Language" SIGN LANGUAGE STUDIES 5:1-19.

1978
LEXICAL BORROWING IN AMERICAN SIGN LANGUAGE. Silver Spring, MD: Linstok Press.

1979
"Lexical Borrowing and Restructuring of Signs" Paper presented at the NATO Advanced Study Institute. "Recent Developments in Language and Cognition: Sign Language Research". Copenhagen, Denmark.

BERGMAN, B
1977 (1979)
SIGNED SWEDISH. Stockholm: National Swedish Board of Education.

1979
LOCALISATION AS A SYNTACTIC PROCESS. Paper presented at the First International Symposium on Sign Language Research, Stockholm 1979.

1982
STUDIES IN SWEDISH SIGN LANGUAGE. Stockholm: University of Stockholm.

BERGMAN, B
& HANSEN, B
1980
"Simultaneity" Informal Presentation at Sign Language Research Workshop, Middleton Hall, Scotland.

BOYES-BRAEM, P
1973
"A Study of the Acquisition of the Dez in American Sign Language" Working Paper, Salk Institute for Biological Studies, La Jolla, California.

1981
"Features of the Handshape in American Sign Language" Ph.D Dissertation. Berkeley: University of California.

BRENNAN, M;
COLVILLE, M D &
LAWSON, L K
1980
WORDS IN HAND (First Edition). Edinburgh: Moray House College of Education.

BRISTOL SIGN
LANGUAGE GROUP
1979
CODING BRITISH SIGN LANGUAGE. Proceedings of the Sign Language Notation Workshop, Newcastle, 11th-13th May, 1979.

BRITISH DEAF
ASSOCIATION
SIGN IT (in preparation).

CARMEL, S J
1975
INTERNATIONAL HAND ALPHABET CHARTS. Maryland: Studio Printing Incorporated.

CARTER, M &
MADDIX, F
1980
"BSL: Contact . . . With Computers" (in print). Available from Bristol Sign Language Group, University of Bristol, England.

COHEN, E; NAMIR, L
& SCHLESINGER, I M
1977
A NEW DICTIONARY OF SIGN LANGUAGE. The Hague: Mouton.

COMRIE, B
1976
ASPECT. Cambridge: Cambridge University Press.

DEUCHAR, M
1978
"Diglossia and British Sign Language" SOCIOLINGUISTICS WORKING PAPER 46. Austin, Texas: Southwest Educational Laboratory.

EDINBURGH BRITISH
SIGN LANGUAGE
PROJECT
1983
SIGN: AN INTRODUCTION TO BRITISH SIGN LANGUAGE (BSL). Videotape Series. Edinburgh: Moray House College.

EKMAN, P &
FRIESEN, W
1978

FACIAL ACTION CODING SYSTEM.   Palo Alto, CA: Consulting Psychologists Press.

FRIEDMAN, L A
1975

"Phonological Processes in American Sign Language" PROCEEDINGS OF THE FIRST ANNUAL MEETING OF THE BERKELEY LINGUISTICS SOCIETY:47-159.

FRIEDMAN, L A (ed)
1977

"Formational Properties of American Sign Language" in L A Friedman (ed) ON THE OTHER HAND. London and New York: Academic Press.

FRIEDMAN, L A &
BATTISON, R M
1973

PHONOLOGICAL STRUCTURES IN AMERICAN SIGN LANGUAGE. NEH Grant Report. AY-8218-73-136.

FRISHBERG, N
1975

"Arbitrariness and Iconicity: Historical Change in American Sign Language" LANGUAGE, 51:696-719.

FROMKIN, V
1971

"The Non-Anomalous Utterances" LANGUAGE, 47:27-54.

HANSEN, B
1980

"Simultaneity" in GRAMMATICAL FEATURES OF DANISH SIGN LANGUAGE by B Hansen, R K Sorenson and E Petersen.

HUGHES, G;
COLVILLE, M D &
BRENNAN, M
1984

"Talking about 'Existence' in British Sign Language (BSL)" in F Loncke; P Boyes-Braem and Y Lebrun (eds) RECENT RESEARCH ON EUROPEAN SIGN LANGUAGE. Holland: SWETS Publishing Service.

HUTCHINSON, A
1977

LABANOTATION: THE SYSTEM OF ANALYZING AND RECORDING MOVEMENT. New York: Theatre Arts Books.

JAKOBSON, R
1979 (1968)

CHILD LANGUAGE, APHASIA AND PHONOLOGICAL UNIVERSALS. The Hague: Mouton.

KEGL, J
1979

VERB STEMS IN ASL. Paper presented at the NATO Advanced Study Institute. "Recent Developments in Language and Cognition: Sign Language Research" Copenhagen, Denmark.

KEGL, J & WILBUR, R
1976
"Where does Structure Stop and Style Begin?: Syntax, Morphology and Phonology vs Stylistic Variation in American Sign Language" in S Mufwene, C Walker and S Steever (eds) PAPERS FROM THE TWELFTH REGIONAL MEETING, CHICAGO LINGUISTICS SOCIETY. The University of Chicago Press.

KLIMA, E & BELLUGI, U
1979
THE SIGNS OF LANGUAGE. Cambridge and London: Harvard University Press.

LABAN, R
1950
THE MASTERY OF MOVEMENT ON THE STAGE. London: McDonald and Evans.

LANE, H; BOYES-BRAEM, P & BELLUGI, U
1976
"Preliminaries to a Distinctive Feature Analysis of American Sign Language". COGNITIVE PSYCHOLOGY, 8:263-289.

LAVER, J
1970
"The Production of Speech" in J Lyons (ed) NEW HORIZONS IN LINGUISTICS. Middlesex, England: Penguin Books.

LAWSON, L
1983
"Multi-Channel Signs" in J Kyle and B Woll (eds) LANGUAGE IN SIGN. London: Croom Helm.

LIDDELL, S
1978
"Non-Manual Signals and Relative Clauses in American Sign Language" in P Siple (ed) UNDERSTANDING LANGUAGE THROUGH SIGN LANGUAGE RESEARCH. London and New York: Academic Press.

1980
AMERICAN SIGN LANGUAGE SYNTAX. The Hague: Mouton.

1983
"Segments and Syllables in ASL" Paper presented at the Third International Symposium on Sign Language Research, Rome.

LOVE, J R B
1941
"Worora Kinship Gestures" reprinted in D Umiker-Sebeok and Thomas A Sebeok (eds) ABORIGINAL SIGN LANGUAGES OF THE AMERICAS AND AUSTRALIA. New York: Plenum Press 1978.

LYONS, J
1977
SEMANTICS. Volume 2. Cambridge: Cambridge University Press.

MCDONALD, B
1982
"Aspects of the American Sign Language Predicate System" Ph.D Thesis. University of Buffalo.

MCINTIRE, M
1974
"A Modified Model for the Description of Language Acquisition" Unpublished MA Thesis. California State University, Northbridge.

MCINTIRE, M
1977
"The Acquisition of ASL Hand Configurations" in SIGN LANGUAGE STUDIES 16:247-266.

MARTINET, A
1960
ELEMENTS OF GENERAL LINGUISTICS. London: Faber and Faber.

MILES, D
1976
GESTURES. Northridge, California: Joyce Motion Picture Incorporated.

MUGDAN, J
1980
"Personal Communication".

SIPLE, P
1978
"Linguistic and Psychological Properties of American Sign Language: An Overview" in P Siple (ed) UNDERSTANDING LANGUAGE THROUGH SIGN LANGUAGE RESEARCH. London and New York: Academic Press.

STOKOE, W C
1960
"Sign Language Structure: An Outline of the Visual Communication System of the American Deaf" STUDIES IN LINGUISTICS, OCCASIONAL PAPER 8. University of Buffalo.

1972 (ed)
SEMIOTICS AND HUMAN SIGN LANGUAGES. Approaches to Semiotics 21. The Hague: Mouton.

1978
SIGN LANGUAGE STRUCTURE. Revised Edition. Silver Spring, MD: Linstok Press.

1978b
"Review of Friedman 'On the Other Hand'". ARS SEMIOTICA, 3:133-147.

1979
"Review of Wilbur 'American Sign Language and Sign Systems'" SIGN LANGUAGE STUDIES, 23:175-189.

STOKOE, W C;
CASTERLINE, D C &
CRONEBERG, C G
1976 (1965)
A DICTIONARY OF AMERICAN SIGN LANGUAGE ON LINGUISTIC PRINCIPLES. Revised Edition. Silver Spring, MD: Linstok Press.

SUPALLA, T & "How Many Seats in a Chair? The Derivation of
NEWPORT, E L Nouns and Verbs in American Sign Language" in P
1978 Siple (ed) UNDERSTANDING LANGUAGE THROUGH SIGN
LANGUAGE RESEARCH. London and New York: Academic
Press.

TODD, P "Interpreting 'The Signs of Language' (Klima and
1980 Bellugi). A Review Article" SIGN LANGUAGE
STUDIES, 28:217-238.

VOGT-SVENDSEN, M "Lip Movements in Norwegian Sign Language" in J
1983 Kyle and B Woll (eds) LANGUAGE IN SIGN. London:
Croom Helm.

WIKSTROM, L A "Lip Movements in Swedish Sign Language"
1979 Unpublished paper presented at the First
International Symposium on Sign Language Research,
Stockholm.

WIKSTROM, L A & "Demonstration of Swedish Finger-Spelling"
BERGMAN, B Unpublished paper presented at the First
1979 International Symposium on Sign Language Research,
Stockholm.

WILBUR, R B AMERICAN SIGN LANGUAGE AND SIGN SYSTEMS.
1979 Baltimore: University Park Press.

WOODWARD, J SIGNS OF SEXUAL BEHAVIOR. Silver Spring, MD: T J
1979 Publishers.

WORLD FEDERATION GESTUNO: INTERNATIONAL SIGN LANGUAGE OF THE DEAF.
OF THE DEAF Carlisle: The British Deaf Association.
1975

Name Index

ABERCROMBIE
123, 124

ALLAN
185

BAKER
2, 26, 179

BATTISON
5, 9, 11, 12, 14, 16, 18, 69, 70

BELLUGI
4, 5, 6, 20, 21, 120, 143, 163, 168, 171, 174, 175, 177, 180, 183, 185

BERGMAN
2, 14, 18, 26, 120, 176, 177, 180

BOYES-BRAEM
13, 174, 175, 176

BRENNAN
189

CARMEL
14

CARTER
57, 126, 135, 170, 171

COHEN
26

COLVILLE
189

COMRIE
183

DEUCHAR
160

EKMAN
26

FISHER
177

FRIEDMAN
5, 41, 45, 47, 49, 54, 68, 70, 94, 132, 140, 143, 148, 156, 163, 171

FRIESEN
26

FRISHBERG
5, 68

FROMKIN
174

HANSEN
180

HUGHES
189

HUTCHINSON
139

JAKOBSON
12

KEGL
174, 175, 176

KLIMA
4, 5, 6, 20, 21, 120, 143, 163, 168, 171, 174, 175, 177, 180, 183, 185

LABAN
139

LANE
175

LAVER
124

LAWSON
2, 26, 57, 189

LIDDELL
2, 120, 179, 180

LOVE
68

LYONS
185

MCDONALD
176

MCINTIRE
13, 174

MADDIX
57, 126, 135, 170, 171

MARTINET
68

MUGDAN
173, 177

NAMIR
26

NEWPORT
184

PADDEN
2, 179

SCHLESINGER
26

SIPLE
68, 69

STOKOE
2, 3, 5, 8, 9, 20, 25, 27, 35, 41, 45, 47, 49, 54, 55, 116, 117, 123, 124, 135, 137, 139, 143, 146, 153, 156, 161, 165, 173, 178

SUPALLA
184

TODD
175

VOGT-SVENDSON
2, 26

WIKSTROM
2, 14

WILBUR
175, 176, 180

WOODWARD
66

198

Subject Index

Allocher
8-9

Allophone
6-9

Alternative Descriptions
173-180

American Sign Language (ASL)
2, 4, 6, 7, 8, 9, 12, 13, 16, 18, 20, 21, 25, 26, 27, 35, 66, 68, 69, 70, 94, 116, 139, 168, 171, 174, 175, 176, 178, 180, 181, 184, 185

Arbitrary Signs
20-21

Articulators
180

Articulatory Constraints
68-69

Aspect
183

Aspects
3-6, 123-137, 163-172

Asymmetrical Signs
58-64

Atypical Signing Space
65-68

Australian Aboriginal Sign Language
68

Borrowings
7, 13, 16-20

Bristol Sign Language Group
57, 170

Catholic Signs
18-20, 80, 92, 102, 112, 113, 116, 119

Chereme
9

Cherology
8-9

Chinese Sign Language (CSL)
6, 199

Chinyanja
4

Classification of Signs
9-10

Classifiers
174, 185

Compound Signs
10, 13, 70, 120, 184-185

Contact (see also Place of Contact and Point of Contact)
9, 39, 140-143, 176-177

Conventionalised Gestures
21

Danish Sign Language (DSL)
4

Deictic Signs
21-22,

Dez (Designation)
3-13, 22-23, 73-121

Diacritics
26, 52-54

Discrete Elements
174

Dominance Constraint
11-12

Double Contact Signs
69, 140, 142

Double Dez Signs 10

Edinburgh BSL Project
26, 176, 180, 185

Eshkol-Wachman Movement Notation System
26

Facial Action Coding System (FACS)
26

Feature Analysis
140, 174-177

Finger-Spelling (see also Manual Alphabet)
13-20

French
4

German
4, 8

Gestuno
158

Hand Arrangement
5, 31-32, 163-168

Historical Change
68

Iconicity
20-24

Idioms
187-189

Initial Dez Signs
26-28

Irish Sign Language (ISL)
80

Labanotation
139-140

Lexical Processes
184-185

Manual Alphabet
13-20

    American
    17, 14-20
    British
    15, 13-20
    Irish
    19, 18-20
    Swedish
    14

Manual Tabs
56-64, 71

Marked/Unmarked
12-13

Methodology
6-8

Minimal Pair Analysis
6-8

Minor Parameters (see also Hand Arrangement and Point of Contact)
5-6, 163-172

Modulations
37, 139, 182-186

Morphological Processes
182-185

    aspectual modulation
    183-184
    derivational
    184
    grammatical
    182-184
    lexical
    184-185
    negative incorporation
    184
    number incorporation
    182
    subject-object incorporation
    182-183

Movement (see also Signation)
3-5, 11-12, 22-24, 139-162, 177

    circular
    149-153
    directional
    139-140, 143-145
    dynamics
    139-140, 161
    interaction
    140, 146-148
    macro
    148-155
    manner
    148-155
    micro
    156-160
    zero
    160

Multi-Channel Signs
178-180, 187-189

Non-Contact Signs
9

Non-Manual Features
2, 26, 178-180, 187-189

Number of Hands
163-165

One-Handed Signs
9

Ori (Orientation)
5-6, 28, 123-137, 163

    finger ori rules
    28, 133-134
    palm ori rules
    28, 132-133
    theoretical issues
    123-125

Parameters (see also Aspects)
5-6, 123-125

Perceptual Constraints
11-13, 68-69

Phonemes
6-9

Phonological Constraints
11-13

    dominance constraint
    11-12
    symmetry condition
    11

Phonological Equivalents in Sign Language
2-9, 173-174

Phonological Processes
180-182

    assimilation
    180-181
    deletion
    181
    liaison
    181
    neutralisation
    181

Phonology in Sign Language
8-10, 173-181

Place of Contact
163, 168-172

Position (see also Tab)
3-5, 6, 35-71, 176-177

Sexual Signs
65-66

Sig (Signation), (see also Movement)
3-5, 11-12, 139-162, 177

Signing Space
35-36

Simultanteity
25, 186

Simultaneous Double Tab Signs
71

Spatiality
25, 186

Stokoe Notation System (SNS)
25-34, 73, 140, 146, 178

Swedish Sign Language (SSL)
2, 18

Symmetrical Sign Dez Signs
58-64

Syntactic Processes
186

Tab (Tabulation), (see also Position)
3-5, 6, 35-71, 176-177

Transcription
25-34, 177-178, 187-189

    conventions
    27-34, 57
    diacritics
    26, 31-34, 52-54, 73-76
    formulae
    27, 32
    phonemic vs phonetic
    25-26
    problems
    71, 56-57, 132-137, 168-172, 173-180

Translucent Signs
21

Transparent Signs
21

Two-Handed Signs
10-13

   asymmetrical single dez
   10, 58-64
   double dez
   10
   symmetrical single dez
   10, 58-64

Typology of Signs
9-10

Word
1, 2-3

World Federation of the Deaf
158

Index of Glosses

A

ABOUT (1)
16

ABOUT (2)
18

ABOUT (3)
18, 154

ABOUT (4)
154

ADDRESS
109

AEROPLANE
23

AFTERNOON
43, 103

AGAINST
148

AGE
90

AGREE
10, 11, 30, 31, 32,
136, 166, 168

ANGRY
95

ANOTHER
64

ANXIOUS
91

APPLE
45, 100

APPRENTICE
56

ARGUE
111

ARRIVE
58, 167

ASK
92

ASTOUNDED
111

ATTEMPT [ASL]
7

AUDIENCE
186

AUDIOLOGY
47

AUNT
77, 104

AWAKE
159, 160

AWFUL
108

B

BABY
102

BAKE
10, 11

BALL
22, 125, 126

BANK
129

BANQUET
130

BASTARD
137

BECAUSE
57

BEFORE
55

BELIEVE
121

BERRY
61

BEST
58

BETWEEN
60

BIRD
22, 105, 106, 159

BIRTH
66

BIRTHDAY (1)
52

BIRTHDAY (2)
53

BISCUIT
55

BLACK
46

BLIND
109, 110

BLINK
164

BLUE
143

BLUSH
46

BOAT
169

BONE
99

BONNET
101, 102

(Underlining indicates a sign illustration)

BOOT
68

BOSS
116

BOTTLE
159

BOUNCE
145

BOW-TIE
48, 107

BOY SCOUT
114

BRA
66

BRAG
83

BREAK
77

BRICK
81

BROADMINDED
146

BROTHER
132, 172

BULL
101

BUSINESS
50

BUT
96, 144

BUTTER
103, 170

BUTTERFLY
86, 171

BUY
79

C

CABBAGE
160

CABINET-MAKER
172

CAKE
10, 59, 136

CALL
161

CAN (1) (noun)
59, 159

CAN (2) (verb)
101

CANNOT
96, 164

CAN'T BE BOTHERED
2

CAPTAIN
111

CAR
22

CARDBOARD
116

CAREFUL
42

CARELESS
109

CASTLE
105

CEILING
65

CENTRE
64, 186

CHAIN
33

CHAIR
130

CHAIRMAN
118, 119, 130

CHEAT
22, 30, 46, 125

CHECK
121, 162, 185

CHEEKY
47

CHERRY
47

CHILD
145

CHINWAG
167

CHOOSE
101, 120

CHURCH
186

CLASS
125, 126

CLEVER
78, 144, 159

CLIMB
91

CLIPE
127

CLOTHES
90

CLOWN
42

COACH
59

COFFEE (1)
31, 80,

COFFEE (2)
81

COLLEGE
18, 153, 154

COME
37, 184

COMMITTEE
18, 153, 154

COMMUNICATION
11, 81

COMPARE
85

COMPETITION
35, 37

COMPUTER
152

CONDOM
66

CONFESS
70

CONFIDENTIAL
161

CONSIDER
96

CONTACT
148

CONTINUE
100, 185

CONTROL
79

CONVERSATION
81

CORPORAL
114

COUGH
172

COUSIN
56

COURTING
53, 86

COW
11, 31, 40

CRANE
155

CRASH
77

CREAM
177

CROWD
154

CROWN
39

CRUEL (1)
44,

CRUEL (2)
49

CYCLE
11, 164

CYCLING
147

D

DANGER
84, 168, 169, 177

DAUGHTER
20, 102

DAY
117

DEAD (1)
103,

DEAD (2)
188

DEAF
47, 181

DECIDE
70

DELAY
93, 127

DELICIOUS
23, 51

DENMARK
108

DEPEND
63

DEPOSIT
154, 155

DEVIL
117, 135, 172

DIFFICULT
22, 31, 136

DIGITAL
157, 184

DIGITAL WATCH
184

DIRTY
60, 92

DISAGREE
119

DISAPPOINT
48

DO
102

DOCTOR (1)
56, 107

DOCTOR (2)
102

DOG
67

DON'T KNOW [SSL]
2

DON'T KNOW
164, 181

DOOR
185

DRAMA
119

DREAM
96, 179, 180

DRINK
93

DROWN
59

DRUNK
109, 110

DRY
158

DUCK
88, 105, 106

DUMMY
178

E

EAR
21

EARLY
140, 141, 142

EAR-RINGS
47

EAT
82, 178

EDUCATION
89

EGG
61, 141, 177

EITHER
63

ELASTIC
98

ELEPHANT
29

ELICIT
110

EMBARRASS
38, 140, 143, 161

EMBROIDER
152

EMPLOYER
23

EMPTY
33, 115

END
23, 63

ENGINEER
147

ENGLAND
60

ENOUGH
2

ESKIMO
83

EVERYDAY [ASL]
168

EXCITING
84

EXPENSIVE
179, 180

EXPLAIN (1)
11,

EXPLAIN (2)
58

EYE
42

F

FAMOUS
119

FAR
35, 37

FEAR
49

FED UP
2

FEEL
95

FILM
170

FINGER-SPELLING
89

FINISH
88

FISH
84

FLAT
149

FLOUR
89, 125

FOCUS
71

FOLLOW
31, 32, 166

FOOLISH
8

FOOTBALL (1)
93

FOOTBALL (2)
172

FOOTBALL PITCH
117

FOR
20

FOREMAN
113

FORGET (1)
30

FORGET (2)
186

FORGIVE
121, 151

FRIDAY
69

FRIEND
78, 168

FRUIT
45

FULL
33, 136, 169

FUNNY
158

G

GAVEL
157

GERMANY
40, 170

GIRL [ASL]
21, 168

GIRLFRIEND
51

GIVE
11

GO
9

GOAL (1)
20, 92, 93

GOAL (2)
64

GOAL (3)
117

GOOD
184

GOSSIP
106

GREEN
55

GROUP
81

GRUMPY
157

GYM
52

H

HALO
39

HANDKERCHIEF
43

HANG
48

HARE
128

HARD
44, 140, 141, 161

HAVE
13, 30, 38, 159

HEAVEN (1)
20, 117

HEAVEN (2)
65

HEAVY
5, 30, 31

HELP
20

HEREDITARY
103, 184

HEREDITARY DEAFNESS
184

HIPPOPOTAMUS
83

HOLIDAY
4, 118

HOME
86

HOPE
112

HORIZONTAL [ASL]
18

HORSE-RIDING
147, 153

HOSPITAL
69

HOUSE
22

HOW
147

HOW MUCH
179, 180

HURRY UP
117

I

I
3, 28, 132, 133, 181

ICE [DSL]
4

ICE-SKATING
129

IDLE
118, 150, 163, 164

IGNORE
47, 48

ILL
23, 30, 31, 134, 135

IMAGINE
179, 180

IMPROVE
61

IN
146, 148

INCENSED
39

INFORMATION
11

INSTEAD
93

INTERESTING
140

INTERVIEW
58, 93

IRELAND
58, 110

IRON
131

ITALY
86

ITCH
55

J

JEALOUS
91

JEANS
97

JOIN
165, 166

JOKE (1)
107

JOKE (2)
108

K

KEEN
84, 184

KEEP
58

KEY
79, 157

KILT
51

KIND
78

KING
28, 39

KISS (1)
70

KISS (2)
116, 178

KITCHEN (1)
40,

KITCHEN (2)
171

KNEEL
110

KNIFE
62

KNITTING-MACHINE
131

KNOW
9, 28, 40, 168

L

LANGUAGE
60

LAST
23, 145

LAST WEEK
182

LAST YEAR
152

LATE
140

LAUGH
100

LAW
85

LAZY (1)
4, 37, 118, 163, 164

LAZY (2)
55

LEARN (1)
70

LEARN (2)
88

LEATHER
18

LEFT
94, 172

LETTER [ASL]
21

LETTER
21

LIFE
49, 142

LIGHT (1)
28, 117

LIGHT (2) (noun)
82

LIKE
49

LIKE [ASL]
176

LIVE
94

LOOK
41, 164, 182, 183

LOUSY
53

LOVELY
(1) 41, 101, (2) 97

LUCKY (1)
38

LUCKY (2)
47

M

MAD
118, 172

MAKE
7, 164

MAN
21

MANGLE
129

MARRY
57

MASTURBATE
66

MAYBE
115

MEASLES
46

MEDICAL EXAMINATION
51

MEET
96, 127, 128, 185

MENU [CSL]
6

MICROSCOPE
61

MINE
7

MINGLING
186

MISER
38

MISERABLE
100

MISS
120

MISTAKE (1)
44

MISTAKE (2)
147

MONEY
158

MORE (1)
31, 32

MORE (2)
167

MOTHER
114, 171

MOUSE
43

MOUTH
21

MUMPS
48

MY
3

MYSELF
95, 99, 134

N

NAIL BRUSH
62

NAME
18, 40, 140, 141

NARROW-MINDED
146

NEARLY
101, 158,

NERVOUS
154

NEVER (1)
57

NEVER (2)
57, 136, 141, 142, 160, 161

NEWS
107

NEXT
78

NEXT YEAR
152, 182

NICE
22

NIGHT (1)
8

NIGHT (2)
109, 110

NIL
82

NO GOOD
184, 185

NOSE
21

NOT
44

NOT KEEN
184, 185

NOT YET [ASL]
2

NOUN
18

NUISANCE
86, 136

NUMBER
43, 77

NUT
83

O

OATH
161

OBJECT
59

OFFICER
50, 111

OLD
42, 109, 110

ONE TWO FIVE
[125 train]
23

ONION
98

OPERATION
50

OPPOSE
147

ORDER
48, 161

OTHERS
60

OVERSLEPT
109

P

PAINT
104

PANTOMIME
131, 167

PANTS
66

PAPERCLIP
106

PARALLEL
166

PARROT
98

PARTICIPATE
59, 146, 148

PARTY
11, 23, 116, 163, 164

PASTE
104

PATIENCE
49

PEACE
131

PEOPLE
185, 186

PENIS
66

PERHAPS
163, 164, 185

PETROL
97

PHOTO
88

PISTON ENGINE
132, 172

PLAN
69

PLAY
150, 152, 153

PLEASE [ASL]
176

POISON
61, 115

POLE
61

POLICE
107

POLITICS
100

POOR
55

PORRIDGE
11

POSH
42, 158

POTATO CHIP
99

POWERFUL
155

PRACTISE
82, 133, 166

PRAY
169

PREGNANT
51

PREPARE
8, 86

PRETEND (1)
42

PRETEND (2)
98

PRINT
7, 80, 129

PRISON
34

PROBLEM
168

PROMISE
10, 13

PROPERLY
130

PROSTITUTE
41

PROVOKE
109

PUBLICISE
71

PULSE
56, 107

PUT
127

Q

QUALIFICATION
18

QUEEN
39

QUESTION
93

QUICK
10, 30, 31, 140, 161

QUIET
131

R

RABBIT
40, 128

RAIN
90

READY (1)
50, 116

READY (2)
112, 119

REAL
130

RECORD [ASL]
18

RED
45

RED INDIAN
40

REFUSE [ASL]
180

REGULAR
10

REJECT
37

RELEASE
165, 166

RELIGION
112

REMAIN
100

REMEMBER (1)
10, 13, 120, 181

REMEMBER (2)
185

REMIND
182

REPORT
45

RESEARCH
105

RESPONSIBILITY
52

REST
112

RETURN TRIP
145

RICH
50

RIGHT (1st Person)
7, 22

RIGHT (2nd Person)
78

ROAD
8

ROB
133

ROCK
77

ROLLER-SKATING
129

ROOF
169

ROWING
153

RUBBER
18

RUN
91

S

SAID
82

SAILOR
67

SALT
158

SAME
127, 128

SAUSAGES
38

SAY
6, 126, 127

SCOTLAND
54

SCREAM
98

SEA
37

SEAL
136

SEARCH [ASL]
20, 180

SEE
6, 29, 41, 126, 127, 185

SEEK
110

SEEM
46

SELL
80

SEND
90, 127

SERGEANT
54, 114

SEVERAL
89

SEW
62

SHAME
172

SHIPYARD
113

SHOE
81

SHOOT
107

SHOP
18

SHOULD
140

SHOW
42

SHUTTLE
24

SHY
116, 172

SIGN
91

SILENT
170

SILLY
118, 134, 135

SISTER
43, 98

SIT
105, 183

SKIRT
53

SLEEP
21, 159, 160

SLEEPY
164

SLY
125

SMART
2

SNOB
101

SNOWBALL
146

SOCIAL WORKER
99

SOLDIER
50, 69, 140, 142

SOME
125

SORE
90

SORRY
51

SPEAK
88

SPECTACLES
108

SPIT
127

SQUIRREL
67

STAR
65, 107

STEEL
44

STOP
161

STORMY SEA
37

STORY
151

STRAWBERRY
106

STRIKE
39

STRIVE [ASL]
7

STRING PUPPET
130

STRONG
54

SUMMARY [CSL]
6

SUMMER (1)
107

SUMMER (2)
159

SUPERB
82

SUSPICIOUS
23, 152

SWEAR
4

SWEAT
102

SWEET (noun)
49, 141

SWIM
150, 151

SWISH
97

SYMPATHETIC
HEARING SCHEME
24

T

TALK
183

TEA (1)
45, 93

TEA (2)
80

TEACHER
45

TEAPOT
23, 97

TEDDY BEAR
39

TELEPHONE
23

TEMPT
92

TEMPTATION
115

TERRIBLE
186

THANK YOU
29, 46

THE
18

THEATRE
94, 143

THEN
63

THIEVE
92

THIN
99

THING
127, 128

THINK
95, 96, 185

THIRSTY
43

THRILL
94

THROB
157

THROUGH
57

THROW
90

TIE
100

TITLE
105

TOGETHER
167

TOMATO
111

TOMORROW
144

TONSILECTOMY
107, 108

TOPIC [CSL]
6

TRAIN
129

TRANSISTOR
91

TRANSLATE
137, 154, 155

TRIP
104, 145

TROUSERS
66

TRUE
10, 11, 31, 85, 136, 137

TRY
60

U

UMBRELLA
33

UNDER
87

UNDERSTAND
41, 101

UNEMPLOYED
118, 150

USE
88

V

VAGINA
66, 97

VALUABLE
146

VERB
18

VICAR
99

VIDEOTAPE
151

VISIT
87

W

WAIT
5, 11

WALES
113, 161

WALK (1)
21, 37

WALK (2)
185

WATCH
108

WATER
44

WAY
113

WE [ASL]
180

WELCOME
87, 156

WELFARE OFFICER
99

WHAT
9, 144

WHERE
150, 153

WHICH
115, 127

WHISKY
100

WHY
9, 112, 132, 177

WILL
77

WISE
144

WISH
112

WITH
106, 166

WITHDRAW
87

WITHOUT
85, 164

WONDER WOMAN
24

WORD (1)
18

WORD (2)
20

WORK
131

WORSE
115

WORST
114, 145

WRIST WATCH
111, 184

WRITE
101

WRONG
114, 136

X

XYLOPHONE
79

Y

YES
156

YESTERDAY
144

YOUR
30, 78